SQUATTER
LIFE

SQUAT LIFE

1

LIFE

ER

PERSISTENCE AT
THE URBAN MARGINS
OF BUENOS AIRES

Javier Auyero
and Sofía Servián

DUKE UNIVERSITY PRESS
Durham and London   2025

Project Editor: Michael Trudeau
Designed by Courtney Leigh Richardson
Typeset in Warnock Pro and Helvetica Inserat LT
by Copperline Book Services

Library of Congress Cataloging-in-Publication Data
Names: Auyero, Javier, author. | Servián, Sofía, [date] author.
Title: Squatter life : persistence at the urban margins of Buenos
Aires / Javier Auyero and Sofía Servián.
Description: Durham : Duke University Press, 2025. | Includes
bibliographical references and index.
Identifiers: LCCN 2024025097 (print)
LCCN 2024025098 (ebook)
ISBN 9781478031505 (paperback)
ISBN 9781478028291 (hardcover)
ISBN 9781478060482 (ebook)
Subjects: LCSH: Squatters—Argentina—Buenos Aires. |
Urban poor—Housing—Argentina—Buenos Aires. | Victims
of violent crimes—Argentina—Buenos Aires. | Marginality,
Social—Argentina—Buenos Aires. | Poor women—Political
activity—Argentina—Buenos Aires. | Women in community
development—Argentina—Buenos Aires.
Classification: LCC HD7287.96.A72 B8425 2025 (print) |
LCC HD7287.96.A72 (ebook) | DDC 307.3/364098212—DC23/
ENG/20241217
LC record available at https://lccn.loc.gov/2024025097
LC ebook record available at https://lccn.loc.gov/2024025098

Cover art: Scavenger in a squatter settlement, Barrio La
Paz, Buenos Aires, November 2022. Photograph courtesy
of Sofía Servián.

TO OUR MOMS, SUSANA AND ANNIE

No matter how much one trains one's attention on the supposedly hard facts of social existence, who owns the means of production, who has the guns, the dossiers, the newspapers, the supposedly soft facts of that existence, what do people imagine human life to be all about, how do they think one ought to live, what grounds belief, legitimizes punishment, sustains hope, or accounts for loss, crowd in to disturb simple pictures of might, desire, calculation, and interest. —CLIFFORD GEERTZ, *After the Fact: Two Countries, Four Decades, One Anthropologist* (1996)

CONTENTS

CONCLUSIONS — 151

It is when they stringently sublimate their social passions into rigorous theory building, robust methodological designs, and scrupulous empirical observation that sociologists best serve the historical interests of the dominated by producing cogent explications of the complex structures that keep them down. —LOÏC WACQUANT, *The Invention of the "Underclass"* (2022)

We first met in June 2018. Sofía was twenty years old and living in La Paz, a low-income neighborhood in Quilmes, a district in the southern suburbs of Buenos Aires. She was about to start her degree in anthropology at the University of Buenos Aires (UBA), a ninety-minute bus ride from home. Javier was fifty-two and living in Austin, Texas. He had been in the United States since he was twenty-seven. He was a professor in the sociology department at the University of Texas (UT). We began to write this preface together in August 2022, and we finished it in November 2023: Sofía in La Paz, now in her last year at the UBA; Javier in Austin, still at UT.

Our first meeting was Sofía's mother's idea. At the time, Susana worked as a domestic worker in Javier's brother's home and, worried as she had always been about Sofía's education and future prospects, she thought Javier could provide some guidance for her daughter during her first year in college. A few months after our first meeting at a coffee shop in Lomas de Zamora, the suburb where Javier was born and where his family still lives, the seeds of the research project that would lead to this book were planted. We began with a very general question: How and why do those with scarce material and symbolic resources put up with, adapt to, or fight against the conditions of social marginalization (low-paying jobs, lack of basic infrastructure, meager social services, etc.), interpersonal violence, and bureaucratic manipulation that produce their suffering? It was, we knew at the time, a very broad question with various ways of approaching it and a multiplicity of possible answers. Over the course of a few more meetings in person and over WhatsApp, we began to narrow it down to something that resembled a "researchable" problem, something that could be scrutinized with the methodological tools of our disciplines.

What "keeps those at the bottom down?" we asked ourselves; why is it that most of the time *los de abajo*, the most marginalized, the utterly destitute, comply with their marginalization? And when and how are they able to "stand up," even if momentarily, to confront the "complex structures" of domination? We had an initial hunch: Those at the bottom rarely explode, seldom rebel against those complex structures and against the individuals or groups that incarnate them, because they are too busy with the task of making ends meet. The urgent demands of a social order that deprives them of their means of sustenance have done the work of symbolic domination. Thus, our initial expansive interrogation began to focus on the ways in which those at the margins seek to acquire their means of subsistence—asking how they manage, individually or collectively, to make ends meet, to acquire land and housing, to get food on the table, to cope with surrounding violence. This was our approach to the general question about the ways in which the wretched of the city experience structural and political determinants.

For Javier, these questions had both academic and political interest and, simultaneously, brought him back to the ethnographic inquiry he carried out for his first book, *Poor People's Politics*. For Sofía, subsistence was not only an (in her case, new) academic or political question. It was a concern that had defined her entire life. For her, "making it to the end of the month" had always been a practical problem—it still is at the time of this writing. This collaborative book meshes academic, political, and vital preoccupations.

In the social sciences there is vast scholarship on what Matthew Desmond (2012) calls "the survival question." For the most part, the emphasis is placed on issues of cooperation and mutual aid that the poor exercise to confront material scarcity. When the state is absent (or the aid it delivers insufficient) and the labor market fails to provide good-enough jobs, most social science research shows that, in order to make ends meet, the poor rely on networks of exchange between relatives and friends. To a great extent, this is still the case in the places where we conducted our research. But the emphasis on collaboration within families and communities tends to obscure relationships of domination and conflict that occur within both. It also tends to overlook the political relationships that the most marginalized establish, often contentiously, with the state.

This book inspects the practices (both licit and illicit) of subsistence. Although we present the voices and actions of individual actors, our units of analysis are the relationships in which these practices are embedded—within families, between people and institutions, and between individuals and the state.

We carried out our research on practices of subsistence for more than a year until, in March 2020, our work took an unexpected turn with the emergence of the COVID-19 pandemic. The very empirical object of our investigation began to rapidly change right before our eyes. Although by then we had some preliminary conclusions regarding the bricolage that the poor assemble to survive, we decided to postpone the writing and to continue the field research.

To research and write about ways of acquiring means of subsistence and managing interpersonal violence means to extricate them of their urgency. It is as if we could stop a movie and then slowly and systematically scrutinize each and every frame. Doing so, that is, attempting to examine and narrate in a careful and attentive way the urgencies of subsistence, runs the risk of destroying the very object under consideration, as plagued as it is by necessities and tensions. To have a dinner of only bread and tea (because there is nothing else to eat) is not the same thing, needless to say, as writing about having a dinner of only bread and tea. We are not sure we have solved this dilemma, but we hope to have inspected and represented to the best of our abilities the difficulties, the conflicts, and the joint ways of subsisting at the urban margins.

ACKNOWLEDGMENTS

First and foremost, we want to thank all the people in La Matera, El Tala, and La Paz who opened their homes and their hearts so that we could conduct our research. In particular, we want to thank "las chicas del comedor" who taught Sofía to cook, to clean, to draw, and to care. Above all, they taught us what a big difference a small gesture of affection can make.

A number of people made sure we never walked alone during these years of research and writing. When this book was a series of scattered notes, we exchanged ideas about the project with Loïc Wacquant, Matthew Desmond, Mario Small, and Jennifer Scott. They recommended plenty of reading and made insightful suggestions on the basic outline of the project. As the writing advanced, Loïc became an informal advisor of sorts—guiding us, with his characteristic brilliance, in many of the decisions (from big to small) that we had to make. *Gracias, Loïc.*

The chapter on neighborhood politics received instructive comments from a group of scholars with whom Javier worked for over three years. As this book goes into production, that collective project, under the title *Portraits of Persistence: Inequality and Hope in Latin America*, is also seeing light. Thanks to Dennis Rodgers, Maricarmen Hernandez, Jennifer Scott, Katherine Sobering, Katherine Jensen, Marcos Perez, Jorge Derpic, Cinthya Ammerman, Alex Diamond, Eldad Levy, and Alison Coffey. You all made the ideal of collective intellectual work come alive—and we are extremely thankful for that.

Many years ago, Dennis Rodgers strongly encouraged Javier to revisit the arguments and empirics of *Poor People's Politics*. This book is not, we are pretty sure, what he had in mind, but that suggestion started the project—so, in a way, *Dennis es el culpable.*

Thanks to Alison Coffey—brilliant scholarly mind and editor extraordinaire. She proofread every single line of this book and made excellent suggestions on both form and content.

An article that Javier published with Faith Deckard in the *Annual Review of Sociology* helped us systematically examine the vast literature on poor people's strategies and then amend the way in which we were constructing our object. Thanks to Faith for pushing us to read literature we didn't know well, and to Douglas Massey and Patrick Sharkey for their suggestions on that piece. Another article published with Maricarmen Hernandez and Sam Law in *Qualitative Sociology* alerted us to other forms of subsistence and collective struggle. Immense thanks to both, and to Claudio Benzecry, editor of *Qualitative Sociology*, for comments and criticisms.

We are also grateful to Mariana Heredia, Alicia Torres, Gabriel Kessler, Luisina Perelmiter, and Gabriel Vommaro. They read parts of the Spanish version of this book and made incredibly useful comments—both about form and content. When we needed to dig deeper into the history of popular housing in Argentina, we were lucky enough to count on the expert knowledge and kind advice of Adriana Massidda. Thank you! And thanks to Claudio Benzecry (again), Daniel Fridman, and Pablo Lapegna not only for being there, in that space of ours, but also for your support and criticism.

We presented chapters of this book at the Seminario del Grupo de Historia Popular at the Instituto Ravignani and at talks at Universidad del País Vasco, Universidad de Antioquía, Universidad de Campinas, University of Michigan, and at New York University's Institute for Public Knowledge. Thanks to Gabriel DiMeglio, Gabriel Gatti, Andrea Delfino, Catalina Tabares Ochoa, Luciana de Souza Leao, Eric Klinenberg, and Gianpaolo Baiocchi for the invitation and to the many participants for their insightful suggestions. We also want to thank the students at the seminar "Fundamentos de Etnografía" at FLACSO-Ecuador, who read the manuscript and provided insightful feedback, and Juan Manuel Solís, Eduard Ballesté, and Miguél Úbeda for their invitation to the seminar "La Trastienda de la Etnografía" at the Universidad de Lleida, where we discussed drafts of two chapters. When we were almost done, we presented the introduction at the Urban Ethnography Lab at the University of Texas (UT) at Austin. Thanks to all the graduate students and faculty who attended and gave us valuable feedback. For the past ten years, the Lab has been a place of fruitful intellectual exchange and scholarly production. It was also a space where we were able to share and debate the emotional ups and downs involved in ethnographic fieldwork. At the Lab, various events, such as brown bags, updates from the field, lectures, and workshops, fed and nurtured our sociological imagination. We are also grateful for the support provided by the Lozano Long Institute for Latin American Studies and the Sociology Department at UT–Austin.

We are immensely grateful to Sean Manning, who carefully and brilliantly translated the two "crónicas" we presented in chapters 6 and 7. It was a treat, a privilege indeed, working with him.

In 2019, the theme of the annual conference at the Lozano Long Institute of Latin American Studies was "Journalism under Siege." A number of talented journalists came to Austin and shared their experiences in reporting and writing. That meeting, and the stimulus provided by a number of other nonfiction writers who came to UT at the invitation of the Spanish Creative Writing Initiative, served as a main inspiration for the narrative form of some of the chapters of this book. Thanks to Florencia Alcaraz, Patricia Nieto, Socorro Venegas, Gabriela Cabezón Cámara, and Cristian Alarcón for (unbeknownst to you all) being the force behind our writing experiment. And thanks to Gabriela Polit for making all this happen, for your advice and support through all these years, and for your incisive writing, which we are trying to emulate here.

María Soledad Lopez also merits special thanks, not only for her unwavering effort on behalf of the wretched of the urban periphery but also for all that she taught us about the daily working of the judiciary in Buenos Aires.

Gisela Fosado and Michael Trudeau at Duke University Press: We are truly thankful for your encouragement and your superb editing. Last but hardly least, another informal advisor, the one and only Lucas Rubinich, merits special mention. It's been many years since a chance encounter right outside the "Marcelo T" building changed Javier's life forever. Since then, Lucas and Javier have been consulting about the content of each other's books, the best way of communicating social science research, and the political intent behind their work. This book was no exception. As we were writing, we found energy and inspiration in his *Contra el Homo Resignatus*.

Gracias, Lucas.

Buenos Aires / Austin, April 2024

INTRODUCTION

The essence of poverty is not simply an economic condition but the linked ecology of social maladies and broken institutions. —MATTHEW DESMOND, "Severe Deprivation in America: An Introduction" (2015)

It is so difficult to talk about the dominated in an accurate or realistic way without seeming either to crush them or exalt them, especially in the eyes of all the do-gooders who will be led by a disappointment or a surprise proportionate to their ignorance to see condemnation or celebration in an informed attempt to describe things as they are. —PIERRE BOURDIEU, *Pascalian Meditations* (2000)

For more than five years, Chela has been coordinating one of the main soup kitchens in La Matera, a squatter settlement in the southern Conurbano Bonaerense.[1] From Monday to Friday, close to one hundred people have their breakfast, lunch, or early dinner in the small room covered with a metal roof right in front of Chela's home. A forty-five-year-old woman, short, stout, and with a dark complexion, Chela seems to have endless energy when it comes to obtaining resources for her soup kitchen: "The federal government sends us stuff, and so do the municipal government and the Catholic Church. I also receive private donations. The local bakery sends us pastries; some others give us [things] for the stew." In May 2019, Chela told us that early in the year only children attended the soup kitchen, but "now there were whole entire families." A year later, in April 2020, as the pandemic began and the Argentine federal government ordered a mandatory lockdown, Chela's soup kitchen started distributing food rations to dozens of families.

The neighborhood "is in really bad shape. Last year, it flooded more than ever. Maybe it's because they never finished the sewer system? You have no idea the number of rats that show up here after each flooding. Here, in the soup kitchen, we put poison and traps everywhere because they are huge!" But Chela does not like to dwell on the problems. She focuses on their possible solutions: "We are going to get ahead," she repeats like a mantra. "Getting ahead" involves the three neighbors who help out in the soup kitchen: "When there is a power outage, we know what to do; when the water is cut off, we know who to call." The four of them start their day early around 7 a.m. and end around 5 p.m. after they have cleaned the kitchen and the dining room.

Soledad is twenty-eight, and she's been working alongside Chela for six months. Soledad's husband works as a butcher an hour away from La Matera. He leaves the neighborhood at 5 a.m.—"he has to wait until there are people in the streets; there are a lot of thieves around," Soledad tells us. They have two children, and the youngest one hopes to become a soccer player. Three times a week, Soledad takes him to practice at two different clubs, a one-hour bus ride from home each way. Twice a week, she takes another thirty-minute ride with her daughter so that she can attend a beautician course. A lot of time and money go into those bus rides: "I spend tons in the SUBE, and the soccer uniform is super expensive."[2]

Soledad tells us, "When I moved to La Matera, my children had to undergo a treatment because the house we moved into had dogs and fleas. It was disgusting. I took them to the hospital and the doctor asked me: 'Mom, where are you living?' Here, you have to burn the trash, because it's infested with rats. My neighbor throws out the garbage and doesn't burn it. When we do burn it, they complain about the smoke." When we ask Soledad if there is any local politician who helps neighbors with their daily problems, she refers to Pocho, a local Peronist broker: "A puntero? There was one who is now in prison."

When we speak to Chela, she is cooking a guiso de mondongo with peas. Amid the clatter of pots and pans, and the voices and laughs of her compañeras, she tells us that she really wants to offer breaded beef cutlets with mashed potatoes. "Milanesas con puré... that's my dream."[3] Chela is not the only one who longs for milanesas. During thirty months of fieldwork in La Matera and in El Tala and La Paz, two adjacent low-income neighborhoods, we repeatedly heard, in formal interviews and informal conversations, expressions such as "a good meal," "a good barbecue," "some good milanesas." Susana, an old-time resident of La Matera, tells us that the minute she receives her AUH payment, she goes and buys "some good, thick beef cutlets."[4] Ana, another resident, hopes that with a new government "we will be able to eat cutlets more often." Dozens of interviewees gave us detailed accounts about the increasing prices of chicken, eggs, butter, milk, and of the "many things that we used to buy with 100 pesos and now you can't buy nothing with that amount of money." "At home," Pedro says, "we drink maté cocido [maté infusion] with milk instead of milk chocolate so that the milk lasts longer." José, in turn, tells us that he gave his daughter "every peso I got collecting metal scraps so that she can treat herself with some milanesas."

Their "milanesa dreams" encapsulate the threefold focus of this book: the material dimension of destitution, poor people's relational ways of dealing with scarcity, and their individual and collective hopes—the relentless hardship, the mutual succor, and the joint persistence at the urban margins. This book examines the subsistence strategies of the urban poor: What do they do to obtain land, housing, and food? How do they deal with the surrounding interpersonal violence—a literal threat to their survival? How and when do the strategies of subsistence and those devoted to protection from physical danger complement each other? When do they conflict with one another? How do those strategies interact with relationships of cooperation, conflict, manipulation, or control between neighbors, parents and children, citizens, local political actors, and the police?

For us ethnographers, the question about the workings of poor people's strategies has to go hand in hand with an interrogation about the ways in which the marginalized think and feel about their own livelihood—the "supposedly soft facts of that existence," as Clifford Geertz puts it in *After the Fact* (1996). Residents of La Matera, El Tala, and La Paz are overwhelmed with the heavy burden of managing daily subsistence, but everyday precarity and insecurity do not paralyze them or make them feel impotent. Their own practices (from taking over land, to building a house, digging a trench for the sewer, paving a sidewalk, sending their children to school, coordinating schedules for a safe passage through the dark streets at night, or working as a volunteer at a soup kitchen) attest not only to the existence of hope in individual and collective improvement but also to something that they can teach those who do not inhabit those relegated territories: persistence in the face of presumably immutable and insurmountable circumstances.

According to the *Oxford English Dictionary*, to persist means to "continue firmly or obstinately in a state, opinion, purpose, or course of action, esp. despite opposition, setback, or failure." Persistence is one of the threads that connects the individual stories and ethnographic reconstructions that we present in this book. As we will discuss in chapter 1, it is now common in poverty research to speak about poor people's "strategies of survival" or "subsistence strategies." Following Loïc Wacquant in *The Zone* (forthcoming), this book shifts to "persistence strategies." This is not merely a semantic move. Studying ways to persist expands the focus beyond material subsistence and *alerts us to the endeavors of the most dispossessed to cultivate or maintain a sense of themselves, of their community, of the meanings of their lives and those of their loved ones, and of their collective purpose in the world.* Examining the forms of persistence enables us to account for the struggle to cling to what it means to be a social being, encompassing its "manifold facets rather than just material sustenance" (Wacquant forthcoming).[5] "Persistence" is thus a more precise and, at the same time, all-encompassing analytic category. It allows us to shed light on the individual and collective efforts made by the residents of the urban margins without losing sight of the objective circumstances beyond their control. This will help us to construct an "accurate and realistic" representation, as Bourdieu advises, without degrading or glorifying those at the bottom of the social and geographical hierarchy.

This book is based on observations and interviews carried out over thirty months of fieldwork, mainly in La Matera (an informal squatter settlement founded in 2001). We also conducted interviews and participant observation in two adjacent low-income neighborhoods, El Tala and La Paz. Both of them were originally squatter settlements (dating back to the early 1980s).[6] Many of La Matera's residents have relatives, attend school, or frequent soup kitchens in one of these two neighborhoods.[7]

Observations and interviews (and dozens of informal conversations) serve to document the depth, intensity, and durable character of urban poverty, as well as the diversity of strategies. Focusing on how residents procure land, build their homes, construct basic infrastructure, and obtain food, our book centers the material dimension of marginality. Concentrating on the way in which these very same residents navigate surrounding violence, we also shed light on their (insecure) physical survival. Examining what they say, think, and feel as they persist in the midst of misery and danger, we draw attention to the symbolic dimension of urban marginality.

We inspect these strategies both synchronically (How do they deal with scarcity and violence in the present?) and diachronically (How have they worked to solve their most urgent problems over the last two decades?). By focusing on the past and present simultaneously, we will see that the *question of subsistence* (How do they provide for themselves and their families in a context of material deprivation and public unsafety?) should not be disentangled from the *question of progress* (How do they try to improve their lives?). As in many other poor neighborhoods (Anderson 2007), "to stay afloat" and "to get ahead" are profoundly intertwined vital issues.

During the past four decades or so, in the Conurbano Bonaerense and particularly in the area where we conducted our fieldwork, transgressive collective action has been a quite successful way of addressing joint problems. Through massive and organized mobilizations, the urban poor have obtained land, shelter, and basic infrastructure in their neighborhoods. Rather than keeping their "heads down," those in need have challenged the political structures producing their suffering. Our first task will be to dissect the form and effects of grassroots mobilization in our field sites. We will see that collective action has been impactful notwithstanding the difficulties in achieving it—complexities that the vast literature on social movements and other forms of episodic contention dissect in detail. We will also see that collective action interacts with ordinary politics. It competes for attention with other (more personalized and, sometimes, morally ambivalent, less disruptive, and physically costly) forms of solving pressing problems.

Road Map

This book is a collaborative product between a student of anthropology who was born, raised, and still lives in La Paz, and a sociologist who has not lived in the Conurbano since 1992 but visits it frequently.[8]

Each chapter presents a story of two or more individuals, a personal testimony, or an ethnographic reconstruction. Although they all center particular individuals or families, they reflect practices and processes that appeared regularly throughout our fieldwork. They all encapsulate the manifold ways in which political, economic, and social forces mold experiences of social marginality, the ways in which exclusion intertwines with individual and collective strategies of persistence.

Chapter 1 briefly summarizes existing literature on "survival strategies." Among several other works on subsistence at the margins, this first chapter returns to classic works by anthropologist Larissa Lomnitz and sociologists

Carol Stack and Cecilia Menjívar. Those who are not interested in the socio-anthropological debates that serve to guide our inquiry and the theories, concepts, and ideas on which we draw (and refine and extend) to order particular circumstances and build our object of study can skip this chapter and go straight to chapter 2. The second chapter begins with a general description of poverty and inequality in Argentina and then briefly describes the history of La Matera and the individual and collective actions that neighbors undertook to build their homes and common infrastructure. We will see that its residents, as well as the urban poor in general, have long known how to cooperate with each other and how to capture resources from the state. This chapter demonstrates that persistence strategies weave horizontal and vertical connections between a diverse set of actors. Obtaining resources from the state is achieved sometimes by collective action (more or less disruptive), other times facilitated by political-partisan intermediation, and in many other instances by a combination of protest and brokerage.

Chapter 3 gets granular while examining the current practices through which poor residents procure their livelihoods. We locate our inquiry at an almost microscopic level, the closest we can get to the rough ground of daily life at society's margins, paying sustained and respectful attention to what Bourdieu (1996, 33) calls "ordinary accounts of ordinary adventures." We focus on a few families to scrutinize the manifold ways in which they obtain essential material resources. If the previous chapter highlights collective action, this one spotlights informal networks of mutual aid. In both, however, we see that political brokerage plays a key role—and that's the reason why chapter 4 focuses on the actions of a neighborhood broker. Here we analyze the functioning and meanings of political practice at the margins. Politics, we will see, operates both as a way to solve pressing everyday problems and as a form of extortion. The chapter empirically tackles this (often-neglected) ambivalence.

Illicit activities are part and parcel of people's strategies at the urban margins. Some of these activities produce violent interactions. Chapter 5 provides an overview of the scholarship on poor people's strategies to navigate everyday violence and presents fresh empirical evidence on the subject. Drawing on deeply personal and intimate encounters with victims and perpetrators of violence, chapters 6 and 7 present two crónicas that focus on the various forms of physical harm that shake the inhabitants of the settlement and surrounding neighborhoods. We also describe an unexpected "use" of one of our crónicas and our intervention in a judicial case.

The indefatigable activity carried out by a group of women in a local community center could only be understood in the context of economic deprivation and insecurity described in the previous chapters. Chapter 8 is based on Sofía's observant participation in this center, where a soup kitchen and a day-care center operate throughout the year. Here we describe a collective livelihood strategy based on community work. This community center not only offers food sustenance to residents in need but also seeks to shelter the youngest inhabitants of the neighborhood—young people whom the women working at the center consider the most vulnerable. The main concerns of this book (food subsistence, physical security, and poor people's search for meaning) converge in this chapter, where we highlight themes such as recognition, community care, and the production of sociability. The last chapter revisits the empirical material presented throughout the book to examine the affective dimension of life at the margins.

In the concluding chapter, we weave together the different chronicles, stories, and ethnographic vignettes, not so much to give them a single meaning but to investigate what they tell us about the central enigma of the book: the complex relationship between persistence strategies and forms of cooperation, conflict, and control among relatives, neighbors, and state actors. The book ends up showing, by way of empirical demonstration, that there should not be a rigid dividing line between works that emphasize economic hardship, suffering, extortion, and violence and others that accentuate hope, collective action, care for others, and dignity. On the contrary, we believe, as anthropologist Sherry Ortner (2016, 61) once said, that it is necessary to integrate these two perspectives, trying to "be realistic about the ugly realities of the world today and hopeful about the possibilities of changing them."

Research, Reflexivity, Writing

Seeing, listening, touching, recording, can be, if done with care and sensitivity, acts of fraternity and sisterhood, acts of solidarity. Above all, they are the work of recognition. Not to look, not to touch, not to record, can be the hostile act, the act of indifference and of turning away. —NANCY SCHEPER-HUGHES, *Death without Weeping* (1993)

The point is not *just* to empathize. Empathy alone has too many limits. The point is to walk alongside the people you spend time with and to do your best to learn from and communicate something about their lives with all the tools that you have. —REUBEN JONATHAN MILLER, *Halfway Home* (2021)

This book attempts to carry out a type of public social science that is localized, rooted in a particular time and place (Collins, Jensen, and Auyero 2017; Burawoy 2016). We do so through the reconstruction of individual and collective stories that are accessible, empirically rooted, and theoretically informed and informing—all written in a way that the general reading public could find both understandable and relevant.

Before writing about the lives of others, it is imperative to spend time with them to figure out, as Clifford Geertz (1973) once said, what they think they are doing. This, time spent, is what defines ethnographic fieldwork (Wolcott 2008; Lareau 2021; Wacquant 2002; Hoang 2015; Desmond 2009). In this sense, the research on which this book is based (long-term engagement and a combination of participant observation and informal and in-depth interviews) emulates what other ethnographers have done before us (more below). However, our fieldwork is different from most social science and investigative research on the topic in one crucial sense. Many of the individuals whom we portray here are Sofía's neighbors or relatives. She was born, raised, and lives in a barrio that borders La Matera. Many of her relatives still live in the squatter settlement. The conversations, in-depth interviews, and life stories that inform the narratives we present were carried out as chats between friends, neighbors, or relatives of very similar social positions. Sofía did not have to "enter the field" and gain the trust and rapport that are often quite elusive, even to the most experienced ethnographer. The challenging task for her was not to "get in" but to "gain distance" from daily life, in order to objectify it, analyze it, and then write about it. The fieldwork for this book thus replicates the methodological strategy one of us deployed in a prior project on environmental suffering (Auyero and Swistun 2009).[9]

"To fully know that game," Matthew Desmond (2009, 294) writes in his detailed and inspiring ethnography of wildland firefighters, "we must play the game. We must eat their food, speak their language, walk on their sidewalks, work in their jobs, fight in their struggles, teach in their schools, live in their houses; and we must do all this until their things, their life—its smell and taste and temperature, its way of reasoning and psychology, its rhythm and tempo and feel—become our things, our life." The fieldwork on which this book is based was carried out by Sofía Servián. To make our arguments, we draw on more than two years of observations and on dozens of interviews and conversations. Sofía did not decide, from one day to the next, to "play the game" in order to understand what subsistence at the urban margins is all about. She shares with residents their food, their sidewalks, their school. It was in La Matera where she flew a kite for the first time (when she was eight); it was there where she had her first pajama party with her cousins; it is there where many of her uncles and aunts live. She never had to "submit [her]self to the fire of action *in situ* ... [or] put [her] own organism, sensibility, and incarnate intelligence at the epicenter of the array of material and symbolic forces" (Wacquant 2006, viii) that shape strategies of persistence, because she and her family have forever been involved in that task. She did not have to intentionally subject herself to a long line in order to receive a welfare check (a percentage of which has to be given to the local broker who facilitated access to such benefits). She didn't have to, because she experienced it firsthand when Susana, her mother, lost her first job. She didn't have to "immerse" herself in a daily life plagued by the risks of assault or robbery, because she has lived with that since birth. In other words, she never had to try to make the "things" that define urban marginality become "her things"—the smells of a putrid stream, the taste of a paltry dinner, the cold temperature in winter, the sound of gunshots, and so on—because, simply put, they have always been. The challenge, as said, was distancing herself from unquestioned ways of thinking and doing. These internalized dispositions, we came to realize, acted as obstacles to fully dig into (to see, to question, to objectify) subsistence strategies—her own, and those of others.

The joint work (between an anthropology student and a sociologist with almost three decades in the trade) was essential to construct subsistence strategies as a "sociological object" (Bourdieu, Chamboderon, and Passeron 1991; Jensen and Auyero 2019). In countless virtual and face-to-face dialogues, we turned the domestic into something "exotic"; we did so by breaking with the "initial relationship of intimacy with modes of life and thought which remain opaque . . . because they are too familiar" (Bourdieu 1990, xi). In the social sciences, reflexivity implies a mental process of directing the analysis not only to the empirical universe under consideration but also, and simultaneously, toward the subject that investigates. We do so in order to understand how our own positions and perspectives affect the evidence we produce and the arguments we construct. This process of looking back at our social selves (*reflection* comes, let's remember, from the Latin *reflectus*, which means to bend backward) was very important while we were doing our fieldwork and while we were writing. The written presentation of this reflexivity will not be relegated (as in many an ethnographic monograph) to a methodological appendix but will be woven throughout the text—sometimes within ethnographic vignettes, other times in the form of slightly edited diary entries.

Throughout these years, our conversations prompted our own exercises in self-analysis. For the anthropology student, this book was an opportunity to reflect on her own trajectory with the help of a sociologist from a different position, both in the academic field and in the social space. For the sociologist, the collaboration with a student deeply embedded in the daily life of a poor neighborhood also offered a reflexive opportunity, in his case, to go back to arguments he had made more than two decades ago in *Poor People's Politics* (2001). Parts of this book, mainly chapter 4, revisit arguments first formulated there. Readers familiar with that book will see that more emphasis is placed here on the manipulative character of "clientelist practices" without losing sight of their ambivalence. Part of this new emphasis might come from the changing reality of grassroots politics. But it also probably stems from the biases and silences that, already present in that study, were unearthed and made evident, thanks to Sofía's constant interrogations about the way of doing politics at the margins—questions that were simultaneously directed to the "field" and to the "expert" on the topic.

Fieldwork Nuts and Bolts

The fieldwork on which this book is based was conducted between March 2019 and December 2021. With the exception of the months of preventive and mandatory social isolation decreed by the Argentine government during the COVID-19 pandemic, Sofía visited La Matera between two and three times a week. Between May and December 2021, she conducted participant observation in Virginia's soup kitchen, working there at least twice a week. In La Matera, she conducted forty-eight in-depth, in-person interviews and another twenty-two telephone interviews during the months of the pandemic. She began the interviews with her former neighbors and family members, and they introduced her to other potential interviewees (further removed from her close circle) in what is known as a "snowball" recruitment method. Sofía also conducted 105 short interviews in two selected areas of La Matera.

At the beginning of our research, as Sofía was conducting preliminary fieldwork and having informal conversations with neighbors, friends and family members, we began to exchange ideas about ways to conduct ethnographic fieldwork, ways to construct socio-anthropological objects, and observation and interviewing techniques. In these months our collaboration was less horizontal, given the difference in training and knowledge. Sofía was at the beginning stages of her degree in anthropology—not yet having taken classes on research methodology. Javier had extensive experience in the field and as a teacher of ethnographic methods. A series of private tutoring classes of sorts unfolded more or less organically, dictated by the need to solve this or that problem, over email, WhatsApp, and then Zoom. We talked and read about the place of theory in ethnography (how the latter is used to extend or refine both substantive and formal sociological and anthropological theories); about La Matera as a possible "strategic research site" (in the words of Robert Merton); about the best way to analytically justify our ethnographic study; about positionality, reflexivity, and the need for constant epistemological vigilance; about possible enigmas we wanted to unravel; about the most effective ways to reconstruct local points of view; and about—and here was where the pedagogical relationship started to become more horizontal, given Sofía's immersion—better ways to produce empirical evidence.

Discussions about the pros and cons of data production techniques (participant observation and interviews) revolved around the problems of inference as well as the limitations of the latter when it comes to addressing issues that the subjects cannot or do not want to talk about. They also addressed more practical issues, among which two stood out: how to take good fieldnotes and how to formulate good questions for the interviewees (questions that were understandable and at the same time produced the information we were looking for). Two classic texts were very useful to us (on ethnographic notes, Emerson 2011; on in-depth interviews, Weiss 1994) in our efforts to distinguish between descriptions of scenes, observed or reported actions, and overheard dialogue, or to move between general themes, particular lines of inquiry, and specific questions to interviewees.

The interviews and observations were conducted with various objectives in mind (to obtain detailed descriptions, to access different perspectives, to pinpoint processes, to understand how they are interpreted, etc.). We discussed how to emphasize some or several of these as Sofía observed and talked with neighbors, friends, and family members. Ethnographic fieldwork is an undertaking characterized by flexibility—we accompanied the subjects and paid attention to those things they paid attention to (such as the direction of a fan, the color of a piece of cardboard, or the price of bread pudding or soap). On more than one occasion we altered both focus and pointed questions. In other words, we were rigid neither about the research design nor about our role as researchers. This is a virtue, not a defect in ethnography (Katz 1982; Lareau 2021). Something analogous could be said of Sofía's closeness with several of the interviewees. The familiarity she had with former neighbors, friends, and relatives was extremely useful in accessing a sphere of intimacy and a level of granularity in the information that is normally very difficult to access, even for the most experienced ethnographer.

All qualitative research work involves a tension between immersion and distancing—the latter was possible thanks to constant epistemological vigilance, which allowed us to break with the actors' common sense and our own. Closeness to the actors, provided it becomes the object of permanent reflection (reflexivity in this case supported and encouraged by collaboration), is an advantage, not an obstacle, in the production of scientific knowledge.

Scholarship on ethnographic fieldwork was, it is important to emphasize, of great use in carrying out this research. But it was the permanent "back and forth," the round-the-clock exchanges (in which Sofía would write and send her notes or transcriptions to Javier, who, at the same time, almost simultaneously, would ask questions and suggest topics to investigate or elaborate on), that made it possible for both fieldnotes and interviews to improve notably during the course of the fieldwork. Between the two of us, we both adjusted our ethnographic "eyes and ears."

As for millions of people, the first months of the COVID-19 pandemic were times of anguish and uncertainty. Sofía was isolated, not leaving her home between March and September 2020. Javier, with fewer mobility restrictions, continued to teach at the University of Texas by Zoom—except for the summer months. At Javier's urging, Sofía kept a journal that was the basis for the "reflective interludes" that appear throughout this text. These were also months in which reading the voluminous literature on poverty and livelihood strategies served to regenerate our perspective—our point of view—on ways of subsisting at the margins. After the pandemic restrictions were lifted, Sofía completed the face-to-face interviews that had been pending and conducted the participant observation on which chapter 8 is based.

1

EXPLICATING SUBSISTENCE
AT THE MARGINS

Fifty-five years ago, anthropologist Larissa Lomnitz conducted the fieldwork research that eventually led to her now-classic *Networks and Marginality: Life in a Mexican Shantytown* (Lomnitz 1977). Published first in Spanish as *¿Cómo sobreviven los marginados?* in 1975, it surfaced almost concurrently with another anthropological classic on the same topic, Carol Stack's *All Our Kin* (1974). Twenty-five years later, Cecilia Menjívar published another now-classic book, *Fragmented Ties: Salvadoran Immigrant Networks in America* (2000), which crucially shaped the research agenda launched by Lomnitz and Stack on the role of reciprocity networks in the survival strategies of the urban poor in Latin America and the United States. That line of empirical inquiry is still quite vigorous throughout the Americas (Alzugaray 2007; Desmond 2012, 2017; Edin, Lein, and Jencks 1997; Edin and Shaefer 2016; Eguía and Ortale 2004, 2007; Fernández-Kelly 2015; González de la Rocha 2001, 2020; Gutiérrez 2004; Jarrett et al. 2014; Lubbers et al. 2020; Newman 2020; Raudenbush 2020; Small 2004; Small and Gose 2020; Svampa 2005). Alongside networks of reciprocal exchange and state aid, research in Latin America has examined patronage or clientelist networks and contentious collective action as prominent ways of obtaining basic needs such as housing, food, and medicine among the urban poor (Álvarez-Rivadulla 2017; Fischer, McCann, and Auyero 2014; Holland 2017; Holston 2009; Perez 2018, 2022; Rossi 2017).[1]

Networks of reciprocal exchange are central to the daily lives of the residents of Cerrada del Cóndor, the shantytown of about two hundred houses in Mexico City where Lomnitz conducted fieldwork between 1969 and 1971. Life for those who lack "any reasonable security features, such as job security, social security, or a reasonably safe monthly level of income" evolves "like a complex design for survival. Age-old institutions, like *compadrazgo* (fictive kinship or godparenthood) and *cuatismo* (a traditional form of male friendship), are mobilized to reinforce and strengthen the structure of local exchange networks" (Lomnitz 1977, 2–3). According to Lomnitz, given the absence of local government action (a context quite different, as we see below, from Stack's), "the basic insecurity of marginal existence can be compensated in only one way: by generating mechanisms of economic solidarity, based on the full mobilization of the social resources of the individual" (91). Exchange networks are defined by "the flow of reciprocal exchange of goods, services, and economically valuable information," including information, job assistance, loans, services, and moral support (201).

Unlike in Cerrada del Cóndor, state aid was quite widespread in the poor neighborhood that Stack (1983) called "the Flats"—many of the African Americans among whom she conducted her fieldwork in the late 1960s "were raised on public welfare, and now, as adults in their twenties to forties, are raising their children on welfare" (27). And yet, residents were keenly aware that "the minimal funds they receive[d] from low-paying jobs or welfare [did] not cover their monthly necessities of life: rent, food, and clothing." The urban poor, in Stack's detailed account, "immerse[d] themselves in a domestic circle of kinfolk who [would] help them" (29).

Thus, much like their counterparts in the Mexican shantytown, Flats residents adopted "strategies for coping with poverty" (9). Among the resources, possessions, and services that kin and friends "swapped" were "food, stamps, rent money, a TV, hats, dice, a car, a nickel here, a cigarette there, food, milk, grits, and children" (33). This reliance on "cooperative support" was, according to Stack, a "resilient response to the social-economic conditions of poverty" (124), and the obligation of reciprocity implicit in those exchange networks was deemed a "profoundly creative adaptation" (43) to conditions of material scarcity. In a paragraph that encapsulates findings analogous to those of Lomnitz, Stack writes, "Men and women in The Flats . . . search for solutions in order to survive. They place their hopes in the scene of their life and action: in the closed community, in the people around them, in kin and friends, and in the new friends they will make to get along" (57).

Based on a thorough and insightful study of social ties among Salvadoran migrants to the United States, Menjívar's *Fragmented Ties* problematizes the shifting nature and value of informal networks—the "web of family, friends, neighbors, and so on, who can provide material, financial, informational, and emotional assistance on a regular basis" (2000, 2). Far from static, "monolithic structures" (117) on which people in need can always rely, networks reflect "dynamic processes" (3). Friends and family members cannot always count on the help of kin and friends: They do so "sporadically, conditionally, and unevenly" (3). Informal networks are created, transformed, strengthened, or weakened depending on both the material conditions of the migrant's existence and the economic and political context. In other words, informal social ties have a "contingent, shifting nature" (116). As Menjívar summarizes it:

> Informal exchanges among immigrants occur in varied, multifaceted ways. Networks of assistance cannot be assumed to be straightforward, smooth interactions that always behave in expected ways. Immigrants do not automatically assist each other simply because they are relatives or friends; having relatives and friends at the place of destination should not be equated with assistance in the settlement process. Exchanging assistance among poor immigrants is a complex often contentious process that may produce contradictory results. . . . Networks [are] not fixed structures—or even attributes—but . . . processes in flux, which thus generated a plurality of experiences. (155)

In this book, we take heed of Menjívar's emphasis on the dynamic and versatile character of informal networks and extend her analysis in two different directions: (1) We inspect the shifting valence of family networks when it comes to dealing with violence, and (2) we examine the changing forms and functions of both party and protest networks.

In a recent review of poverty scholarship in the United States, Matthew Desmond and Bruce Western (2018) advocate for a multidimensional approach, one that understands poverty "not simply [as] an economic condition but [as] the linked ecology of social maladies and broken institutions" (Desmond 2015, 3). Poverty, they emphasize, is "correlated adversity that cuts across multiple dimensions (material, social, bodily, psychological) and institutions (schools, neighborhoods, prisons)" (Desmond and Western 2018, 308). They also warn ethnographers against "reducing people to their hardships" by ignoring the many instances of "resilience and creativity" (Desmond and Western 2018, 310; see also Di Nunzio 2019). In dissecting the various strategies that poor people adopt to not only stay afloat but also improve their lives (to subsist and to get ahead), our book pays attention to those instances while staying both realistic about the harsh experiences of deprivation and hopeful about the possibilities of (partially) overcoming (some of) them (Ortner 2016). Poverty is multidimensional, and so are the strategies poor people use to survive and (seek to) thrive. *Focusing on these strategies allows us to approach urban marginality not only in terms of grievances (and what poor people "lack") but also in terms of their individual and collective efforts to improve their lot.*

Desmond and Western (2018), furthermore, call for a relational approach to poverty, one that focuses on transactions and processes linking actors with unequal power. In this book, we heed this call by zooming in on strategies that connect actors occupying similar positions in the social space (as some of the literature on networks of reciprocity still does) and also on actors with unequal power (poor residents, brokers, state officials). Persistence strategies, our book shows, involve both horizontal and vertical relations—some of them connecting the destitute with established political authorities. We thus place politics (defined as "interactions in which actors make claims bearing on someone else's interest, in which governments appear either as targets, initiators of claims, or third parties" [Tilly 2008, 6]) at the center of discussions about subsistence (Phillips 2018; Small 2004). Poverty is indeed relational, and so are poor people's strategies (see Wacquant 2022).

In the introduction to her insightful ethnography of hunger in Singidia, Tanzania, anthropologist Kristin Phillips (2018, 3) states that in anticipation of resource deprivation "people cast wide webs of connection, obligation, and pressure." Through "acts of both conflict and cooperation, and through networks of both inequality and interdependence" (3), they search for means to solve pressing needs. Our book shows that, although the contexts are quite different, analogous processes of horizontal and vertical entanglement are at work. Their incessant search for food, shelter, and medicine "brings people to each other" and "brings them to their government" (3).[2] This process of "coming closer" to the government in order to procure sustenance became even more pronounced during the long lockdown ordered by state authorities during the COVID-19 pandemic.

We are aware that the concept of "strategy of survival" is not devoid of theoretical glitches.[3] Because both terms (*strategy* and *survival*) could be misconstrued, clarification is in order. On the one hand, *strategy* might evoke images of explicit and deliberate choices made by individuals when, in fact, many of the ways in which the poor manage to cope with deprivation are part of a taken-for-granted, implicit repertoire of action that (1) is not always the product of conscious calculations or overt discussions and (2) emerges out of collectives beyond individuals. The concept of strategies seeks to capture the dynamic interaction between choices (often a product of deep-seated dispositions) and (objective and perceived) constraints, risks, and uncertainties (Bourdieu 1977; Fontaine and Schlumbohm 2000; Hintze 2004; Lamaison and Bourdieu 1986). Scholars working on the topic in Latin America have noted that households and families, not individuals, are the fundamental units out of which these strategies emerge (Chant 2002; Eguía and Ortale 2007; González de la Rocha 2001; Hintze 1989), while also noticing their conflictual features. Stack (1983) also notes that traditional conceptualizations of the nuclear family (father, mother, and child) fail to accurately capture the extended, complex, tension-riddled, and sometimes geographically unbounded units that together devise and deploy strategies. Anthropologist Dennis Rodgers (2007), to offer a particularly luminous example, provides a detailed ethnographic reconstruction of the noncooperative and segmented character of one poor household in urban Nicaragua.

On the other hand, it is certainly true that, except for extreme circumstances (concentration camps, for example), people always do more than merely survive. Concepts such as resiliency or livelihood point to the many other dimensions of poor people's lives. For now, we retain the notion of *survival* because, as we focus on ways of acquiring food, shelter, medicine, and safety, we are zooming in on that "very specific space in which physical persistence is insecure" (Phillips 2018, 8) for those living in the lower regions of the social space. But as we move forward in the book, we will rely more and more on the notion of *persistence* in order to highlight the efforts that those at the margins make, not only to procure material sustenance but also to acquire dignity and respect—to make ends meet and to endow their difficult lives with meaning. These (multidimensional) efforts are in full view in chapters 2, 3, and 8 but are present in the many ethnographic reconstructions throughout this book.[4]

Informal Networks and Organizations

Lomnitz, Stack, and Menjívar are now classic references in the study of how the urban poor manage to subsist when the resources provided by market and state are not enough. They are also our springboard to study how those living at the margins of the Conurbano subsist today—how they did so before the

COVID-19 pandemic, what happened during the long months of mandatory isolation, and how they manage today.

A vast literature in sociology and anthropology, in both Latin America and the United States, examines the role of social networks in helping the poor cope with material scarcity.[5] A recent review (Lubbers et al. 2020, 17) discusses three "contrasting but also partially complementary" approaches to articulating exchange networks among the poor—approaches that are very useful for making sense of the often-ambivalent operation of networks among the Conurbano poor. The first perspective, which Miranda Lubbers and colleagues call "pervasive solidarity," emphasizes the consistent use of extensive kin and friendship networks in order to obtain material resources that neither the state nor wages from informal or formal jobs can provide.

A contrasting perspective, labeled "pervasive isolation," portrays a startingly different reality, emphasizing the erosion of said ties and the isolation of the poor. Along these lines, and already early in the 2000s, sociologist Mercedes González de la Rocha (2001) noted that, due to increasing economic hardship in Mexico, poor people's strategies (based on a diversity of incomes and on networks of mutual help) were no longer viable—that they moved from "resources of poverty" to a "poverty of resources" in her oft-cited formulation. Menjívar (2000) made a similar point when she showed that networks of the most marginalized can "buckle under pressure" (6): The "very conditions that informal networks supposedly mitigate may impede resource-strapped people from assisting one another" (156). Menjívar and other scholars describe not only the depletion of resources that used to circulate within these networks, but also their different valences. Rather than reciprocity, "toxic ties" (Del Real 2019)—ties that, intentionally or not, can become abusive, exploitative, or degrading due to power differences—are said to be quite common among the most vulnerable (in Del Real's case, undocumented migrants). This empirical focus on adverse aspects of social ties is welcome, given the lack of attention to horizontal abuse and lateral animosity in urban poverty research (Wacquant 2015)—an oversight that we intend to rectify in this book.

Lastly, the "selective solidarity" approach highlights the coexistence of isolation and varying uses of ties to seek help among the poor (Raudenbush 2016). In this perspective, those in need do establish networks of reciprocal help, but they selectively restrict with whom they exchange mutual aid.[6]

Ethnographic and qualitative case studies show that, consistent with Lomnitz's and Stack's original findings, the poor still rely on networks of mutual aid to obtain food, shelter, and medicine—though the degree to which these actually serve to make ends meet varies (Jarrett et al. 2014). The extent to which social networks facilitate upward mobility is, even more so, a matter of empirical dispute (Menjívar 2000; Newman 2020; Smith 2016). These reciprocity networks often work in tandem with informal work and illicit work and rely heavily on informal institutions (such as gangs and patronage), a vast array of organizations, and (more or less transgressive) collective action to successfully claim resources held by the state (Diani and McAdam 2003).

In the area where we conducted our fieldwork, there is neither total isolation nor generalized solidarity. Diverse networks coexist: In some, trust and reciprocity abound; others are dominated by abuse and extortion. What is true for some households (such as the ones we examine in chapters 6 and 7, where mutual affection coexists with physical aggression) is also true for more extended networks (where assistance becomes manipulation). This is the case for networks linked to political party organizations that connect brokers and residents—to be inspected in chapter 4. Throughout this book, we will highlight the ambivalence of many of these ties and the many ways in which they are perceived and evaluated.

From the neighborhood's founding to its present, mutual aid networks between neighbors have played, and continue to play, a central role. They were very important in transmitting information among the future occupants before the land was squatted, they were strengthened early on to organize the neighbors for a variety of tasks (opening streets, digging ditches, delimiting land, organizing soup kitchens), and even today they function to ensure daily subsistence (obtaining resources for soup kitchens, sharing information on state social assistance plans, collectively complaining about lacking or malfunctioning infrastructure, coordinating safe movement in and out of the neighborhood, etc.).

Here it is important to highlight the fact that it is not only individuals who create and sustain networks of subsistence. Organizations such as churches, child-care centers, and community centers are direct providers of goods and services for the poor; they are also the places where those still-relevant networks of mutual aid are formed and sustained (Small 2004; Small and Gose 2020). What Small and Gose call "successful brokerage" depends on the extent to which institutional norms "render interaction frequent, long-lasting, focused on others, or centered on joint tasks" (2020, 92). In the following chapters, we will see how different organizations—soup kitchens and those formed around neighborhood political leaders—fulfill an important role in poor people's strategies. Asking "how do the marginalized make ends meet in contemporary Buenos Aires?" will lead us to inspect the functioning of, and relationships between, these organizations, clientelist networks, and collective action.

Succor, Socorrer, Socorro

Stemming from the Latin word *succurrere* ("to run to the help of"), *succor* (in Spanish, socorrer) means to "help or relieve someone when in difficulty." Socorro, in Spanish, also conveys a complementary meaning: It is not only to *offer* help, but also a *cry* for help. Socorrer and socorro: to come to someone's aid, and to ask for assistance. Both terms encapsulate the main theme of this book, which centers not only the manifold ways in which the urban poor assist one another in the daily task of making ends meet and in their persistent attempts to improve their lives, but also the ways in which they demand help from the state and the (sometimes disruptive) means through which they seek to capture government resources.

The acts of socorrer (extending aid) and socorro (asking for it) involve a set of relationships and have a politics. Succor ties and politics are diverse and dynamic. In the chapters that follow, we examine relationships' heterogeneity and their changes over time, scrutinizing their politics to understand how succor, in its dual meaning, is perceived and evaluated at the urban margins. Strategies (getting and offering succor, to obtain resources, to cope with violence) intersect and interact with forms of (class, gender, and political) domination and exploitation. Which relations of domination and exploitation—both direct and indirect—command our socio-anthropological attention?[7] Our ethnographic reconstructions began by placing attention on *precarious exploitation*, the process that defines the relationship between the marginalized and the labor market and which is key to understanding the economic penury that affects poor residents. We also focus on the modes of control and extraction exercised by the state over residents—through elected authorities, officials, police, or local leaders. The exploitation of female labor in the soup kitchen, the appropriation of a portion of state welfare benefits to finance political party activities, the use of residents' labor in electoral campaigns and of their social capital to solve disputes within the political field: We will visit empirically all these examples in the pages that follow. We will pay particular attention to the conflicts and tensions that arise within those relationships, to their sometimes ambivalent character, and to the often paradoxical ways in which they are perceived and evaluated by residents themselves.

But these are not the only relationships we are attuned to. As we conducted our fieldwork, other forms of control warranted consideration: those exercised by police in collusion with actors involved in illicit activities, those that "los pibes" (as residents call some youngsters in the neighborhood) practice when threatening residents in the streets of the neighborhood, those carried out by men over their female partners inside the household, those deployed (sometimes violently) by parents over their children at home.

The people with whom we spoke over the course of two years of fieldwork are neither heroes nor victims. The job of the social scientist is not to celebrate or disparage social actors but to understand and explicate their behavior and the meanings they attribute to it (Wacquant 2002). Our way of avoiding celebration or vilification was to examine a wide range of strategies and relationships in diverse social universes (the neighborhood, the home, the prison, the community center) and to focus on cooperation, conflicts, and ambiguities with the help of existing scholarship that analyzes similar issues in other times and places (Smith 2019).

The conditions of deprivation and insecurity experienced by residents of La Matera, El Tala, and La Paz hamper both their capacities for self-determination (that is, their freedom) and their chances of living a flourishing life (Wright 2021; Sen 1983; Nussbaum 2006; Brady 2019). However, in the midst of hardship and violence, we will see that they yearn for a better life for themselves and their families.[8] Those desires, those aspirations, appear articulated in their words but mainly in their practices—from taking over land to build their homes, to participating in illicit actions such as theft or sale of criminalized drugs, to working daily in a soup kitchen feeding hundreds of families.[9]

The social sciences are on relatively secure ground when it comes to describing and explaining objective inequalities of class, race, and gender; the mechanisms that generate them; and the relations that produce material and symbolic deprivation (Lareau 2003; Massey and Denton 1994; Tilly 1999; Brady 2019).[10] They are on less certain terrain when it comes to understanding the many ways in which individuals, alone or in groups, make sense of and cope with inequality and marginality (Lamont 2009; Levien 2018). These experiences and meanings matter because they often do the cultural work necessary to perpetuate the sociopolitical order, but, at other times, they serve as the basis for challenging it. This book focuses on the experiences and meanings of collective action, violence, fear, labor, and political action. We pay attention to the ways in which misery is lived and felt, highlighting the paradoxical fact that over the last two decades, despite penury, residents believe that they have made "huge progress" in their material living conditions but still feel they are almost totally "unprotected"—a feeling that gives birth to an existential insecurity that manifests itself when women like Chela and Soledad, mentioned in the introduction, describe their diets, their precarious daily routines, and their limited aspirations.

2

COLLECTIVE ACTION AND PARTY POLITICS IN THE MAKINGS OF A SQUATTER SETTLEMENT

This chapter reconstructs the history of the land occupation and settlement of La Matera and describes the ways in which its residents addressed their most pressing problems.[1] Individual and collective actions clearly exemplify the persistence that we mentioned in the introduction. These (more or less transgressive) actions are the incarnations of poor people's hopes for improving their material conditions of existence. We focus here on their hopes, not so much as they articulate them in words, but as they manifest in daily actions and activities (such as building a home or digging a trench) and in particular events (taking part in the land occupation, overcoming the damage produced by a flood).[2]

This chapter also describes how collective action aimed at securing services and infrastructural improvements (a health center, a school, pavement, streetlights, etc.) targets different levels of the state. We argue, by way of historical reconstruction, that as state officials responded to poor people's demands, they sought to control popular contention. We thus focus on collective problem-solving and the ways in which the "hands of the state" shape poor people's strategies (Morgan and Orloff 2017). While this chapter focuses on collective contentious action, the next two zoom in on mutual aid and patronage. Taken together, these three chapters show that persistence strategies operate in a context of pervasive political domination and economic exploitation.

We based our reconstructions on life stories, in-depth interviews, archival research, and Sofía's personal reflections about her (and her family's) own ways of dealing with material scarcity. Before we begin, we briefly describe the evolution of poverty and marginality in Argentina, and in the Conurbano Bonaerense more specifically. This context can help you better comprehend the history of La Matera and the generalized material deprivation in which individual and collective strategies are embedded.

Poverty and Marginality in Argentina

In the mid-1970s, less than 3 percent of the economically active population was unemployed. Less than 5 percent of the total population lived below the poverty line. Approximately 20 percent of the labor force worked in the informal sector or was self-employed.

Fast forward to 2023: Unemployment rates hovered around 10 percent, poverty rates were 44 percent, and almost half of the working force was in the informal sector (where salaries were lower and working conditions more unstable and precarious than in the formal sector of the economy) or were self-employed.[3]

These striking figures capture the drastic transformation in living standards among Argentines. Today, more Argentines are poor, and they continue to have access to fewer and even worse jobs than fifty years ago.

Between the mid-1940s and mid-1970s, Argentines enjoyed some of the highest living standards (and very low levels of inequality) in the region. State-led development, a large light-industry sector oriented to the domestic market, powerful unions, relatively high salaries, and publicly funded education and health-care systems distinguished Argentina from most other countries on the continent.

First introduced by the military dictatorship (1976–83) and then intensified under Carlos Menem's administrations (1989–99), neoliberal reforms drastically changed all that. Neoliberalism emphasized not only the need but also the desirability of "transferring economic power and control from governments to private markets" (Centeno and Cohen 2012, 318). As a political and economic project, neoliberalism comprised a whole gamut of market-based economic policies, including structural adjustment mandated by international financial institutions and the ensuing fiscal austerity, the privatization of public infrastructure and services, flexibilization of labor markets, reduced controls on capital transfers and investments, and deregulation of credit and labor markets.[4]

The results of these policies were everywhere to be seen throughout the region (Portes and Hoffman 2003): Income inequality increased, concentration of wealth in the top decile of the population persisted, the numbers of micro-entrepreneurs and self-employed expanded, and the informal proletariat grew significantly. Argentina was no exception to this regional trend. During the last quarter of the twentieth century, the country became more unequal, while poverty, informality, unemployment, and underemployment skyrocketed (Benza and Kessler 2020; Poy and Salvia 2019).

In the early 2000s, what came to be known as "pink tide" governments came to contest neoliberal thinking and practice by putting in place a set of heterodox policies that both expanded social spending and increased consumption (Weyland, Madrid, and Hunter 2010). In Argentina, between 2003 and 2007, soaring prices of agro-industrial commodities resulted in a period of export-oriented economic growth. Social safety nets were expanded, employment and wages increased, and poverty rates and income inequality reduced. The effects of the boom were short-lived. Since 2010, these improvements slowed down and then stagnated (Benza and Kessler 2020).

In 2010, 31.8 percent of the Argentine population lived below the poverty line. A decade of "stagnation followed by recession" later, 44.7 percent of the population is now income poor (ODSA 2021, 8). In the Conurbano Bonaerense, whose population "shows greater risks of extreme poverty" (7), this decrease in income is even more noticeable. In 2010, 40.9 percent of its population was income poor; in 2019, 51 percent. In 2020, in part as a result of the pandemic, that number grew to 56.5 percent.

Although the Conurbano's population has experienced a generalized deterioration in income since 2010, there has also been substantial improvement in access to decent housing and better infrastructure. In 2010, 38 percent of households in the Conurbano were not connected to water, sewer, or energy utilities. A decade later, it was 30 percent. As we will see later in this chapter, La Matera (like so many other informal settlements) illustrates how this improvement is the product of poor people's social mobilization.

While infrastructural conditions improved between 2010 and 2020, the early 2020s saw a significant deterioration in access to food, health services, employment, and social security—a trend that the COVID-19 pandemic notoriously accelerated. In 2010, a quarter of the people in the suburbs of Bue-

FIGURE 2.1. Precarious, unfinished brick houses in La Matera.

nos Aires (24.2 percent) experienced severe food insecurity (that is, they had involuntarily reduced their food intake and suffered from frequent hunger in the previous twelve months) and lacked access to medical care or medications. In 2020, this percentage grew to 32.2 percent (ODSA 2021, 46).

Poverty levels are not only the result of the logic of the functioning of the economic structure (Salvia 2012). Changes in rates of poverty and marginality also obey political dynamics (Brady 2009, 2019; Huber and Stephens 2012; Wacquant 2022)—both the collective mobilization of the most dispossessed and the social policies formulated in response to it have strong impacts on the extent and severity of material deprivation. In the case of Argentina, this can be seen in the reduction in poverty achieved through income-transfer programs (such as the Asignación Familiar por Hijo, Tarjeta Alimentar, and, during the COVID-19 pandemic, the Ingreso Familiar de Emergencia), conditional cash-transfer programs, and noncontributory pensions.[5] Poverty levels, furthermore, obey more specific, (sometimes) short-term circumstances. As we write this, Argentines are also suffering from runaway inflation and a sharp fall in purchasing power as price hikes outpace wage rises. Inflation (which reached 95 percent in 2022) has hit poor and lower middle-class families particularly hard as the price of food has increased more than other items.

FIGURE 2.2. Unpaved dirt streets in La Matera.

Today, poverty rates are higher than those registered in 1983, the year that democratic rule was reestablished in the country (Gasparini, Tornarolli, and Gluzman 2019, 83). Unemployment and job precarity are also significantly higher.[6] In this context of general impoverishment and deep deterioration of household income among those living at the bottom of the social structure, how do they acquire their means of subsistence? Argentine scholars Amalia Eguía and Susana Ortale (2007, 23) argue that in order to really understand social reproduction among those with scarce material recourses, "we need to grasp both their integration (or lack thereof) into the main mechanism of family reproduction, i.e. labor market, and other complementary resources. The latter include their participation in state welfare programs . . . self-provisioning activities, domestic work, and mutual aid networks among relatives, friends, and neighbors" (see also Alzugaray 2007; Aimetta and Santa María 2007). These will be the foci of the next chapters, where we will explicate past and present strategies, both individual and collective (see figures 2.1 and 2.2). By way of empirical demonstration, we will argue that, in order to truly understand these strategies (and the way they come together as "persistent bricolage" based on all sorts of informal networks), we need to set them in a context not only of generalized poverty and precarious economic exploitation but also of enduring networks of personalized political domination and heightened interpersonal violence.

Squatting: The Beginnings

In the mid-1990s, the government of the province of Buenos Aires began to plan a public housing complex in the area that is now La Matera. Toward the end of the decade, there had been little progress in the construction of the complex, and rumors about the illegal appropriation of the funds abounded. In March 2000, residents of El Tala, the adjacent neighborhood, together with the future beneficiaries of the unfinished housing units, occupied the land. The main organizers were leaders of the unemployed workers' movement (known as piqueteros), along with some others who were part of the Catholic Church and the Peronist party (Nardin 2019). Many had been present during, or had relatives who were part of, the earlier land occupations in nearby areas. Since the 1980s, that area of the southern Conurbano had witnessed massive, highly contentious, and often-successful land takeovers—of both private and public urban land.[7] Examining the squatter settlements that took place in the area between August and December of 1981 (and which included El Tala and La Paz), Maria Cristina Cravino and Pablo Ariel Vommaro (2018, 7) assert that these

> were the result of an organized occupation. . . . The occupants collectively invaded plots of vacant public or private land, on which they quickly built their first houses with precarious materials, which they later improved and built on. . . . The settlements had a defined urban form, with land delimited in plots and the rectangular layout that continues that of the formal city. . . . [These] collective and organized alternatives had better possibilities of resisting eviction attempts due to their visibility and the social organization that supported them. This also explains their location in the urban periphery, as there was less incentive to react on the part of the landowners (whether state or private), and also because they were generally unsuitable for subdivision due to being close to garbage dumps, in flood-prone areas or simply too far away from means of transportation.

March 2002. "Pedro organized folks block by block. He had a lot of experience from other land occupations," María says of her husband. Squatters—known as ocupantes or tomadores—knew (or rapidly recruited those who knew) how to set the boundaries for each private plot, how to open up the streets and dig trenches so water could flow, and how to demarcate and reserve plots for public spaces like the main square, future school, and health center. "Everything we did, we did a pulmón [with a lot of effort]; we got together with other neighbors during weekends and we built the sidewalks." They were also experienced in evading the police to bring in building materials, negotiating with government authorities, and, when necessary, confronting the police who arrived to evict them. "We would put the kids in front of the mounted police so they couldn't attack.... [W]e went through hell...when the bulldozers came to try to destroy our tents."

Mainstream media represented the occupation of La Matera as an extraordinary and transgressive episode carried out by people who were motivated by a basic grievance (lack of housing). This narrative is frequently reiterated, with scant variation, when the urban poor squat land. From this widely shared point of view, the "desperate need" for a home is the main explanatory factor of the "extra-ordinary" way in which the poor demand housing. However, as with many other land occupations that have taken place in the Conurbano and throughout Latin America, this one did not occur outside of (or in opposition to) ordinary political processes, but was deeply enmeshed in them.[8] Squatters' high level of organization, their personal connections with established political authorities, and the fact that squatting was already part of the repertoire of collective action linking the poor and the state all attest to this deep imbrication (Izaguirre and Aristizabal 1988; Fara 1988; Merklen 1991; Cravino and Vommaro 2018).

Those who were present for the land invasion remember that it "was like an empty field...it was all mud...up to your knee." They also remember that the land was occupied by pigs, sheep, and cows, and "you could fish in the creek." To prevent any misunderstanding, this was far from an idyllic "state of nature." "It was all muddy.... The bridges to enter the neighborhood from the creek were made of wood or used tires, *bridges of terror* [we called them], you were afraid to go across" (our emphasis). "We had to carry our own water, but we did it together." Although they remember these initial moments in the life of their neighborhood as times of "union among residents," they also stress that they had to "be very watchful...because if you left your rancho alone, someone would occupy it.... The very same neighbors would take your plot and your home."

Those were days of *collective hope*—hope understood not as an illusory belief that "everything was going to be okay," but as shared perspective, a point of view, with specific possibilities: *this* plot where we are going to build *our* house, this other plot where we will build a plaza, a school, or a health-care center. That hope was made concrete in the act of squatting, in the collective effort of building some basic infrastructure and mobilizing in demand of basic services, and in each family's labor to build their homes. That collective hope is also made evident in the ways residents put up with living conditions (lack of electricity, water, or garbage collection; recurring flood-ings; and so on) that would be considered intolerable or, to put it in crude terms—repulsive—by citizens from other class positions. Collective hope is also expressed in the way in which residents, when comparing past and pres-ent, understand the progress their neighborhood has gone through. As Lucía, an early occupant, states:

> It was hard to level this plot [so it didn't flood]. Truckloads and truck-loads of rubble, dirt, we did a lot. But, hey, it was a struggle . . . we had no water. We had to go and find it on the other side [across the creek], and when it rained the mud covered our boots. It was tough. We cleaned el barrio, we cut weeds, the tall grasses, with a machete. We did so many things.

This tolerance of material scarcity, this "putting up with" poverty, should not be confused with resignation.[9] A few months into the occupation, they had to endure sudden, deeper hardships when their homes and streets flooded—the first in a long stream of floods that still persist. The most traumatic recollec-tion of the first days of the settlement is neither one of food scarcity ("there were plenty of soup kitchens") nor of police violence ("they wanted to evict us, but we managed"), but of the destruction that came in April 2000 with "the water that reached our waists."

"Our Shack Was Halfway Covered with Water"

The rain started on a Thursday night in April 2000. Early Friday morn-ing, Lucas saw that the newly dug ditches had filled with water. The boards they had put down so they wouldn't have to jump over them were gone. The stakes and strings he set up to mark each plot would soon dis-appear under the water. "Gray" is how he remembers the color of the water. Lucas recognized the beginnings of a strong current as it passed through what would soon be the neighborhood's central plaza. He also saw how the tires they laid down to cross the creek were floating by. He and his partner, Alma, decided to weather the storm in their shack—they were afraid that someone would occupy their plot, as had happened to their neighbor Joni when he left the settlement for a few days. Around noon, when Lucas got out of bed to check the water level, his slippers sank into the dirt floor. Twenty minutes later he heard the "plaf, plaf . . ." as Alma crossed the room to make maté. "It's like we're sinking," she thought. Two centimeters of water already covered the floor; in forty-eight hours the water would be up to their knees. Alma and Lucas had already been through a flood together and they knew that if they didn't take care of their mattresses and their clothes, the water would ruin them: "You can always rinse the wood bed, but if water gets to the mattresses they get damaged, and you can't wear your clothes anymore." They put the mattress on top of the dining table and placed the refrigerator on top of a desk. They removed their muddy and soaked slippers, and with their backs against the damp sheet-metal wall, they sat on the mattress to wait—maté and thermos in hand. Alma still remembers the sound of the other three walls of the shack, made of thick fabric, as they flapped to the beat of the strong wind. The storm lasted four days, at the end of which the new settlement was completely covered with five feet of water.

Progress

Surrounded by two creeks that mark the limits between the squatter settlement and two adjacent consolidated neighborhoods, La Matera is, for residents, a *space apart*—an area you "enter into" or "leave from." Although residents perceived the settlement as "isolated," they by no means view it as homogeneous. There are important differences within it—the "area where the Paraguayans live," "the zone where you see more progress has been made," the "blocks where you can buy drugs," and the places "where you get robbed." Much like in other neighborhoods of relegation (Wacquant 2007), borders are highly mutable—they depend on who you ask and the relationships they have (or do not have) in the demarcated area. Despite these internal differences, however, the testimonies that we collected during our fieldwork depict a shared history of progress.

"Two years after the initial settlement, you wouldn't recognize La Matera. It improved a lot," Julio tells us. And most neighbors we speak with agree: "There's huge progress!" This shared viewpoint refers mainly to public infrastructure: a local school, a community center (known as CIC, for Centro de Integración Comunitaria), a health center that functions inside the CIC's premises, a plaza, some paved streets, a bridge that vehicles can use to enter the neighborhood, and the improvement of the other, smaller bridges that cross the creek.

The "bridges of terror" made with truck tires, wood boards, or light posts are now made of concrete. Miguel summarizes the state of the neighborhood in this way: "Years ago, when you were lying down in bed you could see rats this big [opening his arms]. Nobody had a decent home. Now, living here is easy. You have a school, paved streets, you have a health center, a bridge to walk into the neighborhood, another to drive through with your car. Before, cops, ambulances, or firefighters couldn't come into the area." Original settlers also emphasize electricity and potable water—compared to those early days, La Matera is now "another thing. . . . [W]e have water, with good pressure, and public lighting." Antonio, one of the early squatters, puts it this way: "Those of us who have been here from the very beginning have to put up with many, many things. We had no electricity, no water . . . we slowly got connected."

Auto-Construction

With the exception of a small number of housing units built by the state, most homes in La Matera, La Paz, and El Tala were built by residents, in many cases with the help of relatives and friends and with funds coming from a variety of sources (paid jobs, welfare programs, etc.). As in many poor neighborhoods in Latin America, auto-construction is the main way the poor have built their homes (Holston 1991; Ward 2012, 2019; Caldeira 2017).

First, a dining room and kitchen; then there's the bathroom, then the first bedroom, then another one, after that a second story. As tenancy on the land becomes more secure, the more solid and the larger the home gets. In the following note, Sofía describes the process through which her own house was built. Although particular in its details (and in the origins of the funds to buy building materials), she captures the slow process through which residents build out their homes and neighborhoods.

Reflection #1

Originally, my house had a small kitchen–dining room, a room where my mom, dad, and I slept, and a bathroom without a door. The bathroom had only a blue curtain that divided it from the rest of the house. When my brother was born, my parents took out my crib and bought a bunk bed. The bathroom had neither a door nor tiles. Those were difficult times: The country was recovering from the economic crisis of 2001. My brother was born in November, just a month before the "estallido."[10] My dad's salary had been cut in half. We don't even have baby pictures of my brother because there was no money to buy rolls of film.

I had a very close uncle who worked as a driver for a freight company. They transported all kinds of things, including household appliances. In 2002 he had to transport four hundred DVD players. At that time they were very valuable because they had just become popular and were a novelty. When he arrived at his destination with the four hundred players, the appliance house unloaded only two hundred. Apparently, the factory had shipped two hundred too many players by mistake. The delivery note that my uncle had to present to his boss said that they had unloaded two hundred players. There were two hundred left over that no one would claim because they didn't know they existed. My mom tells me that my uncle was desperate to find a place to store them. Before he finished his shift he had to empty the truck. He called a workmate with whom he had a very good relationship and dropped some of them at his house. He gave him a few players in gratitude for the favor. He left others at our house. We kept two and the rest he sold for $400 each (he earned that amount per month!). They sold very quickly. I remember all this because my uncle gave us a good part of that money so that we could build a new bathroom. Until then we had the basics: toilet and sink. We bathed at my grandmother's house, who lived right in front of our house, because we didn't have water inside our bathroom. With the money from the DVDs we bought everything new: toilet, sink, mirror, shower, bidet, and door. We put tiles throughout the bathroom and even had a bathtub installed. When they finished, it suddenly became the most beautiful part of the house. Everything was new; it shined. I was proud to have such a bathroom. It didn't look like any bathroom I knew. Now that I think about it, I don't think I was fully aware of the means we used to build it, even though I remember the image of the many DVD players piling up in the living room. I was only five years old, and I always used to play with two girls who were my neighbors. They almost always came to my house because I had a big yard and lots of toys. On one occasion one of them, while we were fighting over something, told me, "Well, I'm going home, I don't want your uncle, the thief, to see me. My grandmother told me that he stole all those DVD players. She bought one from him, so she knows." She was my age and she only repeated what she heard from the adults around. I also remember my uncle's smile when I told him about my friend. Even today, when he remembers, he laughs.

FIGURE 2.3. Horses and piles of rubble on the dirt streets of La Matera.

Despite Progress

In most residents' recollections, infrastructural improvements are not associated with this or that state official or this or that municipal administration, but with their "struggle" and—as we will see in chapter 4—with the actions of one particular grassroots leader. Despite the undeniable progress in housing and public infrastructure, La Matera is still a quite precarious settlement. More than half of the roughly 1,140 households own neither their home nor the land, and most of the 5,160 residents are poor. According to the last available figures, 55 percent of the population lives below the poverty line (poverty measured by income), and more than 90 percent of the homes are "deficient"— that is, they either have a dirt or loose brick floor (they do not have ceramic, tile, mosaic, marble, wood, or carpeted floors), lack piped water, lack flushable toilets, or are "shacks" or "cardboard homes." A third of households do not have access to water inside their dwellings, a third are overcrowded (more than three people per room), and although most of the houses have access to water from the public network, more than 90 percent of homes do not have a sewer or gas connection (Municipalidad de Quilmes 2010).

FIGURE 2.4. A smelly, garbage-filled creek in La Matera.

Although there is a shared consensus regarding collective progress, residents (both old and new) agree that the recurrent floods threaten their existence, an exception to the otherwise common viewpoint about the barrio's overall infrastructural improvement. In many conversations, residents of La Matera told us about the last storm, the level the water reached, and the furniture it damaged. The lack of garbage collection, the few paved streets, the terrible state of the unpaved roads, and the lack of streetlights in many areas of the settlement are seen as their other main problems (see figures 2.3 and 2.4). The farther one gets from the center of the neighborhood, such as the area around the school and the health center, the more pressing these issues become.[11]

"Ever since I moved here, my house floods," says Rosa, adding, "here you get by the best you can." Ana shares: "We got flooded again this year. There was a time when the floods stopped, but then they started again." Estela emphasizes: "You get tons of rats after each flood." The presence of rodents is also associated with the absence of garbage collection. Neighbors often pay other residents (sometimes youth who work for a political broker) to collect and burn it on the streets or in their own backyards: "You have to burn it, otherwise you get filled with rats, even though smoke bothers everybody."

"There're not enough streetlights.... The streets are dangerous.... It's too dark, there are many youngsters around." This association between the lack of public lighting, the presence of los pibes (youth who are seen as threatening), and public insecurity is something that, as we will later see, dominates the residents' concerns and shapes their daily routines.

But before delving further into their routines and strategies, let us dig deeper into the process through which the settlement was organized and the key role that party politics played in individual and collective problem-solving.

Politics "Down Here"

Those who led the land occupation remember the initial organization of residents—"face-to-face, person to person." During the first months of the settlement, activists linked to progressive sectors of the church and to unemployed workers' organizations (piqueteros) got along well with activists belonging to the Peronist party—the political movement founded in the mid-1940s by Juan Perón. As one of the grassroots leaders remembers, "the leftist ones" and "we, the Peronists," formed a common front (a mesa negociadora, or comisión) that negotiated with police and (Peronist) government officials to avoid evictions, and with other state and municipal officials to obtain goods and services (food for the soup kitchens, zinc sheets for their roofs, mattresses for their homes, etc.). "*Everything* that we got was thanks to the mesa negociadora ... *absolutely everything*," says another of the initial leaders. "We had delegates on every block and we knew that our organization would allow us to reach out to authorities."

As in many other squatter settlements (Merklen 1991; Cravino and Vommaro 2018), the comisión had the difficult task of assigning plots to each family and making sure the layout followed a nascent grid. They did this to avoid the risk of their new settlement resembling a villa (or slum)—an urban form seen by residents and outsiders alike as the opposite of order and progress. "If we were not there," a leader recollects, "this would have been a slum because it was a big mess.... [W]e needed to make sure that areas were reserved for common public spaces, so we had to relocate some settlers. It was hard."

During the early months, problems kept cropping up: Eviction threats were frequent, the "flooding almost covered us all up," and there were logistical issues in manning the many soup kitchens. However, the comisión "remained together ... [as] a very tight group." Osvaldo remembers that "the comisión worked very well. We organized the communal kitchens, we got to demarcate the plots, we got water pumps [they were later stolen], we got the local school, the water, the electricity. We did good work." Pedro, another leader, recalls that a high-level state official—with whom they usually negotiated access to "social aid" programs—threw a wrench into the association between "leftists" and "Peronists." Let's pay close attention to the following recollection of the backstage negotiations between comisión members and state authorities. It reveals how politics, which early on served to aggregate the interests of those seeking land and housing, begins to break up poor people's initial solidarity:

> One day, while we were all flooded and working hard to keep the water out, we got a call from La Plata [the seat of the state government]. We went and we saw that X [the state minister who belongs to the Peronist party] was in the mesa negociadora. He looked at me and he then looked at Manuel [a left-wing leader] and told him, "I don't want to talk to you. . . . I am only going to speak with Pedro and with other members of the Peronist party." The minister is a son of a bitch. He turned around, putting his back to Manuel, and told me: "We don't want a big mess. We want you to make progress, we are going to give you as many hands as we can." That's how we got five hundred welfare subsidies.

It is important to highlight that the story is retold by a leader who is an ally of the minister, not his political enemy. The term "son of a bitch" is meant to denote the minister's political savvy, not his moral caliber. The minister excluded Manuel from that negotiation—and, by extension, the people he represented—because, according to Pedro, he "wasn't part of his people. Manuel was a leftist, a combative one."

What looks like a "divide and conquer" logic is also an (ultimately successful) attempt by a high-level official to become the political sponsor of the grassroots organization. Speaking to some but not to others (because they are seen as rabble-rousers—quilomberos, in the local jargon), and giving welfare handouts to some but not others, is a way of keeping their collective action under the state's tutelage—what Charles Tilly (2006) calls a form of protest patronized by authorities. In this scenario, those partaking in collective action enjoy low levels of autonomy from state officials. This patronage is built around the provision of material resources and does not prevent local mobilization. As Pedro puts it: "From that meeting on, we got subsidies to share.

Later, the municipal government stopped meeting our demands and we began to mobilize. We organized ten or twelve rallies at the municipal building."

Leaders and residents remember the many times they marched the nine kilometers from the settlement to the seat of the municipal government. They also recall the many road blockades they manned to make claims for water and many other infrastructural improvements. Pedro summarizes the interactions between leaders of the squatter organization and state authorities:

> They [state officials] were lying to us and they thought we wouldn't protest because we were working with politicians. We decided that we would blockade traffic to make our claims heard. We blockaded the road for three days. We were unbeatable. The minister then called us and asked us to let the traffic go. We told him that we would stop protesting once the public works [to avoid flooding] began. He organized a meeting and we signed an agreement. Only then did we lift the roadblock. Thanks to our protest they began to work. And we kept at it.

The Hands of the State

Those initial years were marked by frequent and massive mobilizations—rallies, road blockades, and negotiations both between residents and the squatters' leaders and between those leaders and state officials. Looking at contention from the top down, focusing on its public dimension and its transgressive tactics, one would think that mobilizations in the streets were carried out in overt opposition to established authorities. But if we look closer, if we pay attention to what organizers said and did, we see that some state actors fomented squatters' contentious actions in order to accumulate political capital and win disputes that were taking place inside the government. Let's hear from another grassroots leader. He illustrates the workings of the many "hands of the state" (Morgan and Orloff 2017) during a patronized protest.

> We brought news from the state government to the settlers. We negotiated with state officials and informed residents. If officials didn't deliver, they knew we would make a big mess ["íbamos a hacer quilombo"], rally people at the government palace. One day we took almost every La Matera resident there. We didn't have buses to bring them. And they had promised us buses. There should have been fifty buses [for all the residents], and they sent us only seven or eight. It was a mess. We didn't know what to do. Women ended up going in a truck that the Welfare Ministry sent to bring food to the communal kitchens.

Curious about his comment that a state agency promised them buses to mobilize the neighbors for a protest, we asked him if we had heard correctly.

> Yes, because the minister wanted to pressure the governor. The number of people was incredible. The following month we protested again. And we mobilized all the folks thanks to the minister. He told us: "Protest, come over to the government palace, put on the pressure, so that I can push the governor. I will send you the buses [so that you can bring the people]." That protest got us a lot of things.

We should not be surprised that many in the squatter settlement call this particular minister the "Godfather of La Matera." It is not in reference to rumors about his (never-proven) links with organized crime. When residents and local political brokers like Luis and Pocho talk about "the godfather," they are referring to the state official who "provided more solutions to the neighborhood.... He is the one who gave us the most amount of things." This godfather asked them to put pressure on the governor and other state officials through transgressive and disruptive collective actions. We should also not be surprised when we learn that the resources needed for collective action (from buses to food) were coming from the state—something that occurs with regularity in many an episode of popular belligerence (Auyero, Lapegna, and Poma 2009).

The reconstruction of the first days of the occupation not only illustrates the relationship between the logic of patronage and the logic of collective protest, but also reminds us that the state is far from being a unified entity. The state is a space of struggles (Bourdieu 2020; Wacquant 2022). The history of the occupation also demonstrates something that has not been sufficiently analyzed by those who have studied the state as a bureaucratic field: The internal disputes in the field (exemplified in the story of the "pressure" that the minister wanted to exert on the governor) are intimately related to the struggles outside of it (illustrated by the protest that the organizers of the land occupation carried out against state authorities). It is important to take these disputes into account because they highlight how often the outcomes of collective action (in this case, successfully obtaining a plot of land to live on, building a house, and starting a family) depend on exogenous dynamics.

3

PERSISTENCE STRATEGIES

In the task of making ends meet, most residents are hardworking bricoleurs. At the root of this incessant bricolage we find all sorts of informal networks at work. The poor rely on precarious and highly exploitative (formal and informal) jobs. They also rely on patronage and protest, along with always inadequate state aid, and intense participation in networks of reciprocal exchange that sometimes include illicit activities.

Let's start with some basic facts. As mentioned before, between the end of 2021 and the beginnings of 2022 we conducted 105 interviews in La Matera. Thirty-eight of our interviewees were unemployed at the time. Eighteen were working as employees—in commerce, domestic service, and construction. The rest were self-employed, doing odd jobs, and/or were recipients of a state-funded program. As mentioned in the introduction, soup kitchens, both private and publicly funded, were quite common throughout La Matera before the COVID-19 pandemic, and they became even more widespread after its onset. Children and some adults ate their lunch and sometimes even dinner in these comedores. After pandemic restrictions were put in place, residents stopped eating in soup kitchens and, instead, picked up their cooked meals or food rations from community centers and ate at home. Local schools also distributed food rations to their students and families. Local brokers and churches gave away mercadería (foodstuffs) they obtained through their contacts at the municipal and provincial administrations. Before, during, and after the pandemic, state assistance programs also helped residents make ends meet. The Asignación Universal por Hijo (AUH) provided families with USD $30 per child per month; the Tarjeta Alimentaria provided USD $28 per month to pregnant women and mothers of one child (and USD $42 to women with two or more children); and, since April 2020, the Ingreso Familiar de Emergencia (IFE) has offered each family USD $71 per month. Workers with formal employment did not receive the IFE.

This chapter takes a close look at the monthly budgets of a few families. Although the details may be particular to their cases, the many sources they rely on for food illustrate a pattern generalizable to the neighborhood. Going granular on the income and expenses of families allows us to see the individual and collective effort required to subsist at the bottom of the social hierarchy— effort that refutes any argument about passivity, lassitude, or lack of cultura del trabajo presumably generated by state welfare (Wacquant 2022; Fernández-Kelly 2015). A close look at income and expenses also shows where funds distributed by the state are sometimes put to use: Many poor families end up paying for the private education of their children in what amounts to an indirect subsidy to nonpublic schools.[1]

Vanesa (thirty) and Cristian (thirty-two) have been together for fifteen years and have three children: Melanie (fourteen), Uma (eight), and Byron (three). They live in a house that was built by the state and later passed on to them by Cristian's grandfather, Don Javier. Don Javier was one of La Matera's original settlers. As discussed in chapter 2, squatters participated in many rallies and road blockades to secure services and infrastructure. One of their demands was housing, and thanks to collective action, the government built a few units in the settlement. Vanesa and Cristian now own the house where they live. Although Vanesa's household does not need to cover the cost of a mortgage or rent, they still struggle to make ends meet. Cristian works at a slaughterhouse an hour away from home and makes approximately USD $190 per month.[2]

Cristian has an extensive, if checkered, labor trajectory. His current job at the slaughterhouse is his first "trabajo en blanco," as he puts it, that is, a position with all the protections of a formal job. "My uncle got me this job. I really like it here," he tells us. "I started in the offal section, but then I moved to the actual slaughter. . . . At the beginning it was hard to kill animals, but you get used to it."

During his first eight months at the slaughterhouse, Cristian worked "en negro" (that is, not formalized). He was quite used to work without a regular wage, employment benefits such as health insurance, paid vacations, severance, paid sick leave, or advance notice of dismissal. Working "informally" had been his primary experience since getting his first job, through a cousin, as a construction worker at the age of sixteen. Before this first "real job," Cristian used to scavenge for bottles, copper, and aluminum: "I grabbed everything. There used to be a lot of abandoned cars in the nearby creek, and I took everything I could from them."

After an eighteen-month-long stint as a construction worker, he worked at a glass factory, at a business fixing air conditioners, at a printing workshop, at a firm that set up stages for shows ("that job was irregular, but good, they give you a lot of food"), and at a tannery. At this last job, he was fired a few days before his three-month trial period ended, when he was supposed to become formalized. His worst job, "by far, was at the glass factory. I cut my foot disposing bottles in a huge pile of broken glass. I missed one day of work because I had to go to the hospital and when I came back I was fired. . . . They didn't even pay me for the day I was in the hospital."

Material hardship has been a constant in Cristian's life. Money was always scarce. But, he reflects, he "never gave up." Every time he lost a job, he would go out with a friend of his to mow lawns and trim trees. ("When that happens, in the street, it's a real struggle. You don't make enough money. . . . Homeowners bargain with you a lot.")

Vanesa receives two monthly payments from state-sponsored aid programs: The first payment is USD $71 for their three children, and the second is USD $6 for food. Thus, roughly a third of the household income comes from state sources.[3] Without state welfare, their subsistence would be even more arduous ("I get paid every two weeks," says Cristian, "and a few days after I receive the paycheck, I have no more money. You buy food, diapers, and milk for the kids and the money is gone"). However, as we will see, state aid covers only a part of their expenses.

Vanesa cleans her grandmother Catalina's home twice per month—for which she receives USD $4–$5 for two hours of work. Every two weeks, Elena, Cristian's aunt, provides them with milk, noodles, polenta, rice, and corn oil. Elena works at a state-funded local soup kitchen where she receives food, which she then passes on to Vanesa and Cristian. Elena "has a lot of stuff and she shares," Vanesa tells us. Elena is not the only one who helps them make ends meet. Like most of the families we spoke with, Vanesa and Cristian's household is part of an extensive network of intensive exchange. Twice a week,

Vanesa helps her brother Fernando with the sale of clothing he buys in bulk in the city. Fernando often loans her money to buy clothes for the children, and he also helps her with food: "I only buy oranges because they are always on sale. If you come over and see apples or bananas, it's because Fernando came by. I ask him to buy me some potatoes, but he also buys fruit for us," says Vanesa. Once or twice a week, Vanesa also helps her mother, Rosana, who owns a small bakery, in exchange for pizza dough and cookies for the kids. Rosana also reciprocates with clothes and sneakers for Vanesa's children. During the pandemic, Vanesa relied on family members to obtain food. With a portion of the cash Cristian brings home every two weeks, she runs a little store in front of her house where she sells toiletries and cleaning products. She makes an average of USD $2 a day, which she spends on meals for the family: "What I earn, I spend on food. We don't eat too much meat. We eat mainly chicken and noodles... every now and then I make a little more and I buy milanesas."

Along with food, recurrent expenses include paying for internet, cell phones, the gas canister to cook, and the parochial school their children attend—arguably the most important expense aside from food. For perspective, slightly over 10 percent of their income goes to tuition (roughly USD $30 per month). As of February 2021, they owe USD $235 to the school, a debt they make small payments toward each time Vanesa receives her welfare check. We highlight this point because Vanesa and many of the neighbors we interviewed use their welfare payments to cover the cost of their children's education. People like Vanesa and Cristian deposit their hopes for social mobility in education—if not their own, then for that of their children. State aid is thus a component in poor people's strategies not just to stay afloat but also in their aims to thrive. State aid thus contributes to both simple and expanded reproduction.

"To be honest, we never go hungry," Blanca (fifty-two), Vanesa's aunt, tells us. "We might not have all the main dishes, we do not buy milanesas, a good chicken or barbecue like others, but a stew, noodles with tomato sauce... those things I tried to cook every day. But today I can't cook because I am out of gas." It's been ten years since her husband died, and she lives with her thirteen-year-old son and her two granddaughters (Luna and Valentina), who moved in with her after their mother, Eliana, was imprisoned (details of this case are in chapter 6). Blanca used to work at a print shop, packing magazines for delivery, but had to quit her job a year before we interviewed her because of high blood pressure. Blanca's family income is much less than Vanesa's. She received USD $60 a month from the AUH, and USD $7 house-cleaning for Catalina, who, knowing about her precarious living conditions, pays her more than Vanesa. Most of Blanca's income comes from the state.

"I would love to go back in time, when I was working and managing my own money. *Not having to think about it all the time*," Blanca says (emphasis added). Now, she must always think about how to pull together her family's basic needs from various sources. She receives foodstuffs from the school Luna and Valentina attend: noodles, tomato sauce, rice, corn oil. "Sometimes they give you sugar, jelly. They never give meat, but sometimes they give you a chicken." Blanca has fewer expenses than Vanesa but also participates in a strong exchange network—she helps Fernando sell clothes and she assists Rosana at the bakery, and in exchange she receives food and clothing for the children: "Although I do not go around crying or complaining, they know about my situation and they lend a hand."

Blanca's network includes Lili, a local political broker who often provides milk, flour, corn oil, noodles, rice, oats, and "some cans that read 'pan de carne'" (spam). Her network also includes Pocho, the powerful local broker featured in chapter 4. To foreshadow some of the elements that define the resident-broker relationship that will soon occupy our attention, let us cite a conversation (edited for clarity) we had with Blanca—including the dialogues she imagined she would like to have with the local broker:

> I want to ask Pocho for a welfare subsidy. I want to see if he can get me into one of those [state-funded] cooperatives. He knows me well. I am also going to ask Lili. I have time, other than cleaning the house and taking care of the kids, I have nothing to do. If she needs something, I can do it. But I need a subsidy. If Pocho gets me a job at a cooperative but tells me to give him part of what I make there, it's fine. If he tells me, "I signed you up but you don't have to come and work, just give me a part of the subsidy," that's also fine with me. Pocho and Lili make those kinds of arrangements. They have twenty people working like that and they make an income for themselves.

It is not our intention to use Blanca's testimony to criticize brokers' actions. In chapter 4 we will see how extensive these sorts of "arrangements" are in La Matera and we will analyze the diverse ways in which residents evaluate their actions. What we want to emphasize here is that Blanca, like many of her neighbors, counts on brokers to make ends meet—political brokerage is part and parcel of subsistence strategies.

Gustavo (forty-seven) and Olga (forty-five) live with their daughter, Jazmín (seven), a block away from La Matera's public school and main plaza. Their other four grown-up sons are living on their own a few blocks from them. Their youngest son, Franco (twenty-two), built his house in the front part of their lot, where he lives with his partner, Camila (twenty), and their four-year-old daughter. Gustavo and Olga inhabit one of the houses that, after much collective protest, the government built between 2009 and 2011. In 2021, with the roughly USD $200 Olga received from Acompañar, a federal welfare program, they repainted the bedrooms, dining room, and kitchen. The interior of their home now displays vivid violet, yellow, and green colors.[4]

Gustavo is one of the original settlers: "I've been here since La Matera was founded.... I was living a few blocks away. One day, I saw people walking by with the metal sheets and pieces of wood, and, together with my brother, I joined them." Each of them got a plot of land. Like most of the first residents, he sees a lot of improvement in the neighborhood, though public safety is still a serious concern for him. He was robbed four times in the past few years, twice at gunpoint. "To take the bus, I have to cross the bridge early in the morning, and los pibes just surprise you ... they come out of nowhere." He was never hurt during any of these robberies, but he tells us that he is always afraid when coming back from work at night or when leaving early in the morning: "Last time, the robber aimed his gun at me, but after I gave him my wallet I asked him if he could give me back the ID, the SUBE [a transport ticket], and the debit card. And he threw them to me. I only had a few pesos for my sandwich. I think he recognized me. I've been living in the area since I was born.... Everybody knows me, I have lots of friends here."

Gustavo has been working since he was thirteen. He started as a helper at a local grocery store. He worked from 4 a.m. to 10 a.m. and then attended high school at noon. Six months after he started working, he quit school: "I couldn't do it, it was too much.... I couldn't manage my time, it was too tiring." After that first job he was a construction worker, a stevedore at the port, and a tree cutter and brush collector for the municipal government. His worst job, he says, was at the Buenos Aires Central Market: "I had to load and unload sacks of potatoes.... I came back at midnight and had to leave again at 4 a.m. Some days I couldn't even sleep because of back pain.... I got paid by the sack, I had to earn my living day by day ... not like nowadays." Like thousands of other Argentines, he lost his job in 2001—by then he was working at a printing shop. He collected welfare for a year, during which time he and his wife ate at a local soup kitchen.

For the last fifteen years, Gustavo has been working at a transportation company—loading and unloading appliances and doing deliveries. Different from most residents in La Matera we spoke with, Gustavo has what Argentines call a trabajo en blanco, a formal job with health benefits. His own description of a typical day at work, however, speaks about a highly flexible and arbitrary schedule—his job actually lacks the protections afforded by formal employment, which include, prominent among them, defined work hours and workdays. "We work, at least eight hours a day . . . eight hours minimum. Sometimes we work on Saturdays. Other times the boss asks us to stay for another four or five hours." For this second shift, he does not receive overtime pay—only extra cash for the bus and food (called viáticos). The additional days and hours are at the company's discretion, and he tells us it is impossible for him to anticipate if and when he will work more than his mandatory eight-hour shift. Along with the viáticos, Gustavo makes some extra cash by informally selling the worn wooden pallets he uses for loading and unloading. Olga does not work full time but does odd jobs ("changas") once or twice a week at her cousin's local bakery, for which she receives approximately USD $5 a week.

As of August 2022, Gustavo makes between USD $400 and $500 a month. While he and Olga consider this a "good salary," they say that they never "quite make it" to the end of the month. "Don't get me wrong," says Olga, "we are tight, but we eat what we want. . . . If we want a milanesa, we can get a milanesa." Gustavo adds, as if to show that these are indeed better times than most in the past, "When I was working at the printing shop we ate eggs with rice. Nowadays, although our budget is tight, we indulge in certain things . . . for example, this week we are saving to buy some short ribs" ("estamos ahorrando para una tira de asado").

Although they "indulge," money is always scarce. Every month, Gustavo asks for an advance (a vale) from his employer. "Roughly around the twentieth of the month, we run out of money and I ask for a vale of $20,000 [USD $70]. I do it two or three times a month." Most of his and Olga's income goes to food and to pay for the washing machine they bought a year ago. At the beginning of the pandemic, they canceled their two credit cards because they "don't like to get indebted. . . . We sold our car too, so that's one expense less." With the money they both earn they usually help their son Franco with his family's monthly expenses—he has an informal job in construction where he makes USD $200 a month.

Although they want to avoid debt, like many others they owed money to the parochial school their daughter, Jazmín, attends. Early in the pandemic, Olga wanted Jazmín to stay in that school and proposed a payment plan to cancel their debt. But the school told her that they wanted the entire amount she owed ($45,000, at the time, USD $1,000) for Jazmín to be rematriculated. Much to their chagrin, they decided to transfer her to a less expensive school: "I was furious because they won't allow us to pay in installments," Olga says.

As Sofía is leaving their house after the last interview, Franco, their youngest son, comes out of his house and offers her a marijuana plant. "Take it, it will grow," he says. As Sofía declines the offer, Olga says, "I told him that he will need to build a fence. I don't want people who walk by to see the plants. Not sure how much money you can make out of it, but I heard it's quite a bit."

Each marijuana plant can produce between one kilogram (if the plant is outside, in the ground) and six hundred grams (if inside, in a pot), Eduardo tells us, adding, "You can make two joints for every gram. . . . Each joint goes for $800 [USD $3]. My last plant produced a whole kilogram, I didn't know what to do with all the weed. . . . I gave away a lot of it." Eduardo is forty-one and has a stable job at the local municipality. It doesn't pay much (roughly USD $400 a month). He supplements his income selling and trading marijuana, which he has been growing for ten years. After expenses (seeds, soil, herbicides, humidifier, etc.), he estimates that he could make roughly USD $3,200 per year. But he does not sell all of what his plant produces. He keeps some for personal use, he makes oil (used by Nora, his wife who suffers from epilepsy), and he trades much of it with friends and neighbors: "I exchange it for cleaning products, for video games, and sometimes for some jobs I need done. If I need someone to do plumbing, or to fix the AC, or to repair the roof . . . I pay them with weed." Eduardo also gifts some of it to family and friends, especially to those friends who "know much more about marijuana than I do and give me advice on how to take care of the plant and how to improve the quality." Weed, like many other material resources that circulate between friends and relatives, serves to oil the social relationships that help the poor subsist.

Gustavo and Olga remind us about the analytic advantages of inspecting strategies not only synchronically but also diachronically. Even though most of their current expenses are covered by the salary Gustavo earns in his highly exploitative job, once we expand the scope beyond the present, we see that grassroots collective action, state welfare, and networks of kin and friends also figure prominently in their household subsistence. They obtained their land and their house, thanks to transgressive collective action, and public aid helped them navigate a period of joblessness, while local soup kitchens provided sustenance when, during the early 2000s, they had no income. Kin and neighbors are also important: Olga makes extra money working for her cousin, and she found out about the Acompañar welfare program from her neighbors, who assured her it was safe to apply because, they said, there were few controls over the requirements and the use of the funds. Other occasional cash-earning activities (some informal, like the selling of the wooden pallets; others illicit, like the marijuana Franco will soon commercialize) complete the diverse methods through which Gustavo's family seeks to stay afloat and improve their lives.

Precarious exploitation is the process that best captures the relationship between the marginalized and the labor market.[5] The jobs that Gustavo, Cristian, and most of the people we spoke to over the years of our fieldwork carry out are not only highly exploitative (meaning that their effort receives much less reward than the value it contributes) but also insecure, intermittent, and (central to our analysis) not completely reliable for making ends meet.[6]

In her current strategies, Vanesa combines work, state welfare, and mutual aid. In Blanca's case, state welfare and reciprocity are mixed with direct food assistance and what in chapter 4 we will call *clientelist arrangements*. The families of Vanesa, Blanca, and Gustavo illustrate the main ways in which the urban poor stay afloat and seek to get ahead and how their strategies intertwine with state and party politics.

Just like Blanca, Sofía remembers spending much of her time thinking about "making it to the end of the month." The following reflection reiterates the dogged blending of sources of monetary and in-kind income, and it also sheds light on the constant attention that she has paid to every detail of her budget since early in her life, as well as the endless juggling she does to cover her expenses. Throughout our fieldwork, Sofía's sensibility (produced by an early socialization dominated by material scarcity) served us to pay meticulous attention to, and understand the apparently trivial details of, household budgets.

Reflection #2

Mom and Dad split up when I was eight years old. Although my father gave us the allowance every month in a timely manner, the money was never enough. My brother, who was four years old at the time, still remembers how during the last days of each month we would go to sleep after dining on only maté with bread—or maybe a cookie—because we no longer had money. We both quickly adapted to the situation. There was no money, we didn't ask for anything. Once a month, every time my mom collected her welfare check, she bought something for each of us. It was a reward for having spent sometimes more than five hours standing in exhausting queues under the sun to get the welfare check. The rewards were, almost always, food. We went to Coto [the supermarket] and bought the most expensive yogurts, those with colored cereals or chocolate chips. Sometimes my brother would drive my mom crazy to buy him a toy. But, even though he was six years old, he already knew we had no money. So, he would take a toy that he liked and ask my mom: "Is this too expensive, Mom?"

With my dad we behaved differently. We always asked him for the most expensive things because he did have a good job [truck driver]. My mom hardly ever bought us sneakers, and when she did, we were careful to pick the ones she could afford. Even though my dad tried to persuade us to choose secondhand ones (which were cheaper), we always chose the most expensive ones. We didn't even look at the price. When I was nine and my brother was five, he bought each of us a pair. Mine were pink, and a good brand. They lasted me until they did not fit me anymore. The day he bought them, right before I got out of his car, my dad told me that he was going to deduct the cost of the shoes from the monthly allowance he gave my mom. Now that I think about it, and knowing my dad, maybe it was one of the jokes he usually makes. But I genuinely believed him at the time. The following month, we were returning from my grandparents' house and I was telling my mom that my dad had probably already left the money at our house and I reminded her that he was going to leave us less than usual because of the shoe expense. I never forgot that strong anguish I felt knowing that, because of our sneakers, we were going to have less money for the rest of the month (I also remember we were late on our electricity bill). When we got to my house, we saw that the money was on the table. I counted it and told my mom, "Mom! He did not deduct the money from us. Everything is here!!!" We were so happy. I have never forgotten that feeling. I felt it every time we went to buy the yogurts, every time my mother got her salary (she later got a regular job) and took us to eat pizza downtown and bought us clothes at the fair. I still remember those moments in which, for a tiny second, money was not an issue. I never forgot about that.

During one of the first interviews I conducted for this book, Lucas told me how ashamed he was when he had to line up with his mom to pick up foodstuffs. "The queue was a block long. It was ugly." Over these years of research, many people described the food they received from this or that program. But Lucas was the first who talked about being ashamed, feeling uncomfortable, almost undignified. I felt that way too, waiting in line for a welfare check.

When I was a kid I never felt that my friends were as worried about money as I was. Maybe it was because I had to mediate between Mom and Dad. He gave me the money so that I passed it to her and always told me how much money it was, to avoid misunderstandings.

Once a month, he would give us $100 for our expenses. I would put that money into my piggy bank. When my mom and I ran out of money, we use whatever was left in the piggy bank. I was only eight and always worried that my mom would run out of money. I'm twenty-four now and that feeling has never left me.

When I started college, I received the PROGRESAR [a state program for university students]. At that time I got $720 a month. That money was enough to buy photocopies, pay for the bus, and every now and then have a coffee. The most important benefit of the PROGRESAR was the discount I receive to travel with the SUBE. During the first year, college was close to home (in Avellaneda), but the second year I had to travel to the city of Buenos Aires. That was much more expensive— four buses a day, four times a week. I was worried about my classes, and about the money, all the time. In 2018, the government set up a new limit for the beneficiaries of PROGRESAR and I lost access to it. My dad's salary was above the new limit. I remember receiving the email with the bad news while I was in class and immediately forwarded it to my dad. I was so pissed at him. He gave me more money per month but it still wasn't enough. I never asked my mom for more money. I don't know how I managed that year but I do remember I never asked her. The following term, I chose classes so that I only had to attend three times a week—and saved money. I stopped buying photocopies, began to read straight from the computer. I brought food from home so that I didn't have to buy anything. I remember leaving home at 7 a.m. and coming back at 9 p.m. Those were long days, but I didn't have many options (plus I did stay home more days a week and was able to catch up with the readings). Sometimes I had breakfast at home and one snack during the day, or maybe some fruit I would bring from home. My mom

FIGURE 3.1. A male scavenger pushing his cart through the streets of the squatter settlement.

FIGURE 3.2. On a street littered with garbage, a boy with a horse is collecting garbage.

was always waiting for me with dinner ready. I never had money to buy lunch or dinner in college. I counted every penny I had and, occasionally, I would buy something sweet to avoid the headaches I got when I was hungry.

Diego is forty-two years old. He was born and raised in El Tala, two blocks away from one of the bridges that crosses into La Matera. He still lives in the house where he was born—his grandmother was a midwife. Both of his parents passed away a few years ago, and he now lives by himself. Diego worked since he was a kid, but he never held a formal job. For many years, he worked at a sweatshop, manufacturing the soles of shoes, boots, and sandals. He then moved to a car-battery factory and, after a few years there, he worked at a glass factory. When the pandemic hit, he was fired and couldn't get a job for a while. His niece helped him to apply for the IFE (Emergency Family Income—a lump sum distributed by the federal government during the pandemic). The 10,000 pesos came in handy. He bought a cart and started collecting cardboard, glass, scrap metal, and plastic to sell (see figures 3.1 and 3.2). "Copper is the best thing. . . . You can now sell a kilogram of copper for $1,700 [USD $6 as of October 2022]. Sometimes people change the electrical installations at home, and I get a lot of copper. I pile it up, and once I have a kilogram, I sell it." He works Monday to Friday from 8 a.m. to 2 or 3 p.m. "I go around everywhere with my cart. I stop for lunch and then work a few more hours until the wholesaler closes." He estimates he makes USD $5 a day. "That is enough for me to eat and, I won't deny it, to have one or two drinks." He tells us that he wishes he could get a better job: "But I am forty-two, and I doubt anybody is going to hire me. But I really wish I could get a job that pays more than this one."

Individual and Collective Hope

Although unstable and perilous, daily life at the urban margins has its regularities: unpaved streets, recurrent flooding, nonexistent sewers, lack of money (and the surrounding violence that will be the topic of later chapters). This pervasive scarcity and uncertainty present objective chances and obstacles to those at the bottom of the social order—it is worth remembering that opportunities to get a good job, acquire college credentials, or avoid being assaulted are not equally distributed in social and physical space. Subjective hopes—what subjects think and feel about what the future holds for them—*tend* to adjust, according to Pierre Bourdieu, to these objective regularities. This "adjustment" is a propensity, not an a priori conclusion, but something that has to be investigated—practical expectations and hopes do not always correspond to the immanent tendencies of the social world.

What do the voices and, more importantly, the practices of the residents of La Matera tell us about what they believe is to come and about their possibilities to act on that future? The ambition to intervene in the future is, again according to Bourdieu, related to the actual power to control that future—which means, first of all, to have the ability to control the present. In this and the chapters that follow, we see that this capacity, this power, is very limited: What happens both in the streets and inside homes makes people live at the mercy of what each day brings. However, and contrary to what we might suppose, there is a certain hope, a belief in a better future, that still finds some roots in the rough terrain of everyday life in the settlement.

We are not denying the fact that conditions of existence impose constraints and guide the aspirations of residents. But the latter are also shaped by discourses and practices that are exogenous to that social and geographic space. While the urban poor have seen blows to the public education system (which used to be outstanding in the region: see Tenti Fanfani 2021) and experienced the consequences of fragmented and chaotic housing policy, the value of education as a way of seeking material progress and the right to decent housing are still part of their symbolic repertoire—that is, their system of beliefs and dispositions. Only by taking these enduring beliefs into account can we understand why, despite the fact that more than 80 percent of young people between twenty and twenty-four in La Matera have fewer than twelve years of schooling (a very high percentage compared to other popular neighborhoods and therefore an indicator of high educational exclusion), many of our interviewees continue to believe in formal education as a means of improvement for themselves and for their sons and daughters, and act accordingly. Soledad (twenty-eight) tells us that one day she took her daughter to work in order to "teach her what it was like to work and not finish school." Rosalía (forty) attends night classes to complete primary school—"the teacher is very patient with me. I go slowly. One of the teachers congratulated me, saying: 'You finally got school!' I like it. It sometimes gets difficult but I manage." Alejandra (fifty-seven) puts great care in completing the homework that is assigned to her in the adult school. Ana (twenty-seven) tells us that she wanted to be a public notary, and she had started to attend college but had to quit when she got pregnant. She also tells us that her brother-in-law was studying law but had to drop out "because he didn't have the time between study and work.... They also robbed him every time he left the neighborhood; they stole his books, photocopies, everything... he got tired." Ana describes the economic difficulties that prevent her from carrying out her educational aspirations: "When you are poor and want to study, you have many difficulties, many obstacles. Yesterday on TV they told about a boy who sold churros to pay for the photocopies. Now it is impossible; before you could pay for copies with one or two pesos. My brother-in-law received the PROGRESAR but couldn't do much with it. He didn't even have enough money to pay for photocopies: he had to quit."

Confidence in education as a path toward socioeconomic progress is certainly not a monolithic belief. But the practices of many of the families with whom we interacted during these two years (the pecuniary effort they make to send their daughters and sons to a parochial school that they consider superior to public school, their diligence during the pandemic in making sure these children did their homework virtually, despite the lack of personal computers and poor connectivity, etc.) indicate a fairly common shared vision. Sofía's own reflection illustrates the presence of different visions about the value of education within a family and, at the same time, the enduring belief in the value of education (and the actions associated with this belief).

Reflection #3

During the first three years of elementary school, I attended the José Hernández private school near my home. When my parents separated, I had to change schools because my mother couldn't afford the tuition. She transferred me to the Madre Teresa school, a Catholic school that was even closer to my house. The tuition was much cheaper. My dad never cared about our education; my mom usually says that if it had been up to him we would have attended any public school. For her, however, it was always very important that we study in a good school—for her, that meant a private school. She dropped out of school when she was thirteen and she didn't want the same for us. To get a vacancy in the new school, families used to queue very early with tents on the streets to protect themselves from the sun and rain. Since it was a good school and was not very expensive, the queue used to go around the whole block.

In chapter 8 we will see how this belief in education as a tool for individual improvement is expressed in a very powerful way in the work that a group of women carry out in a community center. They invest a good part of their time, and find gratification, in their work as educators.

Hope is not only expressed in aspirations for individual improvement. An important indicator of the existence of a "collective hope" (Braithwaite 2004) is the collaboration expressed in the joint undertaking of squatting land and building neighborhood infrastructure. This enterprise (which, as we described, involved organization and mobilization) illustrates the existence of that hope and also an unquestioned consensus about the right of the poor to their own land and housing—the opposite of the "compliance with dispossession" that Michael Levien describes so insightfully in the case of India (2018). How the inhabitants account for the occupation of public lands, the cooperative construction of infrastructure, and the demand for basic services demonstrates that they believe in a social right that needs to be wrested through collective and contentious effort.

The ordinary functioning of grassroots politics in La Matera also has its regularities: electoral times, times in which "politicians disappear," rumors about economic benefits obtained by this or that politician, and so on. The visions and divisions that politics generates, the consensus and dissent that it produces, constitute the subject of chapter 4.

4

BROKERS AND
THEIR FOLLOWERS

In chapter 1, we mentioned the foundational work of Larissa Lomnitz in Cerrada del Cóndor, a destitute shantytown of about two hundred households on Mexico City's periphery. According to Lomnitz, in order to subsist, those at the margins counted on social resources—kin and friend networks that produced social solidarity. Networks of reciprocal exchange were central in the strategies of the urban poor—as they could not count on state aid to make ends meet. In point of fact, residents of Cerrada del Cóndor lacked contacts with (or knowledge of) state actors. According to Lomnitz, other poor neighborhoods did have contacts with the state through caciques—intermediaries between those at the margins and "modern urban society." In other areas, in Mexico and throughout Latin America, these brokers played (and, as we read in the vast literature on the subject and we will see shortly in La Matera, still play) a fundamental role in poor people's strategies.

That was the case of the shantytown in which one of us carried out the fieldwork that served as the empirical basis for the book *Poor People's Politics*. In a context of growing unemployment and poverty in mid-1990s Argentina, the residents of Villa Paraíso relied on punteros políticos (as local brokers were known at the time) to solve daily problems (access to food, medicine, etc.). This personalized problem-solving served brokers to build and accumulate political capital. *Poor People's Politics* examined the dynamics of this political arrangement between patrons, brokers, and so-called clients while, at the same time, questioning the utility of the very notion of "political clientelism" because of its unilateral emphasis on control and manipulation.

The widespread lack of research on patrons, brokers, and clients in Argentina—which was noted in that book and provided one of its ethnographic warrants—is no longer such. Clientelism and machine politics became the objects of a number of case studies (Calvo and Murillo 2004; Stokes 2005; Weitz-Shapiro 2014; Nichter 2008; Vommaro and Combes 2016). As the studies of this topic have multiplied, so has the examination of poor people's various strategies (reviewed in chapter 1). In order to obtain state aid, to get foodstuffs to feed their families, to fund a soup kitchen, to build a neighborhood school or a health center, to pave or light their streets, the poor sometimes attend a rally, other times blockade a road, and other times march to the municipal building. Many times, they carry out a combination of these (more or less transgressive) protests. Other times, those in need establish a personal (more or less coercive) relationship with a broker. Most of the time, they engage in both individual and collective actions.

The brokers examined in *Poor People's Politics* didn't engage in disruptive contention. Those acting today, like the broker who is the empirical focus of this chapter, combine and simultaneously modify diverse logics of action. Just like the "clients," brokers are also bricoleurs. They fuse various strategies: negotiating with an official, intimidating ("apriete") officials, organizing road blockades, mobilizing followers to attend a partisan rally, or withholding such mobilization when they need to express disapproval for this or that politician. They do all these things to make themselves heard, to gain or defend positions in the local political field while simultaneously attending to their followers' pressing needs and demands. This chapter examines the relationships between a broker named Pocho, his closest followers, and other residents. But, first, let us take a brief detour through the recent scholarly literature on the topic.

Although diverging in methodology, analytic depth, level of analysis, and empirical focus, a typical (more or less explicit) *micro-sociological* sequence can be extracted from most accounts of political clientelism: During electoral campaigns, patrons, through their brokers, distribute goods and services to residents of typically poor communities who, in exchange, give support (in the form of attendance at rallies, for example) and votes. In this process of exchange, citizens become "political clients." While agreeing on "where the (clientelist) action is" (i.e., elections), explanations of clients' behavior diverge: Some point to the existence of a norm of reciprocity driving their actions (e.g., Lawson and Greene 2011) while others highlight rational calculations (e.g., Stokes 2005). When brokers fail to deliver, so most accounts go, clients quit the relationship either because the balance of reciprocity becomes skewed or because it is more rational to pursue other ways of satisfying their interests. What happens between elections when the need to obtain votes vanishes, and what accounts for the enigmatic behavior of those clients who stay in patronage relationships despite brokers' failures to deliver or when better opportunities for solving daily problems present themselves, remains outside the purview of most current studies of contemporary political clientelism.

The abundant recent body of work on clientelist politics expresses a three-decade-long shift away from what, in a now-classic piece, Alex Weingrod called an "anthropological focus" toward a "political science" one. The anthropological perspective on patronage focused on a "particular kind of interpersonal relationship," with an emphasis on inequality and reciprocity. As Weingrod (1977, 324) put it, "The study of patronage as phrased by anthropologists [was] the analysis of how persons of unequal authority, yet linked through ties of interest and friendship, manipulate their relationships in order to attain their ends." While the anthropological perspective examined patronage as a type of social relationship, the new and now-dominant political science approach focuses on a "feature of government" or a characteristic of a political party. As Weingrod (1977, 324) presciently anticipated it, "In political science studies of patronage the key terms are 'bosses' and 'political machines,' or merit versus political appointments. Patronage from this perspective is therefore largely the study of how political party leaders seek to turn public institutions and public resources to their own ends, and how favors of various kinds are exchanged for votes."[1]

This shift of analytical emphasis and empirical focus came at a cost. Scholarship won in precision and calibration—note, for example, the mathematical formulations in Stokes et al. (2013)—while, or probably because, it (a) limited the scope of analysis to elections, (b) narrowed the center of attention to vote buying and turnout buying, and (c) created a strict division between clients and brokers (necessitated by formal modeling).

As a result of their (now almost) exclusive focus on exchanges (and attendant incentives and calculations) taking place before and during elections, most studies tend to disregard an aspect of clientelism first highlighted by anthropological research on the subject: its *embeddedness in everyday life*. As the focus on electoral times came to prevail, the *routine and personal* character of this "lopsided friendship"—as Julian Pitt-Rivers (1954, 23) famously characterized it—key to understanding and explaining the effectiveness and endurance of clientelism, receded to the point of becoming almost nonexistent. Extant scholarship not only suffers from an overwhelming focus on electoral times, but also is premised on a rigid dichotomy between clients and brokers. This strict separation overlooks the crucial role played by the broker's closest followers. These individuals, like Teresa described below, act as brokers' auxiliaries and are also the most loyal clients. Their behavior cannot be accounted for with the usual explanations of rational calculation or reciprocity.

Focusing almost exclusively on electoral times, most of the current scholarship loses sight of the everyday character of clientelism. Premised on a hard dichotomy between clients and brokers, extant scholarship neglects the key role (both structural and symbolic) played by the broker's closest followers. Emphasizing either reciprocity norms or rational calculations as reasons why clients behave as they do, most studies see the voluntaristic choices of individual clients as the mainspring of their actions, thereby disregarding the *dispositional and practical* aspects of clientelist politics.[2]

The one scholar who has best studied the subject in the Conurbano Bonaerense is Rodrigo Zarazaga (2014, 2017). In contrast to the reality described by Lomnitz in Mexico, Zarazaga (2017, 55) asserts that "in areas of high and concentrated poverty, the basic needs of the neighbors are many and the State responds to some of them through brokers' mediation. In this sense, *the neighborhood's brokers represent not the state's absence but its arbitrary presence*" (our emphasis). Brokers distribute a great diversity of resources: "municipal employment, state workfare programs, food, medicine, clothing, footwear, wheelchairs, coffins, school supplies, household appliances, bricks, zinc sheets, cash, marijuana and other illegal drugs. In general, the most coveted by the poorest followers are the jobs in the municipality and the workfare programs that ensure a monthly income" (56). According to Zarazaga, through this distribution, brokers "constitute a minimalist welfare state in areas of poverty. It is minimalist because resources are scarce and solutions are precarious" (50). Let us now delve into the actions and words of Pocho, one of the most prominent brokers in La Matera, a man loved by many and scorned by many others.

Gordo Amor

March 31, 2021, marks the twenty-first anniversary of La Matera. Pocho, the neighborhood's main political broker, wants to organize a massive celebration, but the COVID-19 pandemic thwarts big social gatherings. Instead, he is hanging commemorative banners and painting murals around the neighborhood. Twenty-one years have passed since he joined other Peronist party militants, activists from unemployed workers' organizations (known as piqueteros), and others from Catholic Church groups in the planned squatting of this roughly 2.4-square-kilometer suburban plot.

As we described in chapter 2, back in March 2000 La Matera was all "mud...an empty field." Today, La Matera has an elementary school, a kindergarten, a central square with a play set, a community center building, and more than a few paved streets. As mentioned, infrastructural needs still abound (floods are a recurrent issue, streetlights are scarce, garbage collection is intermittent at best), but most of the longtime residents and original squatters agree that "huge progress has been made." Many credit Pocho for the barrio's improvements.

Amalia, Pocho's current wife, takes pictures while he paints a mural that reads: "Happy Anniversary La Matera. March 31, 2000. March 31, 2021." Despite the heat, he is wearing a shirt and jeans. Under them, an electronic ankle bracelet monitors his movements. Accused of illicit drug trafficking, Pocho was arrested in March 2018 and spent two years in a jail in Greater Buenos Aires. In December 2020 he was released and is currently under the supervision of the prison system. At the time of this writing, he is still awaiting "su juicio"—his trial was first scheduled for May 2021 but, due to the COVID-19 pandemic, it was postponed until May 2022 and then postponed again.

When he is done with the mural, Pocho takes to social media. He posts on his Facebook page: "Hola compañeros. Today is La Matera's birthday. Twenty-one years of much sacrifice. With happiness and with sadness we got where we are today. Due to the pandemic, we cannot celebrate, but, God willing, we will next year. Take good care of yourselves, stay at home, a big hug...the organizing committee is always at the same place in case you have any questions. We will continue to work for our neighborhood." Dozens of comments express the support of his neighbors with hug and love emojis.

In La Matera, Pocho is admired by many yet also criticized by just as many. For many residents, he is a man who "gets things done." He is also a man with loyal followers and fierce detractors; a man who some believe is a drug dealer, others a tireless grassroots activist; a man who professes endless love for La

Matera and who complains that, sometimes, his love is not reciprocated. A father of six children, some say he has many unrecognized offspring in the area and more than one lover.

Most people in Buenos Aires would have trouble pointing to the location of La Matera (and most other marginalized neighborhoods) on a map, but they would be quick to pass judgment on the work of political brokers like Pocho—who are said to manipulate poor people and buy their votes. For La Matera's residents, on the contrary, who Pocho is, what he does, and how he does it are far from settled issues. Delving into the pragmatic possibilities of every-day poor people's politics in contemporary Buenos Aires, this chapter takes a close look at Pocho's actions and at what he says about himself and the neigh-borhood. It also dives into what his loyal followers and his opponents think and feel about him. Delving into the doings and sayings of a broker—from the perspective of his friends and his critics—aims to deepen our understanding of the role that politics plays in the working of subsistence strategies. Pocho il-lustrates how, when seeking to solve pressing problems, residents and brokers alike combine different forms of action: They resort to individualized solu-tions, offering state actors political allegiance in exchange for material support (what the scholarly literature calls "clientelist arrangements"), and/or they rely on (more or less disruptive) collective action. A detailed look at Pocho's ac-tions not only alerts us to this combination of patronage and protest but also sheds much-needed light on "the pervasiveness of horizontal abuse and lateral animosity" (Wacquant 2015, 265) at the urban margins—a reality "little stud-ied even by scholars of urban poverty and the working class because it con-travenes their inclination to valorize a disparaged segment of society" (265).

It was a cold day in August 2019. Between matés and biscuits, Teresa, a neighbor who coordinates one of the several soup kitchens in La Matera, gave us details about what she called Pocho's "tireless" political work on be-half of the barrio. She spoke about the workfare programs and welfare subsi-dies that he distributed among the neighbors, about his many followers, and about the rumors that circulated as to whether or not he was, in fact, a drug dealer—what residents would call a "transa."

"We are just good friends," Teresa said somewhat mischievously. A little later, her cell rang. Sofía glanced at the caller ID as it flashed on the screen; it read "Gordo Amor." It was Pocho, calling from jail. "He gets bored there," Te-resa smilingly told Sofía, "and he calls me to see how things are in the neigh-borhood." This was the first time Pocho talked to Sofía over WhatsApp. An hour and a half later, they hung up. Pocho promised Sofía they would talk again after Teresa vouched for her. Teresa told Pocho that Sofía was "a girl from the neighborhood and is writing a paper for the university about La Matera." Soon after his release from prison, in December 2020, Sofía met with Pocho for a three-hour-long interview. In the months that followed, they would meet a few more times. She twice joined him in his makeshift office, in the front of his house, while he was busy at work—listening to neighbors' complaints, registering them with a workfare program, and informing them about when and where they could obtain food. In March 2022, we conducted a long interview with him.

During dozens of interviews and informal conversations with residents, Pocho often comes up as a topic of debate, the subject of neighbors' scorn or praise. For example, in February 2021, with Pocho out and about, Sofía had this dialogue with her friends and neighbors Noelia and Romi. They told her about the "things" Pocho requested in exchange for his favors.

NOELIA: Romi, Sofía is doing research about La Matera, and I gave her a summary of who Pocho actually is. He is a womanizer. *Re-gato.* "I offer you this thing or a better position, but in exchange you..." Why do you think I won't even come close to him? I don't want anything to do with him. OK, Sofi, get your recorder ready [laughs]. Romi also knows him. Everybody at some point has depended on him, because in economic terms that is useful. You go to him and you ask him for a "plan" [a welfare subsidy, or access to a workfare program].

ROMINA: I once went to see him. I was renting and needed a house. He wanted me to be his woman if he was going to give me a house.

SOFÍA: How did he say it? Do you remember?

ROMINA: He told me "You need to give me some other thing" ["vos me tenés que dar otra cosa"]. And he checked me out ["me miró de arriba abajo"].... I told him thanks but no thanks.

NOELIA: He did that with many girls. They say that he does that to everybody.... Financially, it is useful. The guy will give you a job, or a place in a workfare program... but it's "come into my room first" ["pasá para el cuarto primero"]. It's like that. Many people ask him for stuff. But I will never go. I know how he is. [My husband] Dani and Pocho talk all the time. Dani would follow him because he was always promising stuff but then he wouldn't deliver. But Dani would still follow him like an idiot. He didn't have a job back then, so it was useful for him to follow Pocho. He attended so many rallies. Pocho wanted to have his soldiers; he always played with people, with the money, with their feelings. He was always promising things. That's why nobody likes him. And then there's the issue of all the women. You will find many that will say the same thing. He is a little Pandora's box.

We are not sure if Pocho engaged, as the criminal accusation says, in selling illicit drugs or if the drugs were planted by the law enforcement officers themselves, a fairly widespread practice among the Buenos Aires police (Auyero and Sobering 2019). What we do know is that, through well-oiled connections with municipal and state officials, Pocho obtains material resources (food and access to workfare programs and welfare subsidies) for neighbors in need. Through a combination of personalized negotiation with officials (what he calls "gestión") and organization of street mobilizations (rallies and road blockades), he also puts pressure on the government to provide public works in the neighborhood. His time in prison might have affected his reputation, but not his brokering capacities.

Many residents say that he demands a cash kickback from the state subsidies he procures for them. A few of the neighbors we talked to have personally experienced his predatory behavior. Many others believe that he keeps part of what he obtains for others—for personal gain and to finance his own political career. Despite intuiting that Pocho profits from their misery, despite being aware of his (presumed) illegal actions, many residents support his work because, as we heard dozens of times, brokers "steal, but they give away." For some, his grassroots work is based on love and sacrifice. For others, his grassroots work is driven by his own monetary interests. Not a few have pendulous, ambivalent opinions about him and about the love he professes for his neighborhood.

Pocho According to Pocho

Pocho is a robust man, with long black hair tied in a ponytail, a goatee, and a prominent belly. Born in 1973, the son of a construction worker and a community organizer, he grew up in precarious conditions. "I constantly lived flooded. The water came and took down the shacks. Ever since I can remember, my mother would carry me out of the house when it flooded. . . . [T]he water was always up to her chest. Every time it rained, the water took everything away. That's why I fight so hard so that people don't get flooded, because since I can remember I have lived with flooding. . . . Forty-six years have passed and it is still the same problem."

Pocho began to work at thirteen as a street vendor: "I started with charcoal.... But I also sold bread." He would later become a stevedore in the Buenos Aires Central Market, and he then partnered with a friend to sell candy in bulk. "I always wanted to have my own job... one that didn't depend on the state."

Throughout his extensive political career, Pocho has worked with many municipal, provincial, and national officials. He self-identifies as a Peronist. Pocho has his favorites within the movement: His Facebook page is filled with posts praising past and present figures of Peronismo, as well as pictures of him posing with former president Nestor Kirchner and a few of his ministers. Yet, as he told us, he does not love politicians—"they all lied to my mother.... She was an organizer, and she dealt with a lot of politicians."

"Working with" a politician, for Pocho, means the possibility of accessing material resources for the neighborhood and, by extension (although he doesn't say it), for himself. When he began his activism, alongside a man who would later become an important minister in the federal administration, he received about thirty Barrios Bonaerenses workfare plans with which he put his people to work digging and cleaning ditches. A few years ago, at the height of his power in the neighborhood, he managed about three hundred beneficiaries of workfare programs. Today, recently released from prison, he compiles a list of applicants for state workfare programs he then sends to the mayor's office. Such is the nature of his personal connections with powerful politicians.

Pocho has a prodigious memory when it comes to the history and material needs of La Matera. He knows exactly how many families participated in the initial land invasion, what day of the week they did it, the weather on that day and those that followed, the number of people who joined later. He also remembers each and every one of the claims that he, along with his neighbors, made at the different levels of government: from the earliest efforts (such as opening the streets and bringing in state surveyors) to the most recent ones (paving the roadways, canalizing the stream, and constructing the health center, elementary school, and community center). He can accurately describe the day on which he managed to draw the attention of the Argentine president at a rally. He painted a flag with a misspelled demand for a school and paved roads ("En La Matera, *nesecitamos* escuela y asfalto"). "To La Matera," he recalled the president saying in public, "first we are going to give the school so that they can make a correction to that flag." Pocho can provide details of the neighborhood's many public work projects (start dates, costs, etc.), when and why they were suspended, and the names of the first-, second-, and third-line state officials involved in those projects (both those completed and still unfinished).

"When we started it was a slum ['era una villa'], 2,300 families, on embankments, everywhere. . . . We were moving people, moving houses . . . relocating families. We brought surveyors from the province to measure block by block. It was a ton of work . . . because we did not want to be a slum," Pocho told us. He thus restated the desire of many a squatter to reside in a "barrio" instead of a "villa"—that urban form where spatial stigma and social fears converge.

Much like many other political brokers (both female and male), Pocho presents a larger-than-life image of himself and his actions in the neighborhood. Until he was arrested, he said he was the district commissioner, the firefighter, the nurse, the funeral home director, as well as the supplier of DirectTV, roof shingles, and food. Like so many other political brokers, he places himself at the center of the scene—"If I'm not there, nobody does anything. . . . I built the houses, I laid out the asphalt, I built the school." And he complains somewhat bitterly about the ingratitude of his neighbors: "People forget the things you do."

"I did that asphalt."

"Did you see the school? I got it."

"I'm fighting so that they build the bridge the right way."

"Good morning, Antonio, come over, I'll sign you up [for a workfare program]."

Pocho remembers not only each public work that "he" achieved, but also the "struggle" that each one entailed: the long and contentious march through state institutions to obtain resources for those at the bottom. "Because things don't come along on their own. . . . Before making a mess ['antes de hacer quilombo'], you have to negotiate. You have to go [to the state office], come back, go again, wait to be attended to . . . and all that takes time."

After the land occupation of 2000, the neighbors, led by Pocho, began to demand a health-care center. A short time later, they organized to demand an elementary school: "We presented notes, and then it was the pressure of the people. When we presented the application for the school at the local council, we mobilized with the people, and that's how we got things done." To achieve the canalization of the stream and the construction of houses, they manned traffic blockades on key streets, stopping traffic for hours, "and thus we managed to start the works."

Pocho has an awareness and appreciation for the many tools the poor have at their disposal to make effective claims (going to an event with a visible flag, interrupting traffic on a busy avenue, waiting hours in a public office, making a ruckus with a small but loud and determined group of neighbors). He also has a kind of *intuitive sociology* about who can express these demands and who "takes advantage" of the generalized situation of misery: "The one who really needs is the one who demands the least, because that is the one who has to cope with need every day, to get the children out of the water when it floods.... Those who are in real need are the ones who demand the least.... Those who receive resources are the sly ones ['unos vivos'], they sell the stuff they get, the food, the shingles, the steel beams."

Pocho According to His Neighbors

Outside of neighborhoods like La Matera, state assistance to the poor is criticized for creating a supposed dependency and for discouraging "the culture of work." In the dominant discourse, welfare programs degrade the poor and make them easy objects of political manipulation that determines their electoral behavior. According to this narrative (which takes up some arguments from the so-called culture of poverty), welfare programs and food assistance turn the poor into what some in Argentina call "choriplaneros" for presumably living off a combination of "choris" (sausage sandwiches given away at political rallies) and "planes" (welfare programs). This damning, moralizing, and stigmatizing discourse is hardly unique to Argentina. In the United States, government programs are also criticized by conservatives for presumably producing lassitude and moral deviations—the choriplaneros of Argentina are, analogically speaking, the "welfare queens" or "deadbeat dads" of the United States (Fernández-Kelly 2015).

Within neighborhoods like La Matera, perceptions of state welfare are different—although not a few neighbors reproduce the surrounding stigma. There, "welfare" is closely linked to material subsistence. As we saw in chapter 3, state assistance is an essential part of the monthly budgets of the vast majority of families we spoke with (and had become even more vital during the pandemic). Although not always articulated discursively as "a right," access to aid is seen as something that the state should provide to help those who have less. At the same time, beneficiaries perceive welfare and workfare programs as intricately related to the pernicious functioning of grassroots politics in the neighborhood. For many neighbors, Pocho and other brokers represent those "sly ones" that he himself criticizes, because they either mishandle state aid and distribute it in arbitrary fashion (demanding "things" in exchange) or because they personally and cunningly profit from it.

It is an open secret in poor neighborhoods that many local brokers keep a percentage of the workfare plans they help acquire for their constituents. At least 10 percent of what the beneficiary receives usually returns to the broker. As we heard from many residents, "If you don't give the money to him, he will cross you off the list." It is important here to quote Ana, a longtime resident, at length:

> When the first workfare programs came out, they would be something like 140 pesos. Pocho registered me. I had nothing, I lived in a wooden house. Thanks to him I got the money. I got paid for two months and I had to give half to him. As soon as I got paid the first time, I went to the store and spent everything on bricks and bags of cement. I told him I spent the money. The second month, I did the same, I spent everything. The third month I wasn't paid. And he told me that he was not going to register me for any other state program. "You will never be paid again," he told me, because I did not give him the money he asked for. I reckon he did something to kick me out. I signed up for every possible program, and I never got paid again. Because I didn't give him a cent. He took from everyone he registered, he made a lot of money.... He would pass by me and would be dog-faced. Can you believe that I never got paid again?

"Pocho had six houses in La Matera. Six houses and six women," recalls Alma, referring to Pocho's reputation. "He said that he helped the neighbors. After the first flood, we got slippers, mattresses, beds, and food. He kept a lot of things for himself; he didn't give them away to us." The same suspicion circulates around the public works and housing plans that Pocho obtained for the neighborhood: According to many, he pockets a percentage of the costs. Although they do not normalize this situation, and vent a resigned criticism, neighbors do not have many alternatives in the face of this abuse verging on extortion.

The predatory behavior of many neighborhood political brokers is not limited to profiting from state aid. "Pocho gave us drugs," Juan told Sofía. "I would go to the bar. He would come and throw two tizas [cocaine] on the pool table. He would say: 'Guys, we have to go and put up the posters.' ... Pocho is a son of a bitch."

"Let's go, let's go, I'll bring the dessert," Miguel heard Pocho telling all the youth congregated around the bus. The drums and the banners were ready. Miguel knew what kind of "dessert" Pocho was talking about: a good "rodaja de merca" (cocaine), three or four bottles of red wine, and 100 pesos for each participant. It was 2008, and Miguel was Pocho's righthand man. "Fetch me three or four tizas... you can keep half. Now, let's go." The pills they would get before each political rally, remembered Miguel, "were the most delicious thing."[3]

Not everyone in La Matera is critical of Pocho. There are also several neutral opinions about him ("the times I spoke with him, he treated me well. He had a lot of people working with him; they told me he was kind of a badass but whenever he saw me he greeted me well"), and several other laudatory views ("Pocho gave a lot of welfare subsidies"; "He gave subsidies to people, and they dug the ditches, they cleaned the streets"; "Pocho was in charge of the neighborhood—thanks to him, we have an elementary school, a kindergarten, the community center, the plaza... the neighborhood has advanced a lot").

We spent several afternoons with Teresa before she told us about the heated argument that she and Pocho had had a few days before he was arrested, an altercation that escalated into physical aggression. "He left a purple mark on my neck," she told Sofía, "the first time in eighteen years that he got mad at me. I told him the truth: 'you have your own wife, and I want to meet other people.'"

One morning, while Sofía shared maté with Teresa and her friend Alejandra, one of Pocho's daughters, they both agreed that Pocho and his wife were extremely jealous people: "Now we can't call him [in jail] because he's with her. She doesn't like him saying 'my love' to me. She says that I am a 'fat and old woman,' but Pocho never left '*this*' fat and old lady.' He is in prison and he is going crazy because I am not visiting him." Alejandra laughed when she listed the various women in her dad's life and then added: "I have many half-sisters."

Alejandra doesn't seem to have a moral reaction to her father's lush sex life. Teresa does not elaborate on Gordo Amor's aggressive macho behavior. They are, however, adamant about the unfairness of the accusations of drug dealing that weigh on him: "Do you think that I," queries Alejandra, "would be starving or trying to make ends meet with my little store if my old man were a drug dealer? I would have bought a nice new truck!"

Just as Pocho arouses the affections and jealousy of his various lovers, he generates disparate reactions among many La Matera residents. There are those who, as we just saw, truly appreciate him and his work, despite his alleged crimes. Others, although they criticize him harshly for "what he does to the kids" (i.e., feed them drugs), do not deny that his "tireless political work" has translated into infrastructural improvements—La Matera went from a vacant lot with tents in 2000 to a neighborhood with a plaza, a school, a health center, and several paved streets in 2021.

Whether they valorized or criticized him, our many interviewees agreed that, without Pocho's intervention, resources (the welfare benefits, the public works) would not "have come down to the neighborhood." Pocho can keep food that is destined for soup kitchens, he can appropriate a percentage of the welfare subsidies, he can give paco or marijuana to his young followers, and he can abuse his neighbors.[4] But they all know that without him their lives would be even more fragile and miserable. After all, many of them think, a lot of local politicians and grassroots leaders do some version of what Pocho does—particularly when it comes to keeping a portion of the state aid they distribute.

This dialogue between Sofía's relatives, recorded just under a month after Pocho was released from prison, illustrates the diversity of opinions about him and the ambivalent moral and political assessment of his actions:

BLANCA: Pocho is a son of a bitch, true, but if Pocho hadn't lifted his ass off the chair and mobilized people, there would be no community center, no school, no kindergarten. There would be none of that, because he took the initiative. He mobilized a lot of people to do it.

DANIEL: So what? And the other stuff?

BLANCA: What other stuff? It does not matter.

OLGA: It doesn't matter.

DANIEL: How come it doesn't matter? So, I build a community center for you and I keep ten houses for myself?

OLGA: I don't care. Others also steal but they keep it all. He, at least, stole and half was for us and the other was for him.

DANIEL: You both shake hands, you are two morons.

BLANCA: But we have an elementary school, there is a kindergarten, there is a health center, there is a plaza. Did you see how nice the plaza looks?

The dialogue continued with jokes and laughter. Olga had just found out that Pocho was registering people to receive "some bags of food," and she commented that she was going to sign up. Her sister Susana added, "Everyone should just try to do what they can [to survive]" ("cada uno se salva como puede"). Not missing a beat, her brother-in-law Daniel, who had already criticized Pocho, ironically commented, "That's why we are the way we are." The conversation continued like this:

OLGA: It doesn't matter. If we don't steal, someone else will come and steal.... [Many] say that those of us who receive welfare are lazy....

DANIEL: Why do they have to deduct so much money from my salary to give it to those scoundrels?

SOFÍA: They are not scoundrels!

DANIEL: Yes, they are. Your grandfather worked all his life and receives a $15,000 check, and someone who never contributed to a pension fund received money without working. Is that right or wrong?

SOFÍA: It's wrong.

DANIEL: Well, then . . .

ROXANA: No, but they are not all like that.

DANIEL: The state built their homes. The state built everything for them. What else do you want? That's it! How much more should the state keep giving? That's the way it is in La Matera and in many other places.

BLANCA: Do you think that people don't have needs?

DANIEL: In La Matera, more than a few don't need anything!

BLANCA: Many do! I invite you to count how many people are living in houses that are falling apart.... Pocho signed me up for a housing program and they built my house. I was one of the first who got a home. But there are many people out there who still need one.

The conversation then turned to some neighbors who, according to Daniel, did not "deserve" what they received from the state and then to the case of other local brokers who coordinate soup kitchens and, presumably, also benefit financially from them. While the exchange was friendly, the viewpoints were diverse: The state is seen either as giving "too much" or as not giving enough.

The conversation highlighted an argument that we heard many times during our fieldwork. Nobody denies that politics serves to enrich local political brokers like Pocho. However, the brokers are not judged by what they appropriate, but rather by what they distribute: "He steals, but he gives away." Pocho is no exception.

Perhaps the term *soguero* best captures the ambivalence of neighborhood brokers' actions. Javier first heard the word fifteen years ago when Estela, a resident of a poor neighborhood, La Matanza, used it to refer to a powerful local broker. With that word, Estela described a person who throws a rope (a *soga*) to a neighbor, someone who gives you a hand when you need it—the local broker who helps you and others. Susana illustrated this (helpful) dimension of the broker's actions when she told us that she and her husband, Chori, obtained their house in La Matera thanks to Pocho. "Chori was Pocho's close follower. We got the house because of Pocho. He was involved in politics and had a lot of leverage back then. With Pocho, you got things, medicines, things for your friends, you got things.... It was good to have him as a friend. Even though he had a bad reputation, he did things around the neighborhood."

"Let's tell the truth," Frasca said when Pocho was in prison. "He was the only one who mobilized residents in La Matera. If the power went out, he was the one who called the company or organized a protest until the problem was solved.... The guy did a lot here. And all the people who spoke badly of him are now feeling that because when he is not around things go bad, we get flooded, and nobody pays attention to us. When the guy was around, bulldozers would come and clean the ditches, you would see bulldozers everywhere."

However, the same rope (or the same hand) that is extended to help can also be used to hang you—as Estela illustrated by wrapping the imaginary rope around her neck. The same relations that assist residents with day-to-day problems are also used by brokers to control them. Brokers may demand that their followers do things they otherwise would not, such as attending a rally, or they may extract resources from them, requesting, for example, a percentage of their state assistance subsidies.

Rosario and Mariana, two La Matera residents, illuminated this second meaning of the term *soguero* very clearly. Rosario told us, "When you receive foodstuffs from the broker, you have to go to the rallies, because if you don't, you won't receive the food, they cut you off.... [Food] is helpful, but you have to march." Mariana remembered the long lines to collect a check from a state aid program: "The same day that we got paid, we spent everything.... We bought the things that we normally couldn't eat, yogurt, cereal." Fifty percent of the amount she received, however, had to be given back to "the guy who registered you in that program."

Some neighbors will attend a party organized by their broker because they understand that it is the expectation; others pay brokers a percentage of their subsidy because brokers explicitly demand it. Some do both. Not all brokers engage in predatory or extractive behavior, although all of them expect some kind of reciprocity for their services.

Beyond the two meanings of "soguero" that Estela conveyed, there is a third possible connotation. A rope is used to tie and climb. The aid that brokers like Pocho distribute among neighbors and the infrastructure they obtain for the neighborhood (often through a combination of interpersonal transactions and disruptive collective action, or "negotiations and pressure") serve to enlarge their pool of followers. With a larger number of followers comes greater negotiating capacity and a stronger ability to exert collective pressure—in short, accumulated power. As such, the "rope"—the soguero—also serves to "do politics."

Luciana articulates this third dimension of brokers' actions. She is a municipal employee and tells us that she distributes food to groups and organizations in the neighborhood. She shares "with whoever is in need," but "those resources are also useful during political campaigns. This is a back and forth." Her testimony provides further details about grassroots political practices and about the (in this case, lack of) political orientation or ideology guiding these practices. From her point of view, being a Peronist (an identification she shares with Pocho) makes little difference in the ways in which politics is practiced—in the ways in which material resources are obtained. It is important to cite her because her own words capture the way in which political practice is lived both as a form of exchange and as a way of making ends meet:

> People used to be more grateful. Now it is as if they feel that giving stuff is an obligation. . . . When I started I got welfare plans, I distributed those plans. . . . Now I am well known here in the neighborhood . . . thanks to Pulmón [a municipal official]. We have to be grateful, and I thank Pulmón. He got me my job at the municipality, he taught me how to do this. We are a team. . . . We are Peronists, yes. But in fact there are no more Peronists. It's unfortunate, but there are no Peronists anymore. Each person needs to take care of his or her needs. If you can't keep the refrigerator full for your children, you are not a useful activist. Because I can't fight for another person when I neglect my own children all day and I don't have enough to buy a soda. If those at the top make their own deals and fill their pockets, what remains for us? Should we kill each other defending a party when they, those at the top, eat better than us, drink better than us? There are no more activists as we had

when Perón was alive. These days it all depends on the resources you have.... Everyone boasts "I am a Peronist, I am a Peronist," but it is a lie. This is what I learned: "Do you want me to work for you politically? Well, how much stuff do you have? What resources can you give me and my followers?"

Brokers as Time Goes By

"I learned how to organize a roadblock [a piquete] from my dad," Alejandra (one of Pocho's daughters) proudly stated. Another broker, Lili, described how alongside her neighbors they jointly fought for public lighting and water: "We were the best picketers." In straightforward terms, these two statements capture a key transformation in the brokers' way of doing politics. The brokers portrayed in *Poor People's Politics*, the book on clientelist practices in a Buenos Aires shantytown that one of us authored, were mediators between a patron (a state actor or someone with close links to one) and the neighborhood residents. They were problem-solvers—they would distribute medicine, speed up paperwork, or obtain food for their followers, the "clients." These personalized, individual favors were provided in exchange for political support (attendance at a rally, for example). That assistance, those favors, those always-partial and precarious "solutions" were offered in a context where state services and programs were only starting to be rolled out. The actions of contemporary brokers like Pocho, on the contrary, take place in a context of dense state presence in the form of multiple welfare programs. But this is not the only difference between mid-1990s brokers and contemporary ones. Back then, it was rare for brokers and their clients to resort to contentious collective action—they were not "picketers."

In contemporary Buenos Aires, brokers have adopted many tactics of the existing repertoire of collective action. They assert their claims at party rallies, with flags and drums; they also do so in the streets, blocking traffic on a busy thoroughfare or organizing a protest with "their people" in front of city hall. Today, piqueteros and brokers—actors who at one point defined themselves in opposition to one another—share similar logics of action in their attempts to capture state resources. The actions of Pocho and many other brokers show that clientelist politics and collective action are not opposite or contradictory political phenomena, but rather are dynamic processes that maintain recursive relationships. A brief detour through the scholarly literature will help readers make better sense of this dual logic of action.

Clientelist arrangements have been traditionally understood as separate from, and antagonistic to, most forms of collective action (Auyero, Lapegna, and Page Poma 2009). Most students of patronage politics agree that these hierarchical arrangements inhibit collective organizing and discourage protest. Vertical and asymmetric clientelist relations have been conceptualized as the opposite of the horizontal ties that are seen as the necessary condition for collective action. As we saw in this chapter, clientelist politics and collective action are neither opposing nor contradictory political phenomena. They are dynamic processes that, as Pocho and his followers illustrate, establish recursive relationships. Once we approach them as strategies to solve pressing problems and make claims, we can see the continuities and interconnections between patronage and protest.

In his detailed historical and ethnographic account of the demobilizing process of the MoCaFor (Movimiento Campesino de Formosa), sociologist Pablo Lapegna (2016) examines an opposite process to the one described in this chapter: social movement leaders who, under certain circumstances, work as brokers or intermediaries—that is, they provide personalized solutions to movement participants' daily problems (access to a welfare program, speeding up paperwork at a state agency, etc.). This form of problem-solving is not, according to Lapegna, a form of political cooptation but the product of what he calls double pressure (on the one hand, the claims that social movement members' make to their leaders and, on the other hand, the pressures that state authorities exert on social movement leaders).

The Soccer Field or the Soup Kitchen

Pocho is not the only problem-solver of La Matera. A few other neighbors, some of them participants in the original occupation, possess contacts with state officials and act as intermediaries between them and residents to channel material resources to the neighborhood. In chapter 2, we described how state officials sought to divide and, at the same time, sponsor local collective action. In what follows, we show how state actors use their access to material resources to fragment poor people's demands, to manipulate their political behavior, and to sanction those who seek other relationships to address their pressing needs.

Martín and Nelly have been married for more than a decade. Before the COVID-19 lockdown, they managed a soup kitchen. Twice a week, they had offered dinner to about two dozen residents. A state official "gave us a hand to open it, he sends us resources, we get chickens, rice, gnocchi, oil."

NELLY: The stuff we get is never enough.

MARTÍN: Last night, we made gnocchi but we supplemented with rice because there were a lot of people, and it's not nice when they are in line waiting with their containers in hand.

Martín tells us that, alongside the soup kitchen, he has been trying "another move" with a municipal official. By a "move," he means that he has been trying to obtain funds to improve the local soccer field. Nelly says, "The kids want to have a better field. They got together with my husband, and they want to level it and have some lights so that they can play at night."

According to Martín, this state official asked him to attend a rally. "And I did that. I went with the kids from the soccer field, and I carried a flag that read LA MATERA. I think that those close to the official who is funding the soup kitchen saw me on Facebook at the rally . . . and they took the funds away. I wasn't trying to play with one and not with the other. . . . I was just giving a hand to both state officials."

Martín is hardly the only one who comments on the use of social media to monitor the actions of grassroots organizers like him. Another activist tells us that she hides at rallies because she does not want to be photographed and run the risk of losing her job at the local municipality: "They can fire me . . . and who is going to help me? No compañero is going to pay for my groceries. I have to be careful."

Martín tells us that a few days after the rally they stopped receiving foodstuffs for their soup kitchen. Those were difficult days: "It's really awful when kids come to you with their containers asking for a meal and you have nothing to give." They decided to get in touch with their contact in the government: "The woman told me that if we stay with them, we could reopen the soup kitchen." Nelly explained to her that, in order not to "mix things up," she would "keep the soup kitchen" and Martín, her husband, will "keep the soccer field."

These issues might seem minor or irrelevant to understand popular politics, stories that political analysis tends to discard as "colorful anecdotes." But irrelevant or minor they are not. They illustrate how politics works at the bottom of the social structure and how it is experienced by activists and marginalized residents. Not all politics is like that, of course. But the frequency with which events like these showed up during our fieldwork (and the emotional intensity with which they were recounted) leads us to think about politics as actions that fragment claims and divide local identities. Politics is also an activity that "disciplines and punishes"—monitoring loyalties and sentencing those who, presumably, distance themselves from exclusive political networks.

Politics, according to many neighbors, can be useful to "obtain resources"—as Lucy tells us, "you need to get involved in politics if you want to get stuff for the neighborhood." But politics is also perceived as an activity that encourages divisions among those in need ("either you are with the official that supports the soup kitchen, or you are with the official that gives you resources for the soccer field"). As we saw above, politics is also lived as a form of extortion ("you will have access to this program, if you are with me") and as an activity that feeds suspicions of corruption ("politicians always keep a slice of what they give away"). In all cases, politics is understood as part of a web of relationships of domination on which one can (and often needs to) count to make ends meet.

Pocho for the Time Being

While he awaited his trial, Pocho was required to stay home for all but five hours a day. One hot morning in January 2021, still in the midst of the pandemic, Sofía chatted with him in his "office"—the place where he was arrested. With bare white walls, cement floors, a few plastic chairs, a long desk, and a pool table off to the side, Pocho's place (he calls it "el local") is modest. He was sitting at the head of the table while Toni, one of his loyal followers, prepared some matés. Toni was nineteen, lived adjacent to the office, and acted as a janitor and night watchman of sorts. Neighbors stopped by and Pocho asked them about their health, their latest jobs, their relatives. While chatting with residents, he kept an eye on two of his sons (nine and ten years old) who were mowing the lawn outside the office. Pocho liked to keep them busy—the next time we visited, the two boys were sweeping the sidewalks.

Holding his maté in one hand and his cell phone in the other, Pocho couldn't stop talking about his many "projects." In addition to a shopping center, he wanted to build a pay-by-the-hour hotel ("un hotel para parejas"—locally known as "telos") in the center of La Matera. A few blocks away from where he and Sofía were talking, a bright street banner advertised a recently opened hotel with "new technology for more pleasure." He told Sofía that every neighborhood had a telo and that La Matera deserved one too.

"Wild dreams, I know," he said, "but I'm always thinking about the future. Other people buy new cars. I buy cement bags, because it's all about the future." As noted earlier, many say that Pocho has as many lovers as he has homes in La Matera. We don't know the truth of those claims (though we suspect he obtained a couple of his homes through negotiations with the contractors building new units for a state housing program in La Matera). What we do know is that one of his sources of income is the rent he makes from his properties there. He told us so when describing the way he paid for his lawyer—he sold one of these homes.

But Pocho was not just thinking about money-generating "projects." Shortly after leaving prison, he was already setting up meetings to organize his neighbors to make claims for new infrastructure: drains, sewers, bridges to cross streams, pavement, bus lines, garbage collection. "That's why they say I'm the bad guy . . . because I complain." While he and Sofía chatted, neighbors came by to greet him and he invited them to one of several meetings he was planning. He also wrote their names down for a new workfare program. He would collect personal information from other applicants over the phone, telling Sofía that the mayor's private secretary was the one who asked him to make a list of potential beneficiaries. Even under the supervision of the prison system, Pocho's activity was unremitting.

As Pocho tells it, the infrastructure works he fought for are the reason he ended up in jail. "Politics imprisoned me ['A mí me mete preso la política']. The government sent me to jail. They wanted to build an embankment to stop water from flooding the neighborhood. But they were doing it wrong. I stopped the job. And then I denounced the government in front of the TV cameras from Channel 13. I spoke about the open-air landfill that is right here, in the center of La Matera. I have been fighting for garbage collection. . . . I always fight." Predictably, not all neighbors share his version of the events that ended with him in prison. For many, he is still a drug dealer. As soon as he got out of jail, on the wall of a house near his office, he painted "Pocho wishes you a Happy Holiday." Under his name an anonymous neighbor added "transa" (drug dealer). The accusation did not last more than a couple of hours. Pocho himself covered it up with a coat of fresh paint.

5

LIVES AT RISK

How Do Residents Experience, Explain,
and Deal with Interpersonal Violence?

Academic and policy conversations about the livelihood strategies of the urban poor often concentrate on the ways in which they obtain material resources—primarily food and shelter—while overlooking the ways in which they deal with the very crucial threat to their existence that interpersonal violence represents. Thus far, our analysis has mirrored this way of looking at poor people's lives, focusing on the collective ways in which the inhabitants of La Matera gained access to land and housing (land grabbing and autoconstruction) and the diverse strategies (formal and informal work, political networks, community actions, and state welfare) that its residents, and those of two adjacent neighborhoods, employ to obtain food.

Fifty years after anthropologist Larissa Lomnitz asked the question that inspired our research, relational strategies—poor people's reliance on the help of kin and friends—extend, crucially, beyond the procurement of basic material needs. In a region where interpersonal violence, concentrated in the lowest levels of social space, has been steadily escalating, asking how the marginalized survive also implies asking about what *literally* threatens their survival: the shootings, the street assaults, the fights inside their homes. How do the poor experience, explain, and navigate these daily threats?

Let us briefly review existing scholarship on the topic before presenting our empirical evidence, which is quite consistent with what we know from other parts of the Americas. Ethnographic and qualitative studies in poor neighborhoods describe the widespread fear of violent victimization felt by their residents daily. This generalized concern among the most deprived is consistent with social scientific accounts of the clustering of interpersonal violence in low-income areas in the hemisphere (Moser and McIlwaine 2000; Rodgers, Beall, and Kanbur 2012; Sharkey 2018; Wilding 2012).

Responding to a generalized sense of insecurity over the past three decades, upper and middle classes throughout the Americas have increasingly isolated themselves in gated and walled communities with private security (Adams 2017; Caldeira 2001; Müller 2016; Svampa 2008). They have modified urban space to their advantage. In some cases, such as Managua, elites created security "archipelagos" (Rodgers 2004) connecting heavily guarded housing compounds with commercial centers via high-speed roadways. While poor populations have less capacity to transform urban infrastructure to shield themselves, they still respond to surrounding violence with changes in their built environment. As one of us described in previous work (Auyero and Berti 2016), shantytown and squatter settlement dwellers fortify their dwellings—they "build walls to separate their homes from the streets and alleyways, install stronger doors ('so they can't kick it down and break in'), and add padlocks to their windows. Not only do these investments make residents feel safer when they are at home, but they also make them feel more comfortable in venturing away, which provides peace of mind that the people, and the things they leave behind, will remain safe" (141). Regular seclusion inside homes is one typical way of avoiding violence; another one involves the keeping of regular schedules and strict curfews (see Vega et al. 2019).

Yet, when they must inevitably venture into public spaces, residents of poor, marginalized areas rely on local, tactical knowledge to maintain a minimum degree of safety (Harding 2010; Penglase 2014; Sánchez-Jankowski 2008). "Knowing how to live in Caxambu," writes Ben Penglase (2014, 15), "meant knowing how to live in a highly lethal neighborhood, particularly if you were young, male, and black or of mixed race." Information about the times, places, and circumstances in which residents may encounter potential perpetrators of violence travels through local networks, sometimes in the form of gossip, serving residents as they navigate treacherous public spaces (see Sánchez-Jankowski 2008). David Harding (2010, 44) examines shared understandings of safe or unsafe spaces—"danger zones" where drug dealers congregate—and avoidance tactics among poor youth. This tactical, context-specific knowledge is not merely a diagrammatic representation of risky places and times, but one that informs concrete actions—from hood hopping (lying about your neighborhood of origin to avoid a fight with a youngster from another neighborhood) (Harding 2010) and school choice (Burdick-Will 2017; Denice and Gross 2016; Hailey 2020; Lareau and Goyette 2014; Saporito 2003) to active ignorance (intentionally not hearing or seeing people involved in local criminal activity). As one of Penglase's informants puts it, "You have to respect certain people, even if you don't always agree with what they do. You have to pass by and say 'Hi, how's it going?' Smile, and be friendly. Because small dogs don't pick up fights with big dogs" (2014, 101).

Another concrete precautionary action among poor residents is traveling in groups—in this, they are not alone: citizens of all social classes in Latin America increasingly do so (Villarreal 2024). Both young and old typically avoid traveling alone, especially at night, in the shantytowns of Argentina: "We go to parties with our friends, in a pack...always. You need a big group to go out, and it's better if someone in the group is really a badass, so that...you know...nothing bad happens to you. If you go out in a small group, or worse, by yourself...the thieves would grab you and steal your stuff, your sneakers" (Auyero and Berti 2016, 143). Seeking the protection of other youngsters who "have your back," and prevent others from "messing" with you, is also common in poor neighborhoods in Boston (Harding 2010).

Interpersonal Violence in Six Tales

Sofía's Backpack

In August 2019, Sofía carried in her backpack the recently purchased photocopied readings for her classes as well as a copy of Primo Levi's *Survival in Auschwitz*. A new book, she kept reminding herself, is a luxury for low-income students like her. She had been taking classes at the University of Buenos Aires—a ninety-minute bus ride from her house—for two years. She always made sure her classes did not start too early in the morning or end too late at night. Sofía knew that leaving the neighborhood at dawn or returning after midnight was dangerous. "The kids" stalk the neighbors—the stories of assaults and thefts of cell phones, money, and sneakers were frequent among her friends. She thought that she would never be robbed if she took the necessary precautions: avoid certain hours, walk through the streets that have better lighting, always try to be accompanied by a relative or a friend, and carry few things with her.

That night, she had called her younger brother, Luis, and told him to wait for her at the bus stop. She got off bus 373 at 11:15 p.m. The stop was four blocks from her house, seven from one of the entrances to La Matera. The second she greeted Luis, three youngsters, no older than fifteen, surrounded them. All three were hooded, two showed their knives, and the third brandished a pistol. "The cell phone!" was all they screamed. Her throat went dry and she barely managed to tell them that she had it in the bottom of her backpack. She was afraid that she wouldn't be able to reach it soon enough and thought they were going to hurt her. She put her hand in and there, among the photocopies and Levi's book, was her cell phone—a brand-new Samsung Y6, a birthday present from her mother.

She still remembers the blow to the wrist that one of them gave her when he grabbed her cell phone. He also snatched her backpack. When the three boys ran off, Sofía noticed that her brother no longer had his jacket, T-shirt, or sneakers on.

Two days later, Sofía went to the office of the local Peronist party, where, alongside a group of youngsters, she offered literacy classes for children. Most of the students who attended these classes come from La Matera. During the slightly chaotic two-hour sessions, volunteers like Sofía attempted to inculcate the pleasure of reading to children through different games. Many students attended irregularly; others, like Felix, never missed class.

Felix was really happy at the beginning of the class. He had just turned twelve and was showing everybody his new backpack. It was Sofía's. She felt chills. Her throat went dry again. She smiled and told Felix that she thought it was beautiful. She didn't say or ask anything else.

Teresa's Cell Phone

"I was waiting in line to register Facundo for kindergarten. We were sitting right outside of the school together with Daniela, my neighbor. We went early because we thought there was going to be a lot of people. It was 8 a.m. and nobody was there. I had my wallet, inside of which I was carrying Facundo's vaccination card, his birth certificate, and some other papers. I also had money in it. I had my old cell phone—pictures of my [dead son] Alfredo were in it. I also had pics of Facundo when he was a baby. I don't know . . . one never imagines that it will be stolen. Two kids went by, and then they came back again. When they returned, I thought, 'They are going to rob us.' That's when I threw the wallet away. I didn't hide the old cell phone because they had already seen it. One of the kids faced me and threatened me with a big stick. 'Give me your cell phone,' he shouted. He took it and ran away. You have no idea how much I cried that day, not for the cell phone but for the pictures I lost."

"Here, We Are Forgotten"

Lucy believes that "here, in La Matera, we are forgotten." She is referring to the lack of protection against the violence that she and her family have to endure daily. During the last week of each month, Lucy has to stay awake until late. She won't go to sleep until she hears the sound of her daughter, Paula, closing the front door. During the first weeks of each month, she goes to sleep earlier because Paula takes a car service from the bus stop and that "makes [her] feel at ease." But toward the end of each month, when money is tight, Paula walks the fifteen blocks that separate the bus stop from the house. And Lucy stays awake.

Lucy's son, Juan, "was robbed a few months ago. Four thieves, with knives, they took everything, even his clothes. He came back home naked. . . . I was there when they robbed him." She carries a small knife with her "to feel safe . . . but I didn't react that day because I didn't want them to hurt Juan. . . . I begged them not to hurt my son." Those who assaulted him, Lucy says, "are kids from the neighborhood. They used to play soccer with him, but they still left him with nothing. . . . One of them is in jail now, another one is dead. I was a nervous wreck for months after that assault."

"What If They Kill My Baby?"

"Yesterday night, around 9 p.m., we were coming back from the grocery store with my husband and my son," Caro tells us. "There was a fight among neighbors. They started shooting at each other, and we were stuck in the middle of the shoot-out. I ran to the community center so that they could call the cops. My husband called and they asked him if there were any dead or injured. . . . Do you have to hit someone in the head so that they show up? A bullet grazed my husband's neck. What if they kill my baby son? I can still remember the sound of the bullets. It was crazy. The cops showed up an hour after the incident."

"I Am a Magnet for Thieves"

Rosa is fifty-five years old and has suffered many assaults on the streets of the neighborhood. Once, a very young boy with a knife threatened her. "I don't know if it was a sharp knife because I didn't get to try it. I was distracted. He asked me for my phone.... He had already stolen from me before. The thief had that expression in his face.... Did you see when they are all agitated as if they can't breathe? As if they are in need [of drugs]?" "They are lost with so much paco and pills," Brenda, her twenty-year-old daughter-in-law, adds. On another occasion, Rosa had her sneakers stolen, and a few days later she ran into a neighbor who was wearing them. She confronted her, saying: " 'The paquero [drug addict] who stole from me must have sold them to you.'... But the paquero was her son.... She took off her shoes and threw them at me. And she told me that she was going to tell her son.... She threatened me.... 'Take your filthy sneakers,' she yelled at me. 'Dirty but mine,' I told her. I wasn't going to ask her, but she got upset when I said 'paquero.'" Rosa tells us that she has already lost count of the times she has been robbed on the street: "I am a magnet for thieves."

"Your Heart in Your Throat"

"I've already been robbed about forty times," Daniel tells us. "Do you know how bad it is to cross the street at five o'clock in the morning? Everything is dark, they come out from under the bridge, from the side, they take everything from you, they hit you.... I have seen many people who were robbed in front of me and I turned back.... You have to go with your heart in your throat and there is no lighting at all. Nothing at all."

Interpersonal Violence Continued

The vast majority of our interviewees were, at least once, direct victims of muggings on public roads. A minority told us that they had been "lucky" and did not experience violence in the flesh, although close relatives had suffered it: "My son-in-law was robbed of the horses he used to scavenge.... Luckily we recovered one." "They stole my son's sneakers, his jacket." "Ugly things happen here, lack of safety." Whether direct or indirect victims, all of them feel that they live at the mercy of whatever each day brings. The frequent attacks against their physical integrity do not seem to surprise them.

Constant thefts are not confined to public spaces but also occur inside homes. Soledad, for example, had her gas canister and cell phone stolen one morning when she went to drop her daughters off at school: "When you are robbed, you get the feeling that they are going to come back," she tells us. Soledad is not the only one who had personal items stolen from her home, nor the only one who knew the thieves personally—as we saw in the cases of Lucy, Sofía, and Rosa. Victims and perpetrators often know each other or have family or friends in common.

Social science research has pointed to a number of factors associated with the concentration of violence in marginalized areas, most of which are present in La Matera, El Tala, and La Paz: poverty and unemployment, the accumulation of structural disadvantages, the absence of "collective efficacy" (low social cohesion and few mechanisms of informal social control), the lack of "social infrastructure" (public spaces, libraries, etc.), the influence of the illicit drug market (and the way conflicts in this market tend to be resolved), and the fragile monopoly of violence by the state.[1]

Those who live in the area also have an "explanation" for the violence that impacts their lives. This explanation does not focus on larger structural issues or meso-level factors but on violent perpetrators, particularly on their physical and psychological states. "It's ugly, because they can hurt you for nothing, because the kids are on drugs." Phrases like Mariluz's were related to us, with minimal variations, countless times. All the neighbors associate the assaults and robberies with the psychopharmacological effects of drugs in combination with alcohol. From the neighbors' point of view (which is practically unanimous on this issue), the ingestion of paco, cocaine, or pills along with alcohol irritates, excites, enrages, or emboldens "the kids." And these emotional states translate into violent behavior. For residents, there is so much violence because there are many, too many, violent kids.

How do residents cope with extensive fear and the very real threat of violence? Are they resigned to it and/or paralyzed by it—as the general powerlessness that defines their lives would lead us to believe (Desmond and Travis 2018)? The short answer is no. Like the poor elsewhere, they rely on individual and collective strategies to produce an always-precarious safety for themselves and their loved ones (see Abello Colak et al. 2014).

Faced with constant danger, neighbors in La Matera, La Paz, and El Tala, like their counterparts in other relegated neighborhoods, organize their daily routines to avoid, as far as possible, going out at night when their potential victimizers (los pibes) are usually present. Residents are far from passive in the face of danger and what they see as police abandonment or complicity. Repeated expressions of fear, helplessness, and futility in the face of threats of physical violence coexist with a multitude of ways in which residents attempt to mitigate danger to themselves and their loved ones. Different from other highly violent areas in the Americas, there were not instances of "everyday resistance" to victimization or "vigilantism" (piecemeal or collective) of the kind dissected by political scientist Eduardo Moncada (2022) in Mexico, El Salvador, and Colombia. Nor did we witness strategic negotiations of the kind Verónica Zubillaga and colleagues (2019) examined for the case of mothers of gang members in Venezuela. Instead, we found intermittent seclusion and regular reliance on informal proximity networks.

One common way in which residents attempt to avoid violent encounters on public streets is through regular isolation in their homes ("I stay inside"). The physical structures of their homes, in turn, have over the years been fortified against the outside world with bars, better doors and keys, and padlocks (see figure 5.1).

We know that fear of public violence generates seclusion. But at the same time it engenders regular courses of action (routines) that require connectivity within the household (like when there is a need to coordinate who stays and who leaves so that belongings are safe, and to arrange who goes with whom to or from the bus stop) and also among family, friends, and acquaintances outside the domestic unit (by coordinating schedules for moving within the neighborhood, or leaving and returning to it). Establishing schedules and agreements with family members or neighbors constitutes an attempt to provide some predictability and a sense of control in what is a fundamentally unpredictable environment.

Although it is certainly true that community violence breeds isolation (Pearce 2019; Perlman 2011; Vega et al. 2019), our evidence (and that from many a marginalized community throughout the Americas) shows that violence is also structuring (Rodgers 2000). While they cannot entirely prevent victimization (as we experienced firsthand when one of us was mugged), these routines provide a sort of anchor amid constant risk.[2]

After we incorporate personal safety into the study of poor people's daily strategies, we see the *enduring relevance of kin and friend networks* of the kind analyzed by Carol Stack and Lomnitz to navigate violent environments. Knowledge about the whens, wheres, and whos of violence travels through these informal networks.

What merits more attention, however, is the double-edged character of these informal networks: Just like networks utilized to obtain material re-

FIGURE 5.1. The front of a house fortified with barbed wire.

sources can become skewed, social relations allowing residents to secure protection can also turn into sources of danger. Bandidos, as youngsters involved in drug dealing are known in Rio's favelas (Arias 2009; Gay 2005; D. Goldstein 2013; Penglase 2014), share kinship and friendship ties with residents. These ties can serve residents to "avoid being the target of harassment and violence" (Penglase 2014, 93), but they can also have a negative impact on one's self and immediate family as drug dealers' demands on friends and family turn compromising. Consequently, while kinship and friendship provide some extra safety to some of Penglase's informants, they also worry that "these same connections to drug dealers could expose [their families] to violence" (2014, 99).

We said early on that scholarship on survival strategies has failed to incorporate violence as a risk to subsistence. To criticize this vast (and oftentimes excellent) scholarship for such an oversight is only legitimate if we are able to demonstrate that the failure to consider the threat of violence as a menace to subsistence may cause a misunderstanding of the way in which those strategies work. To a large extent, thus far, we have talked about strategies devoted to material subsistence and those deployed to prevent or protect residents from violence as discrete relational universes. It is important to note, however, that these webs of relations sometimes overlap and complement each other—as when the same tie with a close relative that helps obtain a loan to buy food also serves to coordinate a safe return home late at night when the neighborhood turns dangerous. But these same ties that help a household meet its daily subsistence needs might also bring violence home—as when the cousin who lends you money to pay for your children's clothes gets you in trouble with a local gang because of his participation in the drug trade, or the boyfriend on whom you rely for extra cash or a car puts you in harm's way because of his involvement with criminal activities, or the father who engages in armed robbery to obtain resources for himself and his family provokes a violent reaction from the state or from his competitors, or the brother who, as we will see in the next chapter, "shows up at [a family member's] home" and, as a target, causes others to "shoot up" the house (see also Penglase 2014; Stitt and Auyero 2018; Stuart 2020).

The next two chapters provide empirical evidence about the ways in which the "immersion" of poor people in circles of "kinfolk who [would] help them" subsist (Stack 1983, 29) might also bring unintended consequences that act against their literal survival. Only when we think about material subsistence and personal safety simultaneously are we able to see the complementarity or incompatibility of these social ties.

6

VICTIMS AND PERPETRATORS

There are places where it is more difficult to survive: in a desert, on an uninhabited island, on a mountain peak, on Mars, in a country at war, in the jungle. In my family. —CLAUDIA PIÑEIRO, *Catedrales* (2020)

Interpersonal violence (its uses and the ways in which it is dealt with) needs to be incorporated into inquiries about the strategies of the marginalized. "Surviving" does not only mean obtaining housing, food, and access to health and education, but also avoiding those "sudden reversals of fortune" that interpersonal violence produces (Elias 2000).

Chapter 5 presented a series of short stories about those who have suffered episodes of interpersonal violence. Stories like those abound in territories of urban relegation—in Argentina and in much of Latin America. They are the subject of frequent conversations between neighbors. The presence of imminent danger—threats often created by young residents in the same neighborhood—is a topic of conversation but, as we have pointed out, it also organizes the daily routines of neighbors.

Here we present the stories of Eliana and Damián. Delving into the interactions and biographies of those who simultaneously exercise and suffer violence—victims *and* perpetrators—the chronicle illustrates in fine-grained detail the complex relationship between subsistence strategies and forms of domination and violence at home and in the neighborhood. We will see how family relations can serve as a support for obtaining material resources (either licitly or illicitly) and as a place for caring and protection. We will also show how those close relationships can be the locus where violence and physical harm are produced and reproduced.[1]

Much interpersonal violence is examined as the product of retaliation ("an eye for an eye, a tooth for a tooth"). This retaliatory violence is often encapsulated in dyadic exchanges (Jacobs 2004; Mullins, Wright, and Jacobs 2004; Papachristos 2009). Another strand of social science work has scrutinized the manifold ways in which violent situations (Collins 2008) are linked with one another (Jensen and Rodgers 2022; Auyero and Berti 2016; Stitt and Auyero 2018). Diverse types of violence are concatenated when various kinds of physical aggression—typically conceptualized as discrete and analytically distinct phenomena (because of the place where they occur, because of the actors involved, etc.)—are connected in concrete empirical sequences constituting the "violence stew" (Perlman 2011) that characterizes many poor urban areas. Typically analyzed as discrete forms of violence, their actual empirical links—the ways in which different forms are not only copresent but also connected—usually go undetected. Scholarship on concatenated violence(s) has pushed theoretical and empirical analysis beyond an exclusive focus on one-on-one retaliatory dynamics and into a more socially embedded and intimate examination of interpersonal violence. Taking heed of this scholarship that seeks to transcend the "compartmentalization and balkanization" of violence studies (Jackman 2002, 387), this chapter provides an ethnographic reconstruction of situational concatenations of various types of violence (Gould 2003; Tilly 2003; Collins 2008).

Damián and Eliana

Damián has two photos in his room. In one, his father, Alberto, is wearing a blue and yellow jersey and new stylish shoes. His hair is a bit disheveled, with a look on his face like he has just woken up, and he has a gun in his hand. In the other photo, his brother Albertito is smiling. He is wearing a jersey with the crest of Barcelona FC on it. It was taken the day Albertito left the Juvenile Detention Center, where he had been held for attempted robbery.

Eliana only has the one photo of Albertito. "I don't like looking at the photo because it hurts too much," she tells us. "Sometimes I dream Albertito is hugging me and telling me he's not dead."

In just three years, Damián and Eliana lost their father and then their brother. Both were killed in the streets of La Matera.

Alberto, the father, was killed, seven shots in the back, by a "guy who was out in the neighborhood robbing." "We couldn't believe it," Damián recalls. "I mean, my old man robbed, got into shoot-outs with the cops, and was in worse situations, and some asshole thief comes along and kills him like that."

Albertito died in some confrontation—nobody knows if it was with the police or with a group of thieves or dealers—not far from the house where Damián lives now. "We never found out who did it," says Eliana. "Word is it was a dealer, settling a score." "I'll never get that image out of my head, Albertito lying there in the avenue, dead," Damián tells us. At the wake "there were ten of us from the family and around eighty hoods; he always ran around with a bunch of them."

Damián is thirty-two and married to Natalia. He has three children and a relatively peaceful life. They live on a plot of land they got thanks to Pocho, the neighborhood puntero whom we introduced in an earlier chapter. The little shack he lived in for ten years is now a brick house. Damián works for a construction company, "on the books, with health care, with a pass to use the union swimming pools. I get all the benefits" (something that is not very common in the neighborhood). He works eight and a half hours, Monday to Friday.

Eliana is twenty-four. Her life resembles a roller coaster, filled with jolts and upheavals. Until not long ago she was raising her two young daughters on her own, with the help of a government subsidy and money that her brothers loaned her. She wanted to finish school, which she had left a few years prior. She was waiting to enroll until after her eldest daughter had started kindergarten because "in order to get a job every place requires you to have a high school diploma and it's very expensive to get a fake one.... It costs around 4,000 pesos." Throughout the period of our research, Eliana's ex-husband often showed up at her house unexpectedly, usually at night, normally drunk or under the effects of some drug. He physically and verbally assaulted her. One night, in retaliation, she stabbed and killed him. On April 8, 2022, she was sentenced to eight years in prison.

Like so many other neighbors, Damián and Eliana complained about the violent robberies and flooding in La Matera. But it was their childhood and the relationship with their parents that dominated the majority of the conversations we had with them—a story marked by the criminal activities of her father and brother, filled with violence and hardship. This story vividly illustrates the existence and far-reaching consequences of early traumatic experiences.

"I Had a Childhood.... You Can't Imagine What My Childhood Was Like"

Eliana and Damián's family did not always live in La Matera. They used to live in a neighborhood forty minutes away. A dispute between groups of thieves associated with their father, Alberto, forced them to move: "We had to sell the house," recounts Damián. "My old man told us they were going to kill us all if we didn't."

For as long as they can remember, Alberto made his living stealing: "He used to say: 'I'll be back soon, I'm off to work,' and he'd go out to rob people," Damián tells us. "They'd go out robbing wearing a shirt and tie, dress pants, jacket, and shoes.... I remember being in the kitchen and the old man and his friends he went robbing with would come in and toss all the money on the table ... and I was there under the table hiding."

Damián and Eliana's mother, Rosa, collaborated in other illicit undertakings in the neighborhood: "My mom stored stolen cars for a neighbor who stole—he'd give her a little change and my mom kept them for him. She had about ten cars at the back of the house."

Damián and Eliana have very few good memories of their mother and father. Damián tells us that their dad used to say, "You don't steal from the poor ... they used to smoke anyone caught robbing in the neighborhood," and he describes him as "generous with his neighbors"—recalling that time when he brought the neighborhood a stolen meat truck: "It had like ten half cows.... [A] neighbor ratted him out and the cops showed up. I had to get rid of the truck Dad had boosted.... [T]he police came to the house and took the meat from us. But he'd left half a cow at a friend's house for a barbecue over the holidays. Do you have any idea how great that was?"

But, in general, almost all their memories are tainted by the violence their mother and father periodically and arbitrarily unleashed on them and by the difficulties they suffered during the many years that their father was in prison.

Eliana takes a long silent pause when Sofía asks her to share a "nice memory" from her childhood. "I don't know, I don't remember much ... oh yeah, when my cousins used to come to visit me."

"And what about something positive that your parents passed on to you?"

"Is taking you to a prison, making you freeze your ass off to see a loved one, passing on something positive?" answers Eliana slightly ironically. "When they break a wooden spoon over your head when Mom came home from work? I don't remember anything nice, only that they'd beat me." Eliana also remembers her childhood as a time when her brothers would bring friends over to do drugs and hide from the police, and she says that it is a miracle they did not rape her: "As a woman anything could've happened to me."

"My old man was real rough with us," says Damián. "One time we'd been hanging out in the streets, messing around. My old man looked for us everywhere. When we got home, he told the three of us to go in and wash up, and he grabbed a tree branch and let us have it, whack, whack. . . . Ever since that day I hated him, I couldn't even look at him. . . . I always think back to that day. I had marks all over. My mom had to step in because he wanted to keep going at us. He wanted to do the same thing my grandpa used to do to him; my grandpa'd take a chain into the bathroom . . . and beat the shit out of them with it. My old man wanted to do the same to us. And my mom stopped him in his tracks. . . . My grandma too. 'Do you want to go and do the same garbage your dad did to you?' That's what she said to him. And after that he never hit us again."

Both siblings remember the hunger and the abandonment they felt every time their mother visited their father in prison. Eliana: "My mom worked. The weekend would come around and she'd worry about putting together a bag of things to take to my old man. We'd go hungry. She forgot about us."

"We didn't even have enough to eat," recalls Damián. "My mom worked and everything she made she'd take to my old man. And us, 'you can fuckin' starve.' He ate well in prison; he was better off than us, we were starving to death. On Sundays, my mom would visit him again and you had to make do with some noodles and tomato sauce. As the oldest I used to go out stripping cars, swiping the wheels off cars to bring home something to eat, for me and for my brother and sister. We were starving, super skinny, you could see our bones. My mom got paid on Fridays. She'd buy groceries and take them to my old man. . . . I had to fend for myself. I'd scrounge up something for us to eat. I cooked. When she'd get back and saw I hadn't saved her any . . . whack! She'd beat the shit out of me. She'd smash my head against the wall, beat me with a stick, a belt."

During one of her visits to the prison, Damián said that his mother "told my old man I was stealing and getting high. My old man said he was going to break every bone in my body. I told him: 'You can't say a thing to me because you go out robbing with your friends and now you're in jail and we're starving to death because we don't even have enough to eat. And all your friends, not one ever comes around to ask if we need anything.' I was straight with him. And I told him Mom gave everything to him and made us noodles and tomato sauce once a week. When my mom went to see him, he told her to look after us . . . and then she started to pay attention to us, but by that time everything had already happened. . . . We were already mixed up in all sorts of things . . . headed down a bad path."

The relationship between father and son did not improve when Alberto was released from prison and Damián had his first son: "Not even when I went to ask him for help buying diapers for my son. And on top of that my mom defended him. She would say: 'You see, you asked him when he was drinking, and when he's drinking, he doesn't like to be hassled.' He'd sit around, he liked wine; he'd buy two or three bottles of Michel Torino and listen to rock 'n' roll."

"Albertito Isn't in the Cemetery"

Albertito "was a hothead," Eliana tells us. "He liked easy money. At eleven, he'd already gone out stealing shoes. And that landed him in juvi. The police caught him and let him go. Maybe if they'd left him in jail, he'd still be here with me. He'd have wised up to a few things. He'd be alive and I wouldn't mind going to see him in prison. Not like now, his body in the cemetery where no one goes to see him. I don't want to go to the cemetery. He's not there."

Albertito often went to his brother Damián's house to sleep. It was like his refuge, a break from a life devoted to crime: "Because he'd say that here, he could sleep in peace," his brother recalls. "The police were looking for him everywhere. . . . Albertito was always getting me into trouble."

He liked to steal cars; he would use them for two or three days and then take them apart. He also used to go out robbing with his dad. His father, recounts Damián, used to take him on "break-ins, to rob houses. . . . My old man took him along to straighten him out because his friends had told him he'd better get him in line or else they were going to kill him. And to straighten him out, he took him out on good jobs, not robbing people in the streets or boosting cars. He wanted to show him the right way, robbing those who had money, not the poor, that's what my old man used to tell him: 'You don't rob the poor and you don't rob in the neighborhood because on any given day when the police come looking for you, you'll find nothing but closed doors. Don't eat where you shit.' It's a code of theirs."

But Albertito did not respect that code. Damián told us that neighbors "didn't like him because he robbed the local teachers twice. One day he lost it, grabbed one of them by the hair and pistol-whipped her and took off with her car. Every cop was out looking for him.

"Once I threw him the hell out," says Damián. "I told him that whenever he came by, he brought all his problems with him. And I've got my family here: I don't want anything to do with it. I told him: 'They're coming at you from all sides. And you come to my home and they shoot up my house.' That was the day before they killed him. He asked me if he could sleep over, and I told him to come early. My wife and I waited for him. We made up the bed for him, and he didn't show. The next day I was working with my father-in-law, and Albertito stopped by the house. He was high, boozing, with a group of guys, all of them packing. . . . I told him to watch out for himself."

Robbing to Eat

The first time Damián went out robbing he was sixteen. "I didn't have anything to eat at home. I had two pistols. Each one cost me 15 pesos. . . . With 15 pesos you could eat for a week. A [pack of] Philip Morris cost 80 cents. With 5 pesos you could cook up a great stew. I had to buy the bullets myself. . . . I knew a guy who had a gun shop. The bullets," he tells us, echoing something that we heard on repeated occasions, "you can buy from the police. . . . The cops take your guns and sell them to others. They're all corrupt. If they catch you boosting a car, at the 4th [Precinct], you hand them ten grand, and you're out. The 4th Precinct is full-on corrupt."

The first time you go out stealing, explains Damián, "sure, you're a little scared shitless, the adrenaline hits you, but then it goes away. . . . If you have a gun it takes care of you . . . but lots of times the other guy is packing too, or it's the cops, and if they draw first, you're dead." One time they shot him and the bullet lodged next to his spine: "They almost left me paralyzed. . . . I thought I was dying."

That first time, Damián stole a Ford Sierra. "I chopped it up. I made about 3,000 pesos. I took the money and went to the supermarket, and I told my brother and sister: 'Grab whatever you guys want, jam, candy, cookies . . .' And I went to the butcher's and bought beef and wings, and I put it all in the freezer. . . . All on food . . . I mean, we were starving to death! When my mom got home, she saw all the food and started yelling at me, 'Where the hell did you get the money from!?' And she wanted to hit me. I told her: 'I bought it for my brother and sister, so they could eat.' I bought a bag of potatoes, a bag of onions, I bought boiled maté. . . . Of the 3,000, I spent 800 on food, and with what I had left over I went down to the corner and got loaded, high, and I bought a gun."

The conversation between Sofía and Damián takes place in his bedroom; he is looking at the photos stuck to his mirror. His eyes are fixed on the faces of his dead brother and father, his back almost completely turned to Sofía, reminiscing as if he were alone: "This other time, I was out of work, didn't have a penny for food. My son was out of diapers, so I up and got a friend to go out robbing with me. We robbed some guy who came along on a motorcycle, and then we tried to steal a car, and the police caught me. I spent a month in a cell at the police station; I thought I was never going to get out of there. They beat the shit out of me at the station.

"I tried weed, coke, pills, paco," says Damián. "I was hooked on paco for a year and a half. . . . I changed when I met my wife . . . because she doesn't like drugs, or for me to have a gun. . . . She told me, 'If you love me, you're going to have to quit it all.' I quit, but not all of it. I'd just quit when she got pregnant. . . . Now it's only booze. . . . You'll catch me having a glass of wine with my friends."

"Look What You Made Me Do"

Eliana did not have a partner to "rescue" her but rather had the complete opposite: a husband who tormented her for the better part of the seven years that their marriage lasted. Eliana stabbed that husband in the street on the night of August 31, 2019. Sebastián bled to death in the ambulance on the way to the hospital.

Before violence took over their relationship, there were, Eliana tells us, happier times. For example, when he was working and bringing home money to build their house little by little. Or when they used to take the girls on walks, buy them clothes, and eat at McDonald's. But for the years they lived together, beatings and mutual abuse came first. Eliana called the police several times but never pressed formal charges. There were many calls from neighbors complaining about the yelling and the punching between Sebastián and Eliana's brothers. Sometimes the fights started because they would find out that he had hit her, and other times even they did not know why. They would start "boozing" together, getting high, and then, says Eliana, fists would start flying. Both their girls, now six and three years old, were witnesses to dozens of physical altercations between their mother and father.

"Look what you made me do." That was what Eliana screamed at Sebastián the day she killed him. They had been separated for almost a year. After a lot of back-and-forth attempts to get back together, they had each begun new relationships. He was already expecting a child with another woman, but his abuse toward Eliana had not stopped. He used to track her down with absurd complaints—why was she going out with this guy or that guy, where was she going, with whom was she leaving the girls. Eliana told us that before that tragic night, Sebastián wanted to control her.

On more than one occasion, Eliana left their daughters with Sebastián and disappeared for days at a time. These were days of unbridled drugs and alcohol. She went back to consuming like when she was a teenager and would flee the house to go to the "fucked-up part" of La Matera. She had started drinking and smoking after the death of her father. Her mother tried, as best as she could, to "rescue" her from her addictions: She locked her in the house, left her with her grandparents, and eventually sent her to a rehabilitation center for minors. It was the birth of Eliana's daughter Luna that, according to her mother, decreased her drug use: "Something clicked inside her, a change, and she changed, it was incredible the change she made. She always kept Luna perfectly safe; she took good care of her."

"That Day She Had to Defend Herself"

One Saturday Eliana was at her aunt's house, along with her daughters and current boyfriend, celebrating her cousin's eighth birthday. It was already midnight when an uninvited Sebastián showed up at the party unexpectedly, looking for Eliana to talk about something related to the girls. Eliana's mother says that it was only an excuse to harass her because he knew she was there with her new partner and "that drove him crazy." Eliana and Sebastián started to argue in the hallway at one end of the house, and when he shook her, she punched him. He left the party without saying a word to anyone.

Sometime after 2:00 a.m., Eliana and her daughters returned home. After putting them to bed, she heard an enraged Sebastián pounding on the door. She had the house completely locked up and the windows closed. Sebastián kicked the door, leaving dents in it, and broke the windows. After fifteen minutes, he got tired and left. Furious at what he had done, she went out to look for him. She caught up to him in the neighborhood square. We do not know exactly what they talked about or what happened during the struggle.[2] The only thing we know for certain is that she stabbed him three times in the stomach and once in the leg with a knife he was carrying that night.

Her mother tells us that Eliana "was a woman who suffered from violence. She was violent too, and they would fight, he would hit her, and that day she did nothing more than defend herself. She could've avoided it, but she didn't avoid it, and that day she had to defend herself."

The Use of Our Crónica

Judicial truth does not necessarily deliver the account that rings most true. It does not exclude the possibility of seeking out a different interpretation of the facts. We might call it an ethnographic truth. —DIDIER FASSIN, *Death of a Traveller: A Counter-Investigation* (2021)

Eliana had been in jail for more than two years when, in early October 2021, we got word that the judge was about to make a ruling in her case. The public defender told Eliana's family that Eliana could get up to twenty-five years or life in prison because the murder was "aggravated by the relationship" between them (husband and wife) and such a crime carries a stern sentence in the Argentine penal code. The public defender was worried, and so was Sofía, who delivered the news to Javier. A draft of this chapter had already been written, and a summary of Eliana's story had been published in a social science journal in Buenos Aires in July 2021 (Auyero and Serviän 2021). Triggered by a sense of urgency, Javier thought that if the judge knew her entire story (as he and Sofía were able to reconstruct months before the murder), he might look more favorably on Eliana. He contacted the public defender, Doctor Soledad Lopez. To both his and Sofía's surprise, Doctor Lopez replied immediately and with great interest. Below we reproduce the (slightly edited) exchange between the sociologist and the public defender over WhatsApp. The exchange is important because, in sparking the intersection and interaction between slightly different versions of the events, it ended up determining the fate of Eliana.

October 25, 2021
JAVIER: Hi, Soledad. This is Javier Auyero. I listened again to the interviews we did with Eliana in early 2019. She makes reference to her former husband's drug use and she mentions the violence she was the victim of. I have her authorization to share the interviews with you. . . . Eliana recounts her difficult childhood, her desire to go back to school, the reasons why she dropped out. She also tells us she misses her dead brother, complains about lack of safety in the neighborhood. She speaks about her visits to her dad while he was in prison, about the

day when her brother was killed, about her mother's neglect when she was a kid, and about her brothers' drug use.... She says she does not have any good childhood memories ("I was beaten on the head with a wooden spoon"). She also says that the birth of her daughter changed her life for the better. In the second interview, she tells us she receives no financial help from her husband, and about her divorce. "We fought a lot.... He used to call me 'fatty.'" She describes their relationship as "toxic" and says that he used drugs, drank a lot, and beat her. "Our life was ugly ... he mistreated me."

October 26, 2021
SOLEDAD LOPEZ: This is very useful. I hope to be able to help Eliana. The state should somehow try, through its representatives, to redress what has not been done for her and her environment.

In *Death of a Traveller*, anthropologist Didier Fassin makes an important distinction between judicial and ethnographic truths. The first refers to the version of events that emerges out of a criminal investigation—in the case of his book, the deadly shooting of a man belonging to the Traveller community by members of a special unit of the French police. The ethnographic truth is the account that comes out of systematic sociological inquiry or what he calls a "counter-investigation." Ethnographic truth "is not limited to the individuals questioned but expands its interrogation to the social conditions of possibility of the events concerned" (2021, 9).

The reconstruction we presented in this chapter provides the context needed to understand Eliana's fatal actions. What did the "individuals questioned" say about the events of the night of September 1, 2019?

As we already mentioned, Eliana was sentenced to eight years in prison for the murder of her former husband, Sebastián. The prosecutor and the public defender agreed to what in Argentina is known as a "juicio abreviado"—a shortened judicial process in which testimony is taken but the sentence is agreed upon by both parties in advance and ratified by the judge. There was little disagreement about the facts under consideration. Eliana did kill her former husband. As the judge writes, "On September 1, 2019, at approximately 1:30 a.m., on Calle 816 bis, between 890 and 889, in San Francisco Solano, Eliana Romina Fratti inflicted on Sebastián Alejandro González— father of her two daughters and with whom she had a relationship—a one-centimeter wound on the lateral side of the right buttock and after several minutes she inflicted another injury with a knife, this time on the front side of the thorax, with clear intentions of causing death; and as a result of this injury, at 6 in the morning he died due to traumatic cardiorespiratory arrest."

According to the night watchman of the local community center, at 1:30 a.m., Sebastián approached him and asked for gauze and hydrogen peroxide "because this idiot [referring to Eliana] gave me a puntazo on the leg." The night watchman told the judge that twenty minutes later Sebastián came back and told him that "she gave me a puntazo in the chest." The watchman further reported the discussion that ensued: Sebastián told Eliana to "look at the injury you caused," and Eliana accused him of "ruining the family" while showing a butcher's knife. The watchman also heard Eliana screaming "look what you made me do." Sebastián asked him to "call an ambulance because this idiot ruined me." Eliana also asked him to please call an ambulance.

Although there are no disputes about the actual events of the murder, disagreements abound when it comes to characterizing Eliana and Sebastián. Witnesses for the prosecution describe Eliana as violent, aggressive, jealous, and vindictive and the victim as an "excellent, happy, hardworking person" who was a very good father. Witnesses for the defense use similar language to describe Eliana, and they paint a dark picture of the victim, as someone who was violent, aggressive, addicted to drugs and alcohol, and had repeatedly beaten Eliana. Based on these testimonies, the judge concluded that Eliana and Sebastián had a "traumatic, conflictive, aggressive" relationship, "filled with addictions" (to drugs and alcohol).

Why then the (short, advantageous to Eliana) eight-year sentence? The public defender told us that she knew the circumstances of the case very well. On January 2022, we met her in person and it became clear to us that, despite being overburdened with work, she did indeed know all of its specifics. She also told us that, prior to our intervention, she didn't know much about Eliana's life before that deadly night and that the interviews we summarized for her and the paper we published were "highly influential," she said, in her and the prosecutor's decision to seek an agreement and a reduced sentence. It was her way of telling us that the "ethnographic truth" we were able to reconstruct was instrumental in shaping the judicial outcome of the case.

Residents are not only victims of violence. They are also the perpetrators of physical aggression. As we just saw and we will see in chapter 7 too, violence is used to try to discipline sons and daughters, to try to control wives, to defend against brutal husbands, to obtain material resources, and to abuse and/or extort cellmates. It is deployed not only in the streets, but also in homes, police stations, prisons—in relationships involving actors with different degrees of power (parents and children, police and citizens, inmates, etc.).

Immersing ourselves further in the lives of those who are simultaneously victims and perpetrators, entering their homes and their intimate worlds, helps us to better understand the functioning of physical aggression as an instrumental and normative social relationship, the use of violence as a repertoire of (inter)action. Family relationships, which often serve as a support for strategies (legal or illegal), can be the conduit through which violence penetrates homes and permeates interpersonal relationships.

7

THE STATE OF VIOLENCE, THE VIOLENCE OF THE STATE

Perhaps writing can turn any event, even the most dramatic, into a normal occurrence. —ANNIE ERNAUX, *La Vergüenza* (2022)

"Here, you hear gunshots, and you have to get inside.... The drugs make the kids not know it's you. Drugs are on every corner," Raul tells us, reiterating what we have heard countless times. But then he adds, "The police come to get their bribe; they don't come to get the drugs. They are the ones who bring them in." To the generalized familiarity with violence and the uncertainty it produces (living with "one's heart in one's throat"), and to the association that neighbors make between the violence they suffer and the sale and consumption of drugs, Raúl (like many other neighbors) adds the sense of impotence they feel in the face of police complicity with those who are perceived as the main culprits of public insecurity.

Below we present Elías's testimony. He talks about drug dealing as a way of making ends meet and describes the complicity between state agents and participants in the criminal activities residents constantly complain about.

Elías lives in La Matera. He is 29 years old and is no stranger to the world of illicit drug distribution and use. One of his brothers is in prison for robbery. Another is in a drug treatment facility. His two younger brothers "are already on drugs." Several of his friends deal drugs in the neighborhood. Just a few years ago he used to hang with them on the corner outside his house, where he smoked weed, drank cheap alcohol, and sold "paco and joints" on more than one occasion. "If you have a family," he tells us, "you have to support them, you have to feed them, you have to give them diapers, clothes, pay for electricity, gas, etc. Sometimes things get complicated, the money is not enough, and then a dealer comes and tells you 'sell this for me' and gives you $20,000 [USD $200] a week...." [At the time of this writing, a beneficiary of a state welfare program receives $7,000, or USD $70, a month.] "And sometimes you do it out of necessity, for your family."

Elías knows that the sale of illicit drugs in La Matera, as in so many other neighborhoods, operates with police protection. Every Friday, for instance, he sees the police drive into the neighborhood to receive a packet of money from Fernando, a local dealer. Fernando tells Elías that he gives them 30,000 pesos [USD $300] each week so that they won't bother him. The police, Elías tells us, not only sell protection but also provide weapons and ammunition to the dealers. "It's easy to get weapons.... The police sell them to you. The police provide the weapons. A while ago I bought one for 3,000 pesos, I like to have it to be safe."[1]

Physical aggression in interpersonal relationships sometimes takes the form of chains. These chains can be short sequences in which one violent episode provokes another—a knife attack is retributed by another; an attempted rape prompts neighbors to attack the suspect's house (Auyero and Berti 2016). As we saw in chapter 6, these concatenations can also be temporally extensive sequences, as when violence is transmitted from one generation to another in the form of predispositions that are acquired early on from direct experience within the domestic unit, or as when violent interactions accumulate over time and end up exploding in a lethal outcome, as in Eliana's case.

The story below shows that violence also resembles an oil slick in the ocean. It spreads from inside the home, where Luis, Gonzalo, and Cristina learned to suffer it when they were beaten by their alcoholic father and husband, to the streets where Gonzalo brutally assaults his neighbors, to the police station where police torture detainees, or to the jail where prisoners torment (and are tormented by) other prisoners. The use of violence, in the story that follows, permeates vertical relationships between agents of the state and citizens, men and women, parents and their children, and horizontal ones, among prisoners and neighbors.

The reconstruction that follows may seem idiosyncratic. However, these details lose their particularity once placed in the context of the exponential increase in incarceration rates and the extension of the tentacles of the penal system into the daily lives of the urban poor that we present in the next section.

The Prison and the Police Station at the Margins

Since 2002, the incarceration rate in Argentina has increased from 154 to 209 per 100,000 people. To a large extent this increase is explained, as in the case of the massive growth of US incarceration rates since the mid-1970s, by the so-called war on drugs. Between 2002 and 2018, the population incarcerated for drug offenses soared by 252 percent (Centro de Estudios Legales y Sociales [CELS] 2019, 135). Those at the bottom of the social structure are the most affected by this notable increase. The vast majority of those incarcerated for drugs in 2017 had not completed high school (85 percent), and at the time of their arrest, 36 percent of males and 46 percent of females were unemployed.

The overwhelming majority of those arrested for illicit drug offenses are not the "big narcos" but the most vulnerable actors in this criminalized market, "actors easily replaced within the narcotics trade chain such as 'little soldiers,' retail sellers, people used as couriers or micro-traffickers" (CELS 2019, 136). A large number of these actors await their trial in jail, under preventive detention, for long periods of time.

This explosion in the incarceration rate has translated into, on the one hand, prison overcrowding and, on the other, systematic use of police stations as prolonged detention centers where abuses are frequent and go unpunished. As we will see below, and as has been repeatedly documented by human rights organizations, violence by police officers coexists with abuse and aggression among the incarcerated. Like prisons in the United States, Argentine prisons are "de facto gladiator schools that hone the fighting skills of inmates" and "oblige inmates to be aggressively violent in order to avoid victimization while simultaneously trapping them in a catch-22 feedback loop of solitary confinement, extended prison sentences, and punitive lockdowns" (Bourgois et al. 2019, 29). What anthropologist Philippe Bourgois calls the "institutionalized brutality" of prison in the United States is here amplified by the existence of extortion networks involving prison service agents and inmates—networks that, as we shall see, further encourage interpersonal violence.

It is also important to note that the expansion of incarceration transcends the physical perimeters of confinement centers. Prison is now a constant presence in the daily life of the most marginalized neighborhoods—an institution like the school and the health center with which the poor routinely interact. It is very common (much more common than two decades ago when one of us began his research in relegated urban areas) to meet people whose siblings, children, fathers, mothers, or close relatives are imprisoned in jails or detained in police stations. Many of these people organize their routines (and plan their weekly expenses) around visits to detention centers.

Robbing for Real

"Your son has a guardian angel," the sergeant told Cristina, Gonzalo's mother. "We tried to take him out but couldn't hit him." Cristina was at the police station waiting for them to release her son after he had tried to rob the owners of a pizzeria.

Gonzalo knew he would not spend more than a night in that dark, damp, filthy cell: "That's why I went out robbing, because I knew, at fifteen years old, they wouldn't keep me in jail long." Still feeling the effects of the pills he had taken before going out to rob and with his head bloodied from the beating the police had given him once they arrested him, Gonzalo was bragging to the other inmates: "I'm in here because I got into a shoot-out with the cops. I was out robbing for real." That night had been his first time. Before then he had mugged people at the bus stop, using only his fists. But "thieving" is something very different from "robbing for real," gun in hand.

That night was different, planned. With three of his friends, they called the pizzeria, pretending to order a large cheese pizza, and found out when it was closing: "There were three of them, a family of Paraguayans. The guy who made the pizzas, the mom, and a little brother." They had to calculate the robbery for the precise moment after the patrol car would pass on its rounds but before the family reached the avenue—where the traffic and streetlights would make it difficult to rob them. They met up at the corner and drank several Coca-Colas with beer. Gonzalo put half a strip of Rivotril in his glass. Six pills. All in one gulp.

Gonzalo and Maribel hid their guns. Toto and Mario grabbed their sticks and bottles. Sometime after midnight, once they saw the lights of the patrol car fading in the distance, they jumped the family from behind a tree. "Don't move, this is a robbery," Gonzalo yelled at the owner of the pizzeria. When the man tried to run away, Gonzalo smacked the mother, grabbed her by the hair, and threw her to the ground. Toto struck the young boy over the head with his stick. "Stop, don't hurt her," begged the owner and pulled a wad of money from his pocket. Gonzalo sensed that there was more and fired once at the ground, a few feet from the mother, whose hair he was still gripping tightly. The shot galvanized the fourth assailant who, breaking a bottle over the boy's head, started to yell, "I'm gonna kill him, I'll kill him." When the woman saw that Gonzalo was pointing a gun at her son's head, she reached into her bra and threw another, larger wad of bills on the sidewalk. While some of them gathered up the money, the others took the youngest victim's new soccer jersey and his shiny new shoes.

Less than three blocks from the robbery, when the four of them were scurrying away in the opposite direction of the avenue, a police car appeared. Gonzalo remembers running, the money falling from his pockets, the shootout, the gun he tossed into a ditch, the four police cars cutting him off, and the final scene when he tried to scale a wall "to start jumping from house to house . . . and the two bullets that made me fall back."

Gonzalo shows us the scar on his cheek that he has had since that night. His "guardian angel" had saved him from dying, but not from the beating he received from those uniformed men during the hours that he was at the station.

"Five Months in the Pen"

More than a year had passed since that first robbery. "So you're Gonzalito? So you're the famous Gonzalito?" three policemen yelled at him as they slapped him across the face and punched him in the ribs. They had him hanging from a gas pipe in the basement of the station. A few hours later, they transferred him to the penitentiary where he would spend five months, accused of a homicide that he did not commit. "I was hurting all over."

Neither Gonzalo nor Luis, his younger brother, really know the source of the confusion that led to him being put behind bars. "I spent five months, fighting, surviving. I spent a month fighting almost every day, someone would come along and, bam bam, I was fighting, another would come along and, smash smash, I was fighting. They'd take me out of one cell and send me to another because I'd enter a cell and there might be three guys there, and I'm not gonna let nobody intimidate me . . . and so fists would start flying." Luis remembers his visits to the penitentiary: "It was so horrible going to see him. . . . He suffered a lot in there. They were always fighting. I remember the smell of blood in the prison every time me and my mom went to see him."

After a week in prison, Gonzalo met a man from the northeastern province Corrientes, whom they aptly called "Correntino." To the best of his memory, this is how his first conversation with him went:

c: What's up, brother?

g: Who you calling brother, motherfucker!

c: Hey, hold up, I didn't say nothing bad to you, don't disrespect me because I didn't disrespect you.... Have a seat. Are you hungry?

g: And what's it to you if I'm hungry?

c: I'll tell you again, I'm not disrespecting you, don't disrespect me, because if you want to fight, we'll fight, but if you don't want to fight, sit down, and if you're hungry, eat something.

g: Yeah, tell you the truth, I'm spent, man. I'm in here doing time for nothing.

Gonzalo broke down in front of Correntino. He cried for a long while.

I'm in here and I didn't do nothing, and they're beating the shit outta me, man.

c: Yeah, I heard you all night. They were moving you from cell to cell, all night long. I couldn't get any sleep because of you. But you know what? In three of those cells, you're the one who started the fight, and in the other three cells, you made them respect you.

g: If I don't, I'm gonna end up being someone's bitch or someone's wife.

Thanks to Correntino, Gonzalo was able to get some rest. He slept almost two days straight, exhausted from all the fighting. A few days later, another inmate tipped them off that a dealer had arrived at the penitentiary. "Selling drugs and rape are the worst things you can do," says Gonzalo. "Prison is meant for guys that rob, not for a drug addict or a rapist." The same day they found out, Correntino asked Gonzalo to get "the pigeon" ready—a bedsheet cut into strips that they used to tie the dealer to the cell toilet. "We pigeoned him up, put a blanket over his head, and started punching him." In prison "you can [have been] a small-time thief, you can lift chains [steal cars], rob old ladies, kill, get into shoot-outs," but you cannot have sold drugs. A dealer is seen as someone who "ruins dudes."

Being at the very bottom of that convict totem pole means suffering violence from the more dominant inmates and also being a tool to satisfy the material and corporeal needs of those who call the shots in prison. For two nights, Gonzalo and Correntino forced the dealer to phone his relatives: "Tell your family to bring me a TV, a PlayStation, a tape recorder.... Tell your wife to request a private visit with me."

Throughout the months of Gonzalo's incarceration, he was always prepared for a fight. Starting at seven in the morning, he would head to the showers with his towel and soap, keeping his underwear on as he washed. That is where he hid his knife. Many of the brawls that occurred between prisoners came in response to extortion involving their girlfriends and mothers: "You try to do that to him and the dude is gonna want to fight you: 'You might kill me, but you don't mess with my family'..., and you have to fight. But that's how it is, that's life on the inside."

The dealer was transferred off the block, and a few weeks later another prisoner took his place. Gonzalo liked the new arrival. He claimed to have "caught a robbery rap," to have important contacts. "But prison is a small world," Gonzalo tells us. "If you lie, you're the worst, because sooner or later someone comes along and spills on you. Another prisoner ratted on him." Word got out that the new inmate had raped a six-year-old girl. It did not take long for them to "pigeon him up."

Gonzalo grabbed him by the hair, furious at having been deceived for several days, and with a few of the others, forced him to call one of his daughters: "We're taking good care of your dad. He has every comfort here, but he needs food. In an hour, we're gonna get you a list of the meals your dad is gonna eat. Your dad's gonna put together a little list and we'll get it to you. When you come on Tuesday, don't forget to bring the food."

They also demanded marijuana and cocaine. "No, but how am I supposed to pass you the stuff?" the daughter replied desperately. Gonzalo explained to her: "Listen, you're gonna get a condom, you'll use your mouth to blow it up, in it you'll put a 25 [25 grams of marijuana] and the blow.... You'll tie it in a knot, you'll put another condom over it the other way and you'll tie it again, then you end up with a little block.... You're gonna spread your legs real wide and stick it inside; you'll come here and don't forget to put in one of those tampon things women use. Don't forget to put that in you or else the drugs are gonna fall out while you're walking. When you get here, you give it to your dad, and he'll give it to us."

After spelling out their orders for her, Gonzalo and his partners continued with their threats: "If you don't do everything I tell you... listen to your dad's face." The punches and shouts rang out from the other end of the line. "The girl brought us food from the list, Oreos, alfajores Guaymallén, juice, all sorts of cookies, three tubes of toothpaste, three bottles of shampoo, conditioner, noodles, sugar, rice...lots of food. That's life for a rapist, someone who's a dealer...they all live that way."

"Collecting for the Lawyer"

Cristina, Gonzalo's mother, took care of finding the money to pay for a private lawyer—they did not trust the public defender, who they thought wanted him to go to jail. In order to get the 35,000 pesos that the lawyer was asking, they sold their furniture, the refrigerator, and the television.

They never had extra money lying around in the house. Cristina remembers the mornings in the city center when she would stand in line in exchange for money: "We used to sell spots outside Nation Bank. You would get to the bank early in the morning and stand in line like normal, like you were going to buy dollars. We had a sign and offered the spot for 8 pesos. With 1 peso, you could buy three kilos of flour; with 6, you could buy [a tank of] gas." She also recalls the different state welfare programs and food kitchens that helped her make it to the end of the month each time she or her husband lost their job. She remembers the strips of sheet metal she received from the city to build their house and the boxes of food she had access to, thanks to her friendship with Pocho, the neighborhood puntero. She also remembers asking her husband, José, how to go about selling marijuana and cocaine in the neighborhood: "I swear I considered dealing out of sheer desperation."

The family budget always had to consider José's addiction to alcohol and cocaine. He secretly spent all the savings they had put aside for a used washing machine. Cristina had to make several payments to buy her youngest daughter a dress and shoes for her fifteenth birthday, using the extra money that she made selling food to the neighbors. She did not ask José for a cent: "He says we throw money away and doesn't see how much he spends on booze and drugs."

Released into the Countryside and Hugging Your Brother

Every extra peso that Cristina did not use—"we played eeny, meeny, miny, moe to decide what we'd pay for and what we wouldn't"—ended up in the pockets of the lawyer. It was money well spent; a few days after he had done his five months in prison, Gonzalo was released.

They let him out at midnight. "They made me sign some papers, opened up the gate, and sent me out into the countryside, to the road." Gonzalo did not know how to get home. He walked for two hours until he saw a sign and realized he had been going in the wrong direction. He managed to convince a bus driver to drop him off not far from his house for free, arriving very early in the morning. There he hugged Cristina and Luis. José, his father, had left early for work.

The first night in his house, he dreamed that "they were coming to get me, that I was gonna get shanked. I could hear the sounds of the bars. I could hear the guys yelling. I'd wake up at night and lie there staring at the door, thinking the police were about to bust in looking for me."

Luis's face lights up when he remembers the day Gonzalo came home from the penitentiary. They celebrated their reunion, he recalls, with bread and Coca-Cola. "You have no idea, Sofi, how much I cried when I saw him again."

"I'd Rather Be Embarrassed and Not Be Hungry"

Throughout their childhood and adolescence, the brothers had been inseparable. They slept in each other's arms in a twin bed, and together they suffered their father's violent attacks: "My old man was a real piece of shit, an asshole. He didn't give my mom money for food: He'd hit her, he beat the shit out of us . . . he drank a lot, got high . . . I was embarrassed." That is how Luis remembers his father.

The same goes for Gonzalo: "I don't have any nice memories of my dad. I don't remember playing with my dad. My mom says I did, but I don't remember my dad ever taking my hand and going for a walk or taking me shopping . . . never. I only remember him always hitting me, that he was drunk, partying. Anyone who slipped up, he'd hit them."

When he was six, Gonzalo was already making the rounds to the local food kitchens asking for a plate of food—his father was out of work or would spend everything he earned on drugs or alcohol. He started collecting bottles or cardboard when he was seven or eight years old. He remembers the humiliation he and his brother were subjected to. When Luis asked at a bakery if there was any bread left over, the owner, in front of several customers, yelled at them that they were a couple of slackers: "Tell your dad to get a job." Luis started to cry and told his brother that he did not like begging, that it was embarrassing. "Me neither," Gonzalo replied on their way home, "but I'd rather be embarrassed and not be hungry."

One year, for Epiphany, me and Luis went to play at our grandpa's house. All the cousins were there.... We went home in tears, we got there, and my dad was drunk... for a change, right? And, so, we sat down crying in front of him. My dad asked us why we were crying and we said: "Because we don't have any toys and all our cousins do." My dad hugged us and started to cry too. He told us he was sorry and said he couldn't buy toys, that he had his welfare check and a few side hustles but it wasn't enough. Then he said, "I'll be right back," and he left. We sat there and a little while later, my dad comes back with a bag this big. I don't really remember, but I think it had a ball and two water guns. The next day my mom told us my dad had gone around the corner from our house to a store where they know him and asked them to put the toys on his tab and that he would pay them later.

"That sounds like a nice memory," says Sofía.
"It's the only one I have. He treated us real bad."

Polito and the Fan

"When I was a kid, I used to get down on my knees in front of my old man and beg him not to drink anymore," recalls Luis. "Once he was so strung out, at a party, he didn't recognize us, and he pointed a rifle at us.... An uncle of mine came over and punched him and knocked him out and they tied him to a bed." And what was for Luis perhaps the most definitive proof that he had not had a father around to take care of him, to look after him, he says, "Last Saturday I went to the movies for the first time. I'm twenty-five years old; I went with my son.... That's so sad. Every Friday there was a fight, my old man with one of my brothers. He would also hit my mom. I was five, I'll never forget it."

Cristina will never forget it either. She suffered José's insults and beatings in silence for many years. "He insulted me and I sat there quietly.... He'd go crazy when he was on drugs; he was like another person. When that craziness takes hold of him, he doesn't care about anything."

On more than one occasion, Cristina had to take her children and flee the house for fear that José would hurt her or one of them. She usually went to her father's house to spend the night until her husband had calmed down. One Saturday afternoon, when José was very drunk and especially violent, Cristina switched up her usual refuge. She ran with her children to her sister's place about twenty blocks away, where José would never think to look for her. In her haste to leave the house, Cristina, Gonzalo, Luis, and their two younger sisters forgot about Polito, the family parrot. They all loved that bird, recalls a close relative: "Every time we'd go to their house, they'd show us some funny new trick it was learning, like saying 'hello' or asking for 'a little water' when it was thirsty." This relative gives us an account of what happened when Gonzalo went back for Polito:

> Since he didn't know if his dad was still off his head, he decided to go in through the back door . . . just in case, so he wouldn't see him. He grabbed his parrot along with its cage and saw his dad was lying on the bed, sleeping. It was summer and very hot. José had the fan on, but the air wasn't blowing directly on him. Gonzalo saw he was sweating a lot. He went into the bedroom and turned it so it was pointing directly at him.

Cristina once chose not to stay quiet and not to flee. "One day everything went bad between us. I put him in his place. I'd made up my mind, if he came at me, I was going to break his skull. I was going to kick him out of the house. I told him to stop treating me like garbage. The next day he asked me to forgive him. He realized I wasn't going to back down." However, to this day, she still suffers the occasional beating from José.

Parental and marital violence marked the childhood and adolescence of the siblings and the adult life of Cristina. In the above narrative, violence coexists with the memory of a son's caring gesture toward his father "who was going crazy," and with the hugging and crying of this same "piece of shit" father when he had no money to buy gifts. This coexistence captures how torturous it has been for the siblings—and still is for Cristina—to deal with this father and this husband.

The beatings, the threats, the yelling, the drugs, and the alcohol have sculpted not only Gonzalo's, Luis's, and Cristina's pasts, but also their aspirations and their hopes. Without giving us details, but knowing that we understood what she was talking about (because we knew her story), Cristina told us that she wished the future "wasn't so much like the past." When, in another conversation during the pandemic, we asked her what she wished for her daughter, Micaela (now twelve years old), we were surprised (although we shouldn't have been) by her answer: Unlike many other parents who talked about their children's future career or education, Cristina said that what she really wanted was for Micaela to find someone who "wouldn't mistreat her." Only by delving into her history and her present of violence can we truly comprehend this particular and urgent plea.

Rather than isolating episodes as if they belong to different spheres (public or private), we decided to present the story on the basis of multiple accounts so that readers can observe not only the form that violence takes in the home and in the street, but also the effects of early exposure to it and the participation of state agents in its exercise. Vertical violence between state agents and detainees, horizontal violence between inmates and between members of the domestic unit: Both coexist in this story, forming concatenations of physical aggression.

The pibes, whom the neighbors point to as the main culprits of the violence that plagues them, have histories. Reconstructing Gonzalo's story does not seek to exonerate him from the brutal violence he exercised with his friends on the owners of the pizzeria or with his cellmates on other inmates and their relatives. It is not the task of the social sciences to put individuals on trial but rather to understand, through a radical contextualization, the web of relationships that produces this daily violence: absent and abusive parents, environments in which access to addiction treatment is nonexistent, "law enforcement" agents who act as armed thugs (protectors of some illegal enterprises, and suppliers of the weapons with which the robberies are carried out), and prisons in which networks of extortion and abuse are part of their ordinary functioning. Of course, not all (or, as far as our evidence shows, most) of the residents are involved in violent worlds like Gonzalo and Luis, or Damián and Eliana, but pibes like them set the tone and pace of life in marginalized neighborhoods.

The Limits of Understanding

I have electric dreams. Where my dad, when he can't fix something, smashes it into the ground. He gets angry, shouts, calls names. We scream our love for each other, sometimes with blows. That's what we are. A pack of wild animals with dreams of humanity. Sometimes one needs several lives to comprehend this. The rage that runs through us doesn't belong to us. —From the film *I Have Electric Dreams* (dir. Valentina Maurel, 2022)

"We knew how to hear what was not said, how to understand silence," writes Jesmyn Ward in *Mother Swamp* (2022, 4), her moving fictional account of nine generations of women who have survived enslavement, hunger, and sickness. That sentence came to mind as we were trying to understand what these stories' "complex specificness, their circumstantiality" (Geertz 1973, 23) say about life at the margins and what they silence. Are we equipped to get to the heart of these stories, what they say and what they can't quite articulate? And what is their "heart" anyway?

What happens every time Eliana looks at her dead brother Albertito's picture? And when she remembers a wooden spoon cracking on her head? And when Damian feels, because we think he can still feel, the tree branches breaking on his back? And what kind of mark has that glass bottle left on the pizzeria boy? Or the cops' punches on Gonzalo's ribs and face? How many sufferings does Eliana articulate as she screams at her dying former husband, "Look what you made me do"? These stories, although as extensive, detailed, and profound as we were able to reconstruct, only scratch the surface of the actual impacts and meanings of violence. It would be intellectually arrogant to argue otherwise.

These stories show us that violence is deployed in a diversity of interactions. It is used to procure material resources, to exercise (or attempt to exercise) discipline within the home, to control a partner, to retaliate for a previous offense, to defend oneself, and to resist or reinforce authority in private and in public, in the household, in the prison, or in the streets. Sometimes it emerges with malicious intent and sometimes it is, as the neighbors pointed out when talking about "how crazy the kids get with drugs," a by-product of alcohol or psychoactive drugs. Gonzalo intuitively knew this when he went out to "rob for real," high on a mix of alcohol and Rivotril pills. Many of these distinctions, as it is clear from our reconstructions, dissolve in the whirlwind of physical fury in which people like Damián, Eliana, and Gonzalo have been socialized and which to this day marks their lives.

Bringing in the larger structural and political factors that shape their experiences and enable their reproduction—the high levels of poverty and the misery it entails, the growth in the illicit drug market and the economic opportunities it presents for urban youth, the involvement of police forces in the regulation of this market, their levels of brutality, the increasing rates of incarceration, the absence of effective social policies, and so on—is certainly needed to better comprehend what is going on.

And still . . . Damián seems to be doing okay now; Eliana is behind bars for killing her former partner. Early exposure to violence shapes dispositions to physical aggression, but it does not dictate a definite outcome. Other interactions matter too: a partner and a child who "save you," a lawyer that takes you under her wing, a friend who leads you into even further trouble. We deal with tendencies and possible trajectories; constraints, not determinations.

Sofía kept digging into the many twists and turns of these stories because we knew that the long-term relationships she had with Gonzalo, Gonzalo's mother, Damián, and Eliana were the basis of a deep trust. Such trust, in turn, is the condition of possibility for the kind of personal, meaningful answers she obtained in often very difficult conversations. As we listened to the recordings, we thought that it was our job to "write it all down" and construct as accurately as possible interpretive accounts—inscriptions, as Geertz (1973) would put it—that can also be reinterpreted by others as they are reading them. We also knew that we were never going to get to the bottom of these stories, to provide a definitive understanding. That certainty, which one of the protagonists of Ward's short story talks about, is beyond us.

8

WOMEN AT WORK
The Social Life of a Community Center

It is necessary, as Flaubert taught us, to learn to bring to bear on Yvetot the look that one affords so willingly to Constantinople: to learn, for example, to give the marriage of a woman teacher to a post office worker the attention and interest that would have been lent to the literary account of a misalliance, and to offer to the statements of a steelworker the thoughtful reception which a certain tradition of reading reserves for the highest forms of poetry or philosophy. —PIERRE BOURDIEU, "Understanding" (1996)

"My legs hurt, particularly my knees. I've only been working for a day doing what these women do four times a week. I'm exhausted." This is Sofía's entry from her fieldwork diary on July 1, 2021. She is describing her first day of participant observation at the "Comedor de Virginia." Virginia is the name of one of the founding members of the community center where Sofía volunteered over the course of six months. From Monday to Thursday, a group that oscillates between six and eighteen women distributes food rations to roughly 160 families from La Matera and El Tala. The food is, in part, provided by the mu-

FIGURE 8.1. Food at the comedor: one package of crackers, two carrots, two onions, two potatoes, one bottle of oil (1 L), one carton of tomato puree, one carton of milk (1 L), two bags of pasta, one bag of polenta (18 oz.), six eggs, one bag of sugar (18 oz.), one bag of lentils (18 oz.), one package of powdered milk (500 g), and two cans of tuna.

nicipal government and private donors and, in part, purchased by the women at the center (see figure 8.1). Food rations include fresh produce, such as potatoes, carrots, and onions. They also include various types of dry goods, such as noodles, rice, powdered milk, polenta, sugar, flour, eggs, a quince paste, and one fresh chicken. Every week, Tacho, the only man in the group, unloads the chickens from the municipal truck and stores them in the center's freezer until the day of the distribution.

SOFÍA'S FIELDWORK DIARY, JULY 1, 2021. *When we finished packing everything, Claudia put together a list of people who could not come to pick up the food (they were sick, no adult was available, etc.). Together with Brenda, María, Fernanda, and Julia, we take the food packages to them in two carts. Felipe, an old man we brought food to, gave us a bag with chocolates and candies in return. According to Brenda, he always gives them a little present.*

FIGURE 8.2. Six residents line up outside the soup kitchen to receive food.

Sofía's first note captures the grueling physical labor that goes into preparing the rations—from unloading the heavy bags from the truck that brings them to the community center, to setting them up in the main room, to packing them up for distribution (which involves spending hours squatting) and bringing them to those who cannot pick them up in person. That day Sofía participates by packing merchandise. A few days later, on the sidewalk of the center, she sits next to two of the "chicas del comedor" (as the women from the center are known) to distribute food rations. Every week, keeping the appropriate social distance imposed by the pandemic, neighbors form a line outside the center to pick up their rations—neatly arranged to avoid damaging the most fragile products (see figure 8.2).

Less than three months after visiting the center for the first time, Sofía is already part of its daily dynamics, working alongside the core group of women—to the point that they decide that she should be compensated for her commitment. One day after lunch, early in October 2021, one of the coordinators and Sofía have the following conversation. We reproduce it because it illustrates the ethnographer's position—at once achieved and bestowed through her sustained engagement—and also because it anticipates one of the themes that we will explore in this chapter: the material and symbolic rewards obtained in (and conferred by) this collective care work (which includes but also exceeds the mere distribution of food). Like many of the fieldnotes presented throughout this chapter, we edited them for clarity. We also decided to keep many of the apparently trivial details in the text so that readers can actually witness the interactions taking place in real time and see the role of the ethnographer in the production of the data (the emphasis is ours).[1]

SILVIA [one of the center's coordinators]: Sofi, who do you live with?

SOFÍA: With my mother and brother. My parents have been divorced for a long time. It's only us three.

SILVIA: Does your mom work?

SOFÍA: Yes, she is a domestic worker. She works four times a week. All is good.

SILVIA: I ask because Virginia was talking about giving you food rations every week.

SOFÍA: But... well, I benefit from coming here; you know I am doing research. So, I don't think I should be given food rations.

SILVIA: Yes, we know your research, don't waste your time telling us. But, beyond that, *you are putting in your time here, and that has a certain value.* Even if it is one hour, or two, or an entire day. You may not realize, but there are some activities that we wouldn't be able to carry out without you. *You give the children who come here your time, a look, a smile, a hug.... That has value, and we want to acknowledge that.* Even though we do not have much to give, even if it is only a pack of noodles, it is our way of recognizing you, because your time is valuable and we want to thank you. And, on top of that, well, for me, you are already one of us. Every day I ask about you because I'm used to seeing you. It [the food ration] is a recognition for the time you put in here.

Reflection #4

FEBRUARY 2, 2022. I didn't really want to accept the food rations. I know it was their way of compensating me for my help. The soon-to-be-an-anthropologist Sofía knows that it is perfectly okay to receive food, that it is something "dignified." But the Sofía of the past, the girl who waited in long lines for many hours along with her mother to receive "social assistance" (the Sofía that still lives in me), feels ashamed. It was hard for that Sofía to accept the food rations that the women at the center were so generously offering.

It didn't take us long to realize that, although packaging and distributing food rations was a key part of the work these women carry out on a daily basis, these activities are not the ones from which they derive most of their gratification and recognition. The community center is a site of intense neighborhood sociability—where women like Silvia, Macarena, Majo, Claudia, Silvi, and Patricia not only feed children and adults, but also educate kids and youth and share vital (and sometimes intimate) information with their neighbors and among themselves.

At the Comedor de Virginia, these women teach reading and craft classes, prepare breakfast and snacks for the participants, make gifts and souvenirs for the students on national holidays or for other celebrations (Children's Day, Mother's Day, etc.), and organize outings (during our fieldwork, children visited the Ciudad de los Niños in La Plata, less than an hour away). These activities require constant rearrangement and cleaning of the center's multipurpose room and kitchen (more than once, Sofía was in charge of sweeping and wiping everything down after each class). The group also manages a day-care center located half a block from the center (Virginia's daughter, Silvi, is the main coordinator). The administrative work is also unremitting: Coordinators must organize and communicate the shifts to ensure that all activities (packaging, distribution, cleaning, cooking, classes, etc.) are covered, while constantly seeking out additional donations of food and clothing. The food sent by the municipal government is never enough; every week they supplement the rations with fresh produce they themselves purchase or obtain from private donors.

In addition to their jobs (a majority have informal jobs as domestic workers, shop attendants, etc.) and the "double shift" they carry out at home (cooking, cleaning their houses, and raising their children—tasks that include, as mentioned in a previous chapter, strong routines of protection against the interpersonal violence around them), these women complete a "third shift" at the center. They thus offer a clear illustration of women's triple role, first identified by Caroline Moser: productive, reproductive, and community.[2] As Moser (1993, 28–29) puts it in her now-classic book:

FIGURE 8.3. A female cook serves soft drinks at the soup kitchen.

In most low-income Third World households women have a triple role. "Women's work" includes not only reproductive work, the childbearing and rearing responsibilities, required to guarantee the maintenance and reproduction of the labor force. It also includes productive work, often as secondary income earners. In rural areas this usually takes the form of agricultural work. In urban areas women frequently work in informal sector enterprises located either in the home or the neighborhood. Also, women undertake community managing work around the provision of items of collective consumption, undertaken in the local community in both urban and rural contexts.

At the center, from Monday through Thursday, they take care of others beyond their immediate and extended families (see figures 8.3 and 8.4). In exchange for their work, the state grants them an "incentive" of 15,500 pesos per month (10,500 from a welfare program, and 5,000 for participating in the soup kitchen). They do not receive a salary in exchange for the hours of work they put in, but an "incentive," not a juicy amount (as those who criticize the alleged generosity of state assistance plans seem to believe), but less

FIGURE 8.4. The inside of the main room of the soup kitchen. Big bags of onions are ready to cook

than one-fifth of what is needed to cover the basic food basket according to INDEC (the National Institute of Statistics and Census). As this exchange between one of the center's coordinators and the man who unloads the produce from the municipal truck illustrates, these women are very aware of their meager stipends:

SOFÍA'S FIELDNOTES, JULY 14, 2021. *In between jokes, one of the men who unloads the truck tells Majo: "Come on now, stop bothering me. Do you know how much they pay me for doing this?" Majo replies: "Do you want to know how much I get paid? You earn more than I do!"*

Along with the money they get paid as "incentive," each woman receives a bag of produce and a fresh chicken every week—the same food ration they distribute among neighbors. In order to get the extra 5,000 pesos, they need to produce receipts (they call them "tickets"). These receipts should only be for food. Given that they sometimes use the extra cash to pay for a variety of things (medicine, cell-phone charges, debts, etc.), they are always in search of "good tickets" to justify the funds received.

SOFÍA'S FIELDNOTES, JULY 6, 2021. *"Yesterday while we were walking to La Matera," says Mariana, "I picked up a lot of receipts. I crouched down so many times, I think half the neighborhood saw my ass," she adds with a laugh. "Without them we don't get paid, there is no money," says Mary, who explains, "We have to present them to be able to justify the money they give us so that they can reconcile the funds with those on top."*

AUGUST 31, 2021. *Majo (who handles some of the administrative tasks at the center) is doing accounts with the calculator on her cell phone. The women who work at the center are about to receive their 5,000 pesos incentive and they must, like they do every month, bring supermarket receipts. "Oh, you're quite an accountant," Mary tells her. "These receipts are really good. Leila [my daughter] told me that later she will bring me more," Mary says. "Ah, okay," Majo replies, "but with the ones you already gave me you are well covered."*

Routines in Context

These women's routines must be understood in the context of the economic hardship and interpersonal violence described in earlier chapters. The emphasis that they place on apparently minor details of their tasks (the number of items that a goodie bag should contain, the way to cut the cardboard for crafts that will accompany a gift for Family Day) and the meaning that they imprint on their activities must, in turn, be understood within the framework of the devaluation of care work and the stigma that weighs on those who receive state assistance. They may not discursively articulate these ideas, but the logic of their actions (the arrangement of their schedules, the organized execution of their tasks, the dedication to details that they themselves recognize their students will not pay much attention to) indicates that they are constructing a meaningful world.[3] In what follows, we argue through ethnographic documentation that these women's everyday praxis is a *relational way of persisting*. We pay attention to apparently unimportant circumstances of their joint caregiving tasks, and we demonstrate how and why these women not only take care *of* others, but also care deeply *about* them. We also show that in establishing routines and sustaining relationships (which are not exempt from conflicts and tensions) they exercise a "popular ethic"—that is, an effort to collectively do what they believe is the right thing in a context that constantly pushes against it (Das 2012; Lambek 2010).

Our observations record both our initial impressions (how tired we are after a day's work, for example) as well as particular moments or incidents (the day devoted to helping a girl do her homework, the day the current mayor visits the center). But, above all, our observations focus on what the women at the center experience on a daily basis as well as what they consider significant or important (the care they put into each task, the attention to routines that organize the life of the center, what they say to each other in the daily work, etc.) (Emerson 2011). In formal and informal interviews, we avoid asking, "Why do you do this or that?" Because these questions often produce self-justifying narratives, we focus instead on questions such as "How do you do this? And after doing this, what else do you do?" These interrogations usually generate detailed reports of the ways that experiences develop. These reports and our observations uncover illuminating moments that help us understand what actually happens at the center and how these women think and feel about their work—practices, thoughts, and feelings that are, after all, the empirical object of all ethnographic work.

The community center is not a place devoid of tensions. The most significant strains occur between the longtime coordinators and those newer to the center, who sometimes clash over the schedules everyone must comply with, the work with the youngsters, or what they consider the best ways to carry out certain tasks. We emphasize their collective work—and the sociability and recognition that they create—not because we intend to exalt these women or praise their tasks. It is not, as we said at the beginning of this book, the task of sociology or anthropology to pass moral or political judgments or build heroic characters. Six months of systematic participatory observation serve as the basis for building a realistic narrative—a narrative that pays simultaneous attention to interactive and affective dynamics and to the local context of vital uncertainty in which these occur. It is only through this contextualization that we can hope to understand these women's thoughts, feelings, and practices.

Ordinary Days

The activities at the center are quite diverse, and the center's workers become frantic when there is a special event, such as an outing or a visit from a public official. The following fieldnotes capture the daily routines during a typical day at the center.

SOFÍA'S FIELDNOTES, JULY 29, 2021. *When I arrive, they are just starting their activities. There are three groups. Brenda, Mary, and Betty have returned from the grocery store and are packing the food rations. Every time they pack ten rations, they separate them and write it down on a list to keep track. They have to put together 160 bags. The second group (Camila, Macarena, and Anahí) are in the library unpacking the boxes of merchandise (sent by the municipal government) to prepare the rations. A third group (Claudia, Yesica, and I) are putting together school kits for the children. As of Monday, face-to-face classes at the center are back, and so are classes at the local school (after the first wave of infections during the COVID-19 epidemic). Claudia thinks it is a good idea to give the kids some basic supplies to start classes. For the elementary school boys and girls, we put together a kit that includes a folder, lined paper, pencils, erasers, a ruler, and a notebook. There are also new overalls, as well as folders, paper, pencils, and notebooks set aside for the high school students. While Claudia is putting together the kits, Yesi and I assemble the folders with sheets of paper. We are missing some sheets and we go and buy them. While we are doing this, Majo, Silvia, and Susi arrive. The latter join the group that is preparing the food rations.*

AUGUST 3, 2021. *Eleven elementary schoolchildren arrive around 2 p.m. As they enter, Majo takes their temperature and writes it down with the child's name. Children sit at their tables, and Majo and Priscila tell them that, since the afternoon is sunny, they will be playing outside. . . . We are outside for two hours. When we go back into the library, Eli, who is in charge of the kitchen, begins to prepare snacks for them: maté or tea with milk and two servings of bread and butter. Some children ask for seconds. At 4 p.m. parents or guardians come to pick them up. Once the day is over we begin to clean. Eli takes charge of washing the glasses and dishes. Priscila and I sweep and bleach the*

*library and dining room. Majo and Claudia go to shop for cardboard
and glue to make some crafts to celebrate Children's Day.*

Contrary to what the habitual nature of these activities would lead us to
think, what most caught our attention during our six months of observation
was the consideration they gave to presumably trivial details. The following
notes illustrate this attention to detail and indicate, at the same time, the
meaning and value they give to their work (our emphasis):

SOFÍA'S FIELDNOTES, JULY 14, 2021. *Majo is in charge of drawing, cutting, and gluing sixty-nine cardboard hands that adorn the
goodie bags that will be given to the children at the center. Yesterday,
she stayed along with Priscila until 7 p.m. making the stencils for the
little hands. At home, she stayed up until 2 a.m. cutting them. "I had
time to finish. I didn't make dinner," she tells me. While we are cutting cardboard flowers and hats, I ask her: "You are really devoted to
this. Do you enjoy doing crafts?" "No, not at all," Majo replies. "I do it
but it's not something I do well." Claudia intervenes and says, "Sure, I
don't think anyone here does it very well, but we* make a good effort.
We force ourselves to do things. Usually we wait for Miss Patri [one of
the teachers] to make the stencils for us but sometimes we can't wait."
*At that point, Maca comes into the room and tells Majo: "Everything
is divine, but you do know that after getting the candy the kids will be
throwing all these hands in the garbage, right? "Yes, I know," Majo replies, "but it doesn't matter. I know that the children will appreciate
the work we put into them."*

AUGUST 10, 2021. *We are preparing goodie bags for the kids. Majo
and Virginia say in unison that something is missing from the bags.
They want to add colored cheese puffs. Virginia brings some small
transparent bags from her house to put the puffs in. Virginia is always checking on us. As I fill the bags with treats, I feel her eyes on me.
When she thinks I put too many or too few treats in them, she tells me
so. She does the same with Macarena. "You are really good at this," she
tells me. "Yes," I reply, "because last time with Susi we did about eighty
of these." "Poor Sofi, since she got here we've always asked her to do
something, just like everyone else," adds Majo. And Virginia concludes:*

"We are always doing something, for Children's Day, and then Family Day, and then Christmas Day…"

As mentioned previously, once a week the center distributes food to 160 families and offers after-school classes to boys and girls from the neighborhood. These classes are held in two shifts (morning and afternoon), during which students receive breakfast or snacks. The women who work at the center (and sometimes their relatives) have lunch there every day—as a result, the activity in the kitchen is always frenetic. Procuring, preparing, and distributing food takes up a good deal of time. However, the women did not find most of their satisfaction and recognition in these activities. Women at the center care the most about—and build their identity as "protectors" around—the education of girls and boys. Just like feeding families in the neighborhood, educating the children was conducted by the women as a joint enterprise.

Although an extreme case—due to the number of women involved in the task of helping a single girl—the next ethnographic note that we present illustrates very well this collective aspect of their work. It is important to emphasize that by the time Sofía records this episode she is already part of the operation of the center, fulfilling daily tasks in after-school classes and helping to clean the premises:

SOFÍA'S FIELDNOTES, AUGUST 17, 2021. *On August 17, Argentines commemorate the death of General San Martín, known as the "liberator of the country." I arrive at about 11 a.m. Susi, Eli, and Mary are the only adults present. Susi is outside playing with six children from the morning shift. As soon as I walk in, Bianca, Mary's niece, comes running to hug me. Bianca is nine years old; her dad is in jail and her mom apparently has addiction problems and can't take care of her. She is in Mary's charge. I greet Mary and, instantly, she says to me, "Are you good at drawing?" "I'm okay…not great," I reply. "Bianca has to hand in a paper on San Martín, and she needs a drawing or a photocopy to paste. I'm going to make a photocopy of San Martín. Can you make the cardboard?" she asks me. "Yes, of course," I answer.*

While Bianca finishes copying a short text about San Martín, which Silvi found among the books in the library, I write, "August 17, day of the liberator General San Martín" on a piece of cardboard. Virginia shows up and says out loud: "This girl has a lot of homework. All of us helped her: We are going to make her a good student." While I am working on the cardboard, Bianca wastes a lot of time talking. "You do like to play with fire," I tell her. "There are two hours left before you go to school and we still have a lot to do." "You are right," she replies with a mischievous smile. "Maybe I should skip school." From the kitchen, Mary yells at her: "What are you talking about!? Finish up!!" "All of us helped her," Mary tells me, laughing. "Silvi looked up the information for her homework; Virginia helped her with her math exercises." When we are done with the San Martín project, we glue everything and Mary goes outside to show it to Virginia: "Oh, it's beautiful, very nice," she says approvingly.

After a while, Susi and Eli go out to deliver a bag of food to a neighbor. Mary asks them if on the way they can make a photocopy for Bianca's homework. "My homework is looking really good. I am going to get an A," Bianca tells me, and I immediately reply, "We are going to get an A." Not losing a beat, Mary jumps in and exclaims: "Yes! We are all going to pass the grade!!! All of us into fourth grade!!!"

It is thirty minutes before the school bell. Bianca is having a quick lunch, while Mary is becoming impatient. Eli is not back and they are missing the photocopy. "We can't hand it in like this," Mary says, "It looks incomplete."

AUGUST 19, 2021. *Early in the morning, I arrive at the center and Majo, Silvia, Brenda, and Bianca are already having breakfast. Silvia is helping Bianca practice reading, and she asks: "Bianca, I heard you got a lot of help with your homework. Is that true?" "I did it all by myself," she replies playfully. Mary, Silvia, Majo, and I laugh out loud.*

Women at the center understand themselves as educators and as guardians—as providers of protection. And although they do not receive a salary for their work (only an "incentive"), they think of their labor as work ("I like to do this but it is also my job"). The following note best captures the *identity* of these women (that is, the way in which they understand themselves) and the *meaning* they assign to their work.

SOFÍA'S FIELDNOTES, AUGUST 9, 2021. *Majo, Priscila, and I are finishing up the crafts when Silvi [Virginia's eldest daughter, who coordinates the day care] arrives and, leaning on the stove, starts talking with Silvia and Virginia. Silvia has just finished a Zoom meeting with coordinators of other soup kitchens. She comments on some of the meeting's highlights. Silvi, in turn, begins to talk about a workshop she attended with some other women from the center last Friday. The workshop was called "networks for parenting" and brought together different female "popular educators" (her words) from soup kitchens in the province of Buenos Aires. During the workshop participants were asked to make a doll with whatever material they wanted. The doll had to be a "quita penas" (a doll to get rid of your sorrow)—the one you "put under the pillow to take away the sorrows when you go to sleep," Silvi says. The doll had to represent both the guardian of their lives and the one who takes their sorrows away. When they met in the workshop, by Zoom, they had to introduce the doll, give it a name, and say why it was their guardian. Silvi recounts that "Yami [a center participant] said that I was her guardian, because I was the one who took her off the street, who taught her a trade and taught her how to be a mother." Almost unable to hold back her tears, she continues, "It was very moving, because you know Yami, she is always teasing people, she never says how she feels, and the fact that she said that was very touching." None of us listening to this story can hold back our tears.*

SILVI: *Just now I'm finding out about this.*

VIRGINIA, tears in her eyes: *Oh, this Yami was terrible; she changed a lot.*

SILVI, also in tears: *I have felt like the guardian of many young people.*

SILVIA, also crying: *Yes, me too. I was the guardian of many young people who were in the streets. . . . They had to be taken in from there.*

This dialogue occurred, we reiterate, not as a product of an interrogation (by the ethnographer) but in the natural course of events that take place at the center. It encapsulates, in a particularly vivid way, the view that many women have of themselves and of their work. Toward the end of the field-note is a theme that appears frequently in both our observations and interviews: Women understand that one of the missions of the center is to "rescue" young people from the "streets"—a place where, according to them and many of their neighbors, delinquency and drug addiction germinate. The center is a place not only to "rescue" others but also to "rescue oneself" (rescatarse).

In early August 2021, a women's organization invites Silvi to do an interview about her work as an educator. Silvi and her mother, Virginia, talk after lunch about the interview.

SILVI: I don't know what to say. I have ideas in my mind I don't know how to express. Besides, I don't know what they're going to ask me.

VIRGINIA: They are going to ask you about your work as a caregiver, why you do what you do, if you like it and stuff.

SILVI, laughing: Well, I don't know. If they ask me why I do what I do, I'm going to tell them that when I was fifteen you grabbed me and told me: "Instead of hanging out in the street, you are going to work at the center." And every time I want to leave, you tell me: "You are not going anywhere!"

The opposition between "the center" (as a place of routines and stability) and "the street" (as a place of danger and perdition, from which they have to "rescue" youth) appears so often it takes the form of a taxonomic scheme. This scheme serves to give meaning to the work women do at the center and the work of other neighborhood institutions (soccer clubs, for example). As seen below, these institutions are understood as schools of morality, shelters to protect residents from the risks that plague the neighborhood. As Susana tells us when recalling her first years at the center, "My daughter was really rebellious. She was never at home; she didn't pay any attention to me. She liked to be in the street. These ladies told me to bring her here. They talked to her, and thanks to them she is not a slob. She now has her own family."[4]

The center is not just a place that provides food, care, and education. It is also, as Sofía herself experienced during her six months there, a place of sociability where the women can discuss the issues that most concern them in a frank and relaxed way—from intimate relationships to parenting, from household economics (and the always-present debt) to issues of public safety:

SOFÍA'S FIELDNOTES, JULY 1, 2021. *Lunchtime is so much fun. The whole time they are making jokes about work, food, and their partners. They talk about their plans for the weekend. Julia, who lives in La Matera, says that tonight she is going to go to a friend's house to get high and then have a night of sex with her boyfriend.*

JULY 6, 2021. *During almost the entire meal we are talking about two topics: braces and thefts. Three days ago, Priscila went to the dentist to have braces put on. She was charged 10,500 and she must pay 1,500 per month. Brenda also has braces but she says that sometimes she has to skip a visit to the dentist for a readjustment because she has no money. We also talk about the recurring robberies. Brenda first says that she has never been robbed and, after a few seconds, she remembers: "Oh no, wait. I was robbed three times. Once when I first moved to La Matera..."*

JULY 14, 2021. *Camila, one of the younger women at the center, didn't come to work because she had a migraine and didn't have money to purchase her prescribed medication. Majo says that Camila is awaiting the "incentive" to buy the medicine. Virginia asks Majo: "Why doesn't Camila ask us? We can buy the medicine for her. We want her to work, but we also want her to feel well. We are not going to leave her on her own!"*

JULY 29, 2021. *While we are packing the food rations, the topics of conversation are sex education and diapers. All of them agree on the importance of having sex education in schools in order to prevent pregnancies and abuse. Several of them are deeply concerned about their daughters suffering abuse. Every time we get to work, we talk about husbands, the price of household items, the price of diapers, the violence in the streets, and so on. They never talk about politics.*

During their daily activities, women create sociability—that experience of being *with* others and *for* others, as Georg Simmel once said (1964). They also exchange vital information. The following notes describe how intimate conversations could circulate news that was crucial for navigating challenging circumstances.

SOFÍA'S FIELDNOTES, JULY 6, 2021. *Betty is my neighbor. As we are packing food rations, she tells me that she kicked out her husband a long time ago because he was very controlling, jealous, and a hitter. "What use is he to me?" she says, looking at me. She lives alone with her twenty-eight-year-old son, who was diagnosed with schizophrenia four years ago. Betty stops Silvia on her way out to ask her what*

*they can do about her situation. Her son had a crisis very recently and
required hospitalization but, due to* COVID *protocols and the lack of
ambulances to transport him, she couldn't hospitalize him. Apparently
he is in a violent phase of the disease. Betty tells Silvia that she has
been calling the hospital but no one is giving her a solution. Silvia asks
her if Betty told them she was calling from the center and, when Betty
tells her that she did not, Silvia says she is going to call herself: "When
we tell them that we are from the center, they will attend to us quickly.
They already know us."*

AUGUST 10, 2021. *Mary asks Virginia if they can play music in the
kitchen. "Yes, it's too quiet," Virginia replies. Those things are common
in the kitchen: Mary puts on music to make cooking more entertain-
ing and, from time to time, they dance with each other. On this occasion, she puts on a cumbia and Majo joins in dancing with them. [Two
hours later,] Mary is not feeling well, so Majo calls her daughter-in-
law Camila and asks her if she can accompany the "chubby" [la
gorda]—Mary—to the hospital because she thinks she has a urinary
tract infection. "Go to the Solano hospital, which is the only one that
has a gynecologist on call," Macarena tells her. Majo agrees. "Mmm,
I do not know. The Solano hospital doesn't give me much confidence,"
Mary replies. "Go there. It's closer than going to Quilmes and they'll see
you faster. If they want to hospitalize you, you tell them that you are
alone, that you come back later and that's it." Even though it is obvi-
ous that she is a little scared, Mary goes to the Solano hospital. Before
Mary leaves for the hospital, Majo tells her naughtily: "But do tell the
doctor* everything." *"Everything?" she asks her while smiling. Toward
the end of the day Majo's phone rings. It is Mary: She is awaiting the
lab tests, but the doctor confirms she is not pregnant. Majo confesses
to me that she was worried about that. "Vamos gorda!" Majo happily
yells at her through the phone.*

Information about health services, food distribution, and other state services
not only circulates among the women who work at the center. The center is,
in fact, a hub for the diffusion of much-needed news among residents who
come by even if they do not work there.

SOFÍA'S FIELDNOTES, JULY 29, 2021. *While they deliver food rations, Silvia and Claudia sit at a table outside in the sun to fill out administrative forms ("do paperwork"). They know the name of each person who stops by: They ask about their sons and daughters, their families, and their work. A woman gets her ration and Silvia asks her how her son, who has autism and attends kindergarten, is doing. She asks if she has already seen the educational psychologist [EP] who attends to the kindergarteners. Once the boy is diagnosed by the EP, Silvia says, he can be referred for services at the neighborhood CIC [Community Integration Center].*

Extraordinary Days

Less than a month after the ruling party's defeat in the September 2021 primaries, and perhaps in an attempt to obtain more votes in the legislative elections of November, the mayor of Quilmes, Mayra Mendoza, announces her visit to the Comedor de Virginia. The coordinators of five other community centers that form a network with this one (a "collective") will also be present at the meeting. The account that follows, built on the basis of extensive fieldnotes, describes the days leading up to the (failed) visit.

According to Robert Zussman (2004, 362), "Successful case studies look at extremes, unusual circumstances, and analytically clear examples, all of which are important not because they are representative but because they show a process or a problem in particularly clear relief." We use an analogous logic to warrant the reconstruction of these extraordinary days. These days do not represent the daily operation of the center. Instead, they capture several of its most salient aspects: the collective dimension of the work, the emphasis on caring for children (care that is expressed in the dedication they put into the preparation of gifts, for example), the attention to the small details of the physical space (photos, a tablecloth), and the recognition that these women avidly seek and build together. At the same time, the reconstruction highlights a theme that we have emphasized throughout this book: the dire needs that, stemming from the rise of un(der)employment, precarious work, and the malfunctioning of the state, pervade daily life at the urban margins. Finally, it is important to highlight that, although the activity of these women is eminently political, the reconstruction of these extraordinary days shows how they strategically avoid linking the center with any particular political group or faction.

SOFÍA'S FIELDNOTES, OCTOBER 12, 2021. *I show up at the center around 10 a.m. When I get there, Maca is in the library making paper puppets with the twelve students from the morning shift. The desks are in a different position because on Friday there was a big cleaning to prepare for Mayra's visit. Lots of things were moved around. On the wall of the main room there is a huge handmade, colored cardboard tree with the alphabet. Coordinators take it down and replace it with framed awards given to the center, and pictures of themselves and the center's founding members. Cleaning supplies, plants, children's toys, and tableware are also rearranged.*

Majo arrives freshly bathed, with her hair loose, groomed and wearing very nice clothes. It is evident that she is dressed for the important visit. When the students leave, we begin to clean. With so many crafts, the boys left a mess on the floor. I sweep and pick up the chairs; Maca wipes them down. While we let the floor dry, we sit for a while in the dining room with the others. Since Sunday is Mother's Day, they are already preparing little gifts for the students' mothers. Majo is preparing the stencils to make a little book with two cardboard arms around it, inside of which we will paste a drawing made by the students. They will also prepare daily planners to give away. Many of the women at the center seem worried that they won't be able to finish all the presents due to the mayor's visit. Majo approaches us and laughing at herself, tells us: "I thought Mayra [the mayor] was coming today. That's why I got ready . . . and took a bath." "I put on perfume because I thought today was the day," I reply. We are now finding out that the mayor's visit is tomorrow.

The next day I arrive at the center at 11 a.m., knowing that I am going to stay late. They are all sitting at the table preparing the presents for Mother's Day. Virginia, Silvia, Claudia, and Majo are making the daily planners and, at a separate desk, Maca is pasting the children's drawings on the little books. "We were waiting for you," Claudia tells me. I immediately get to work along with Maca. Mayra will arrive at 4 p.m. We all talk about how busy we are. "Today is going to be a long day. Only after Mayra leaves will we be able to get back to finishing all these [presents for Mother's Day]. Oh, God, in the end, Mayra comes to keep us busy more than to do us a favor," says Virginia. "When she leaves, we'll get hard to work on all this," replies Majo. On her desk they have something resembling an assembly line: One paints, another folds, another cuts, and the last one glues.

After working for a while we stop and set the table to eat. At 12 o'clock we have rice stew for lunch. We are a big group: Virginia, Claudia and her husband and her son, Silvia, Susana, Mary, Betty with her two daughters, Tacho, and Majo with her son. When we are finishing lunch, Silvi arrives very well dressed. Silvi reiterates that Mayra is coming at 4 p.m. and she has "a tight schedule." At this moment, Virginia raises her voice and asks the group: "How come we didn't think of buying something to share a maté with her, some croissants, for example?" "I can make bread in a second," says Claudia. Then they start talking about all the things that they need to do before the visit. Virginia interrupts and says: "Okay, enough sitting around. Let's go to work." Maca and I finish our cards and start helping the others to set up the place. I take out the tablecloths to clean them up.

After clearing the table we begin to clean the dining room. Claudia prepares the homemade bread. While I sweep, Maca cleans the library. Virginia asks me to please take care of the letters of the alphabet on the main blackboard while Majo tells me to make sure every letter is well glued.

It is 1 p.m. and there are three hours left before Mayra's visit. Virginia instructs us to arrange the chairs in a circle and, in the middle, two tables where they are going to put the maté equipment, homemade bread, glasses, juice, and so forth. We never stay still. We hang a whiteboard right next to the front door. Then Virginia tells me: "You have nice handwriting, girl, please write this: 'Friday 15th, food rations. Wednesday 13th, Mayra Mendoza's visit. Come on, come on, girls, we have to sell our work!" Virginia says as she claps her hands. We put the tablecloths, glasses, and napkins on the table.

It's now 2 p.m. and we are done. We sit down to drink maté: "I'm going to have some maté and then I'm going to go home to change my clothes," says Virginia. At 2:15 p.m. Claudia receives a WhatsApp message. Mayra is cancelling her schedule for seventy-two hours due to the murder of a seventeen-year-old boy outside a school in the center of Quilmes.

[The secretary of public works shows up on behalf of the mayor. A two-hour-long meeting ensues where Virginia, Majo, Mary, and others talk with the secretary about the many needs of the center and the neighborhood's residents.]

We finish around 8 p.m. I help tidy up the place a bit and get ready to go home. I'm exhausted. They are going to stay up late finishing the *presents for Mother's Day. "My apologies, but I can't stay. I have a class today," I tell Majo. "Go, take it easy, girl. Thank you for everything," she replies. On the way out, I overhear this conversation:*

PRISCILA: *Who is the center with?*

MAJO: *The center is with no one. With no political party.*

PRISCILA: *Well, but at the same time, we try to make a deal with whoever is in power.*

MAJO: *Yes, well, the doors are open to everyone, but we are not with anyone.*

Claudia's Love

We conclude this chapter with the story of Claudia, the woman in charge of the center's administrative tasks. Her story vividly encapsulates the main themes of both this chapter and the book as a whole.

Claudia is fifty years old and has been working at the center for more than thirty years. She arrived in El Tala at the age of seventeen from the northwest province of Santiago del Estero. At the time she was pregnant with her first child. Amelia, her sister-in-law, put her up for her first three years in Buenos Aires. At that time, the center was mainly a soup kitchen operating out of Amelia's house. Claudia remembers being welcomed by Amelia and the women who worked at the soup kitchen as a "second daughter." She started helping in the kitchen and she also participated in the "casitas solidarias"—grassroots day-care centers in the neighborhood. The first years at the center were, according to Claudia, very difficult—"we cooked with what we had, each one put in a little, with what came in the PAN box. The few who had formal jobs collaborated with food so that we could cook."[5]

In a couple of interviews, Claudia explained what those first years of the community center were like, the collections they organized to buy materials to build the first dining hall, the donations of bricks from neighbors, and the monetary contributions of a local NGO: "The construction of the dining room was all done by hand; it was a common effort."

At the center, she and several other families found out about the occupation of La Matera: "We only had a few wood sticks and some ropes [to mark the plots]. I remember that Don Ramos, who had already worked on the occupation of El Tala, told us how to demarcate the plots so that it would not become a slum, so that there would be streets, blocks, so that it would be a real neighborhood. That is how we got our little piece of land. At that time, buying was impossible." Echoing many of the stories we summarized in chapter 2, Claudia mentions several other leaders who had been organizers in El Tala and who were organizing the takeover of La Matera ("they knew how to do things"), the clearing of the land, and the layout of its streets. Among those leaders was Pocho. In line with many of the criticisms described in chapter 4, Claudia immediately expresses reservations about him: "He was a leader only in his area of La Matera. We had no relationship with him. He believed that he was the boss of all of La Matera, but he was only from one sector. . . . He used the opportunity to get his own house." Although she has her political sympathies (she identifies as a Peronist), the mention of Pocho makes Claudia reiterate something that we heard many times in the center: "We have welcomed many politicians, but we do not marry anyone. We are always independent, no matter who is governing."

In his illuminating analysis of wildland firefighters, Matthew Desmond (2009, 86) draws on Erving Goffman's work to assert that "people tend to find the good in dire situations; this certainly applies even (perhaps especially) to dominated groups who not only accept conditions that other groups would despise and reject but find ways to remain content—sometimes even happy—in those conditions." This is certainly useful for understanding the predicaments of Claudia and her compañeras—poor women who feed and educate children at the bottom of the social structure and feel a sincere joy for their work and love for those who attend the center. As Claudia told us,

> I have a vocation to serve. . . . I came here for emotional reasons. I came from Santiago del Estero, I was uprooted, I left my mom. I came alone, with my husband, and got the love of my sister-in-law. I came to this space looking for some kind of refuge. Amelia, the cook, was like my mom while I was pregnant. From day one I began to feel that love. She adopted me as her youngest daughter. I like what I do in the dining room. There I raised my children, there I bathed them, I changed their clothes.

When we last talked to her, the center was on summer break. Despite being closed for the month of January and part of February, the weekly food distribution continued. Therefore, Claudia had to keep up with the many administrative tasks: She had to distribute the "incentives," do paperwork, and pay suppliers ("I think I rested eight out of the thirty-one days in January"). Toward the end of the interview, with a huge smile, she told us that she was about to go to the beach in San Clemente for four days: "Four days without thinking about numbers, chickens, bills, or people."

Claudia foreshadows a theme that will be developed in chapter 9, the affective dimension of daily life at the margins (see Jaffe et al. 2020). For now, let's just point out that the women's emotional bond with the center (that "love" that Claudia articulates so well) is both the product of their participation in it and the reason why they return day after day ("I wake up every day excited to come back here," Claudia tells us). However, the reasons why these women find satisfaction and recognition in their tasks, and why they persist in their daily work at the community center (like Claudia, allowing themselves only a short respite from the intense activity), are not to be found exclusively in social dynamics of that specific universe. We can only make sense of their actions in the context of profound hardship experienced at the urban margins. Misery highlights the centrality of food; the surrounding violence is a risk that accentuates the relevance of care. The reasons why they keep at it can also be found in the rewards offered by the state, however meager (Claudia maintains that "the money that the girls receive" is "miserable"), as well as in the strongly structured gender expectations that weigh on care work.

The love these women feel for their work then has to be understood as *an affection shaped (in part) by a process of adaptation to social, political, and economic conditions over which they have little control.* The origin and the form that this affect acquires further underpin the central argument of this book: Persistence strategies are deeply intertwined with existing forms of political, social, and economic domination.

Claudia has experienced a significant improvement in her living conditions. She arrived in Buenos Aires "with nothing" and today owns her house in La Matera. Two of her children, educated in nearby private schools, are now members of the federal police. Her youngest son also attends a private high school near her home. The community center, in these thirty years, has grown significantly—from occupying the living room of a private house to having its own well-equipped site. Claudia would like the center to continue to improve and one day become a place of recreation where "kids come not only because they lack a plate of food, but because they find a job opportunity here. I wish that in the future they can learn something useful here, a trade, for example. I wish we can offer workshops for them. . . . That is my hope."

9

HOW DOES
MARGINALITY FEEL?

Brenda is twenty-seven years old. Born and raised in El Tala, she moved with her husband, Maxi, to La Matera. She lived there for a few years until she moved back to her mother's home in El Tala right before the pandemic began in March 2020. From where she lives now, it is a short walk to the Comedor de Virginia, where she works caring for children, cleaning the premises, and, occasionally, cooking. In her own voice, she summarizes some of the main themes covered thus far: poor people's relentless material scarcity, their (individual and collective) ways of dealing with it, kin-based subsistence networks, their job precarity, the violence and infrastructural deprivation that pervade the urban margins, and the persistence of those who live there despite it all. She also illuminates an aspect of marginalization that, implicitly present throughout our descriptions and analysis, is the explicit focus of this chapter: its affective dimension.

I had my first job at seventeen as a babysitter for my neighbor. She had three kids and I took care of them. I was living with my mom. She had separated from my dad, and she was working every day, from Monday to Monday, no rest. . . . I told her I wanted to quit school and she told me: "If you drop out of school, you have to work: You are not going to be idle all day." She tried to persuade me to stay in school but I didn't want to. I started babysitting for many other neighbors. A few months later, when I was eighteen, I got pregnant. I stopped working. Maxi, my partner, was working. He was doing odd jobs, then he worked as a waiter. . . . I didn't have a job until Zoe, my daughter, was three years old. For her first three years, I was cooking, doing laundry, all day long. I was homebound! And my mom told me that I had to get out of the house, either to work or to study. She offered to pay for a manicurist course, like the one my sister took. She couldn't see me inside the house all day, so she took me to work with her. She was a cleaning lady in several homes in the center of Lomas de Zamora. One of her bosses, Carina, got me a cleaning job in the home of her cousin. In that home I was doing everything, and occasionally my boss paid me a little extra for bathing the kids, or for cooking . . . not much, just a little extra. I was doing a lot. I did laundry, cooked, took care of the kids, cleaned the whole house. . . . She wanted me there full-time but I didn't want to quit my other cleaning jobs. Carina then got me another job with another one of her relatives. So I ended up working the entire week in different homes, working for different people, from Monday to Saturday. . . . I had so many debts! Although both Maxi and I were working, he was paying the installments for a car, and I was paying for a refrigerator, an oven, and our bed. . . . Every penny I earned went to pay for those things. My mom helped me a lot: she would buy groceries for Zoe because all our money was tied up in debt. . . . One of my bosses, Dolores, was a language professor and she persuaded me to go back to school, to finish high school. So, after work, three times a week, I went to school. I came back home around 10 or 11 p.m. . . . dead, super tired. And when there was a train strike, I'd wait for the bus and that took even longer. While I was living in La Matera, I had to take a car service from the bus stop to my house. And if none were available, I had to walk all by myself. Fortunately nothing ever happened to me . . . but some areas in the neighborhood are now really hot, picantes. A few months ago, I was working for the census and we couldn't get in because neighbors were fighting, shooting at each other. . . . While we were living in La Matera, we got flooded very often. In one year, I think it was like five times. We lost our washing machine, our bed, our closet. The water destroyed all of Zoe's clothes. We lost all her toys too. . . .

My sister-in-law was living in a shack right here, on our same plot. Someone broke into her house and stole the electric kettle and something else. Even though nothing ever happened to me, I got scared. My mom told me to leave La Matera and come back to live with her. We got back to her house a month before the pandemic began. [Since March 2020] nobody could go out to work.... Carina, one of my bosses, sent me some money every now and then. Dolores also sent me money every week. It wasn't a lot but it helped.... During the pandemic, my mom got sick with cancer. I stayed with her during those ten months until she died. It was so difficult [*crying*], I had to ask for special permits to move around, pay for car services.... It was tough....

After Mom died, I became depressed. I didn't leave the house for four months. Not even to take Zoe to school. I had panic attacks.... María, Virginia's daughter [the coordinator of El Tala's local community center], came to hang out quite often and she told me that it was not worth it to be inside all day. She told me to get out, to try to finish school. I had one more year to complete. I couldn't do it while my mom was sick. I swear I tried but [*crying*] I just couldn't. So then, in 2021, I started volunteering at the center's soup kitchen. And, well, you know, the comedor is like *another world* [her emphasis]. And I began to feel better. The women there helped me a lot. I started to work at Carina's twice a week, but then I quit again when I took over the center's day care. I started working for 4,000 a month, but I also got foodstuffs, and Zoe and I ate there every day. At the day-care center I not only was in charge of caring for the kids but I was also helping in the kitchen . . . peeling potatoes, chopping onions, picking up produce from the community center, et cetera. Even though I started working for almost nothing, I was, and I still am, happy there. I now receive a social welfare plan and an "incentive" for my work.... I am sometimes in charge of twelve or thirteen children, all by myself. I manage because I really like the kids. I grew up at the center, my mom was also an attendant there [a cuidador]. She had my same job. The center is a *community* center [her emphasis]. The very words say it: community. You are caring for a child, but if the bathroom is dirty, you have to clean it. If one of the cooks gets sick, you have to chop onion to make a stew....

[A few months ago], Maxi lost his job. He'd been working en blanco [i.e., in a formal job] for five years. I was beside myself. How are we going to pay our bills? How are we going to pay our credit cards? We are so indebted. But . . . we have a positive attitude. We are going to make it.

We are not going to give up. Maxi told me he was going to get out and take whatever odd job he could get. A friend of my sister who works as a janitor in a couple of buildings in the city offered him a painting job, and then he started laying tile, doing some plumbing. Maxi now works for him en negro [i.e., off the books, no benefits]. My brother works at Banfield Football Club and he helps us a lot: He buys me soap, toilet paper; he gets groceries when he sees our fridge is empty; he buys us meat. And my aunt also helps us out. Every time she receives her pension check, I ask her to go to the butcher.

When they are often hungry, precariously exploited, frequently preyed on by local politicians, other times extorted by police agents, constantly surrounded by violence, what do poor people do? How are their actions and beliefs shaped by local history and politics? How are these, in turn, shaped by poor people's behaviors and experiences? Seeking answers to these questions, adapted and reformulated from E. P. Thompson's classic "The Moral Economy of the English Crowd in the Eighteenth Century," led us to scrutinize poor people's strategies—ways of making ends meet in a context of high marginality. But how do hunger, exploitation, political control, extortion, and violence *feel* at the margins?

Brenda encapsulates marginality's affective dimension (the realm that encompasses affects, emotions, and feelings [Cvetkovich 2012]). Early on we asserted that managing daily subsistence amid precarity and violence makes residents feel overwhelmed. We will now expand and qualify this statement. As Brenda expresses well, poverty is indeed exhausting (Desmond 2023), because of draining work schedules, long commutes, piled-up debt, and so on. Poverty is also dangerous—there are multiple risks and a plethora of emotions that emerge while experiencing them, among them anxiety about being mugged or robbed, or sadness at losing the few things you own during a flood. But we need to move beyond the tropes of exhaustion, danger, and the attendant powerlessness if we want to capture the full affective complexity of life at the margins. Brenda offers us a blueprint: Poor people's daily lives are a *patchwork of negative and positive emotions* that includes tiredness, fear, and sadness, but also joy, pride, sense of accomplishment, and hopefulness. Furthermore, Brenda illustrates that all these emotional states emerge in specific social situations, in relational settings, traversed by those living in relegated neighborhoods: at home, on the streets, at the community center.

Let's now take a closer look at the affective dimension of life at the urban margins by inspecting how fear, anger, frustration, and sadness, but also pride, trust, gratefulness, and joy show up and permeate specific situations and interactions. We will leave aside individual emotional states (for example, delight at the sight and flavor of an expensive yogurt, or admiration for the radiance of new bathroom tiles) to concentrate on those shared by many of the residents we spoke to.

Tired, Fearful, and Angry

Financial worries have, needless to say, a constant presence among the poor. This feeling is well articulated when Sofía remembers her concerns about "Mom running out of money." It is also expressed when people say that they would rather not "think about it all the time," or when they talk about the "sheer desperation" that the lack of money produces. Scarcity is also occasionally associated with other emotions: shame for receiving food at a state pantry, or embarrassment about having to beg for food.

There is little question that the lack of material resources exhausts people, but it also prompts them to carry out (also exhausting) a constant juggling of strategies (the bricolage). But, as said, this is not the only (negative) affective dimension of living at the margins. As mentioned in previous chapters, feelings of fear manifested again and again during fieldwork. This category encompasses worry, anxiety, and panic. Residents are scared at the prospect of being robbed or assaulted ("your heart in your throat" when you leave for work early in the morning or come back home late at night); terrified after a violent event ("I was a nervous wreck," "the feeling that they are going to come back"); and sad when losing pictures of loved ones stored in a stolen phone ("You have no idea how much I cried that day") or when someone takes a brand-new phone that was a birthday present. Residents' narratives about specific events and their aftermaths demonstrate that these feelings linger as bodily sensations ("chills," "dry throats," "nervios," "becoming hysterical").

Many emotions are tied to a causal attribution made by the subjects. As we said, "los pibes"—a general category that encompasses youngsters who hang out on street corners, some of them consumers of alcohol and drugs—are seen as the cause of the fear they feel. This fear, as we see in the narratives of street assault, is the result of an interaction (real or potential) in which residents are subject to a power greater than their own—that of youngsters, like Gonzalo and his friends who brutally assaulted the owners of a local pizzeria.

The sense of powerlessness (absent when they recount the origins of the settlement or when organizing community actions) is palpable. They feel, truly feel, that they are at the arbitrary mercy of forceful others.

Anger and frustration about politics are also emotions that are attributed to specific actors and actions: We heard many neighbors criticize, sometimes with fury, other times with resignation, the actions of local brokers who use people to their advantage, who profit from their actions, who demand things (money, sex) from them in order to access a welfare program. As we also noted, brokers, at the same time, receive feelings of gratefulness—mainly from those who have benefited from their actions.

Paradoxically, we did not hear any contempt, frustration, or anger about their employers or firms in which many residents work. If anything, we actually heard praise for this or that good (flexible, accommodating, encouraging) boss—especially from women who work as domestic employees. We say paradoxically, because many a casual conversation about politics among the Argentine middle classes and upper-middle classes (of the kind one of us repeatedly heard) would not fail to mention the behavior of the poor, their lack of willingness to work, their lassitude, and the pernicious impact of welfare programs (wrongly thought to be very generous) for the fiscal health of the nation. The nonpoor talk constantly about the poor—more often than not to criticize their actions and beliefs—and the emotion articulated in that talk is one of hostility, what Spanish philosopher Adela Cortina (2022) calls *aporophobia* (hate, repugnancy, toward the áporos, the indigent, the poor). The poor, on the contrary, rarely (to our knowledge, almost never) talk about the well-to-do in negative, hostile terms. One could speculate about the relationships between this lack of hostility against the well-to-do and compliance with the established order, but one thing is clear: The negative emotions (anger, frustration, resentment) are directed at those living in the same social and geographic space—youngsters, brokers, and occasionally a corrupt neighborhood cop—and do not take the form of an affective critique of class inequality.

Overwhelmed by State Paperwork

"The first time she sees her she is immediately struck by her fragility and helplessness. She is not a completely blind woman, but she carries a cane and wears thick glasses. She is sitting on the ground with her legs curled up, under the eaves of a bank building, taking up as little space as possible to protect herself from the rain. On a piece of cardboard next to her, she has written that she is a 'woman without resources.' She asks for 'work and food.'" This is how Spanish writer Sara Mesa begins her poignant work *Silencio administrativo: La pobreza en el laberinto democrático* (Administrative silence: poverty in the bureaucratic labyrinth) (2019, 2). In it, she describes the predicament of Carmen, a thirty-seven-year-old destitute, homeless woman, who seeks to obtain state aid (renta mínima de inserción social) in Sevilla, Spain. The book vividly portrays the emotional undertones of the excruciating journey involved in seeking state aid, both on the part of the applicant ("accustomed to being denied and dispatched") and on the part of those who, like the author and her friends, try to help Carmen ("feelings of frustration and failure") (7).

Let us go back to Brenda's story. Since her mother died, she had to take charge of her aunt and her two cousins, the three of them suffering various degrees of mental disability. Her prolonged pilgrimage through the state offices to obtain guardianship and receive disability payments uncannily mirrors the one described by Mesa. She also illustrates a process that characterizes many interactions between marginalized citizens and state agencies. Through endless, uncertain, and arbitrary waiting times, through constant delays, postponements, and random rectifications, people like Brenda become "patients of the state" (Auyero 2012). Lastly, her story captures another layer of the affective dimension of life at the margins, that of feeling overwhelmed not only by the arduous task of subsistence amid precarity and violence, but also by the bureaucratic, time-consuming demands of the state that is presumably acting to alleviate suffering.

"It took my mom almost fifteen years to obtain the guardianship of her sister and the kids. Two months after she died, they stopped receiving payments," Brenda tells Sofía. In her view, all her mother's information was "erased" from the office in charge of making payments. "When she was already sick with cancer, my mom told me, 'Bren, I leave you in charge of the kids. Grab that blue bag.' And in the bag, she had all the paperwork, even the bus route she took to the state office." When Brenda went to the state office to claim the reinstatement of disability payments, an officer told her that first she needed to go to the children's special education school and ask for a note certifying that the children were living with her.

> I got the note and went back to the office. There they told me that everything was okay but that the proof of disability was expired. The officer was kind enough to put the application through, even though the proof of disability was expired. Many months later I began to receive payments. But now I have to renew the certificate proving that they

are all disabled, my aunt and her two daughters. I went to the children's public hospital in the city of Buenos Aires where their neurologist works. In order to get the proof, the neurologist needs to consult with a board. But the neurologist only sees patients twice a week, and there are only four slots. So you have to go to the hospital at dawn, or better, sleep there, right outside. After that consultation goes through, I need to come here, to Quilmes, to get some other papers to get the certificate. And then there is the fact that the girls are now over eighteen. I went to the hospital's information desk and they sent me to the second floor but there they sent me downstairs again. They couldn't give me the information. So I'll have to go again.

The "demoniac bureaucratic labyrinth" (Mesa 2019, 27) exhausts the energies of those who need the state the most, the Carmens and Brendas dwelling in the cities' margins—even when they try hard to dutifully follow all the state's rules. "My mom," Brenda resignedly tells Sofía, "did everything so that they have their proofs of disability. I didn't know that renewing them was so difficult ['tanto quilombo']. And, on top of this, I have to renew it every four years."

Fear of victimization, anger and frustration about politics, and fatigue with the state are certainly quite negative emotions. But to exclusively focus on fear, anger, exhaustion, and frustration is a distortion that disfigures the affective life at the margins. These emotions coexist with a positive affect: *pride* at joint accomplishments and *joy* with the rewards produced by community work—of the kind Claudia described in a previous chapter when referring to the "love" she feels for her work, and when Brenda expressed her happiness when working at the community center.

Pride in Community: The Little Things

When narrating the history of the settlement and the specific actions each person carried out during the early days of the occupation, residents express pride in their accomplishments, their level of organization, and their collective efforts ("a pulmón"). Listening to their recollections, we couldn't help but detect another emotion: hopefulness at the prospect of a better life, one with a home of their own, and with a school for their children, a health center for their new neighborhood, and so forth. As described in chapter 2, this hope was created and sustained by their own (more or less transgressive, more or less belligerent) collective actions. Pride shows up again and again when residents stress the infrastructural progress made in the neighborhood thanks to their "struggles."

Specific needs and interests drive individuals to join with others in common action: in the case of "la toma," the need for housing; or, in the case of the Comedor de Virginia, obtaining and providing material sustenance in the context of pervasive food shortages. But many groups or associations are also characterized by "a feeling, among their members, of being sociated and by the satisfaction derived from this" (Simmel 1964, 44). The community center produces a sociability that is a value in and of itself, above and beyond the interests and needs that it satisfies.

The "little" things women at the center carry out in daily activities and the personal language they use can be misleading in their significance. Their involvement in (and excitement about) a girl's homework, the methodical cleaning of the dining room and kitchen, the care put into this or that gift, and how they converse with each other and refer to one another can, if well interpreted, speak to more general themes. They are, paraphrasing Rosine Christin (2000), saturated with a collective history (a history of marginality and stigmatization, and also of struggle and search for respect) and with a shared affect.

Through all the activities described in chapter 8, the women of the center build an experience of *collective care*—caring for others and for each other. How does it feel, what does it mean, to take care of others? They experience care both as dignified *work* and as a set of *relationships* that serve to protect others and protect themselves (Ruddick 1988). "To the extent that caring is devalued, invisible, underpaid, and penalized, it is relegated to those who lack economic, political, and social power and status," writes sociologist Evelyn Nakano Glenn (2000, 84–85), adding, "to the extent that those who engage in caring are drawn disproportionately from among disadvantaged groups (women, people of color, and immigrants), their activity of caring is further degraded." The women at the center carry out work that is not only devalued, made invisible, and poorly paid, but also stigmatized—insofar as those who carry it out are beneficiaries of welfare programs that, according to prevailing discourse, not only produce fiscal imbalances but also discourage a "culture of work."

Despite the lack of material and symbolic recognition for their work, and without much hope that a radically different societal recognition will raise their status or their rewards, these women create a sense of dignity and community centered on the value of their work—which extends beyond food distribution to the education of boys and girls, "rescuing" them from the dangers of "the street." We do not think it would be far-fetched to thus interpret their actions as a collective way of counteracting the stigma that falls on recipients of state aid. We would even argue that as they create themselves as educators and guardians of a community at risk, they are re-discovering what sociologist Doug McAdam (1988, 138) once called a powerful sociological truth: "The most satisfying selves we will ever know are those that attach to communities and purposes outside of ourselves."

A shorter version of this book was published in Spanish in July 2023 under the title *¿Cómo hacen los pobres para sobrevivir?* Book in hand, we visited the Comedor de Virginia one last time to bring several copies of the book. Virginia, Brenda, Claudia, and others were delighted. They received us with open arms and expressed joy at their work being depicted in detail in a "good-looking" book. They had told us to come around 11:30 a.m., and we showed up on time. After briefly catching up and taking several pictures, we both noticed that it was our time to go. Happy as they were with the book, they were not distracted. It was time for them to serve lunch—dozens of kids were eagerly waiting, and the book authors were not going to interrupt their work. They didn't tell us it was time for us to leave, but we could read it in their hurried bodies and facial expressions—it was time to go back to do what they love the most.

CONCLUSIONS

Digo mirar con carácter, digo contar un mundo, digo tratar de entender.
—LEILA GUERRIERO, *Zona de obras* (2015)

Be specific. Go granular.
—COLUM McCANN, *Letters to a Young Writer* (2018)

El punto exacto está en un detalle, hay que ser observador.
—SAMANTA SCHWEBLIN, *Distancia de Rescate* (2020)

In this book, we took a deep dive into different universes of urban marginality. What general panorama should readers gain from our journey through these diverse scenarios? What substantive as well as methodological lessons do we learn about persistence at the bottom of the social space?

Quite often, entire and internally diverse categories ("the urban poor," "poor youth," "vulnerable women") are reduced to one or two salient features ("recipients of state aid," "grassroots activists," "illicit drug dealer and/or user," etc.). Their complex and changing lives are encapsulated in what novelist Chimamanda Ngozi Adichie (2009) calls "a single story" or to what sociologist Patricia Fernández-Kelly describes as "flat representations of social problems" (2015, 17). This book tells multiple stories about poor people's strategies and their intersection with forms of domination, highlighting the internal heterogeneity of life at the margins.

The inhabitants of the urban periphery are *bricoleurs*. To persist, they rely on relatives, neighbors, brokers, and state officials; they combine mutual aid, state assistance, formal and informal work, and illicit ventures; they merge transgressive collective action with their participation in clientelist networks. This web of relationships can and should be characterized objectively: Some relationships are more horizontal than others; some relationships are of cooperation, others of exploitation or manipulation; and some relationships of reciprocity and others are characterized by highly unequal exchanges. Just as we can say that a job whose salary is not enough to satisfy basic needs (like the ones most people have) is a "poorly paid job," we can also define the "incentive" that the women in the soup kitchen receive as "meager"—and interpret it as an indicator of exploitation of their work by the state. A local broker who keeps a percentage of the social welfare benefits that neighbors receive or who promises access to these same benefits in exchange for sex or for attending a partisan rally, a policeman who collects a bribe from a local drug dealer in exchange for "looking the other way," another police officer who beats a young man hanging from a pipe in the basement of a precinct, a husband who punches his wife every time he gets drunk: There is no intellectual dishonesty or interpretive bias in characterizing these relations as ones of domination, predation, extortion, manipulation, or violence, provided that we show (rather than simply tell) the empirical evidence drawn on to produce those claims.

Many of these relationships have an ambivalent character. The state, through some of its officials, may try to "divide and conquer" the neighbors (as we saw in chapter 2). These same neighbors may gain from this political relationship (such as with access to land or infrastructure)—these advantages influence how this relationship is perceived. The same can be said of the gain that a state agency obtains from the labor of the women in the soup kitchen: Thanks to them, social assistance is delivered in a quite efficient way. These women not only receive material resources in exchange for their participation (in a context of food scarcity, the "incentive" and access to daily lunch and dinner are not benefits to be undervalued) but also (as we saw in chapter 8) find gratification and recognition in it. The broker might extort and manipulate residents but, at the same time, she or he solves their daily pressing problems (provides access to a new social program, facilitates paperwork at a state agency, and so forth).

In other words, relations with the state or its representatives are not one-dimensional: they help to obtain essential resources for subsistence but, at the same time, they are conduits for manipulation and abuse. Relationships within the neighborhood and the family are not a monolithically positive force either: As we saw in chapters 6 and 7, reciprocity and cooperation can put family members at risk.

Unearthing this ambivalence, seeking to understand how and why it works, allowed us to take a more realistic view of life at the margins, or "describe things as they are," as Pierre Bourdieu advocates in the quote with which we began this book. What anthropologist Ruth Benedict (2006, 228) stated in her descriptions of the Zuñi or Kwakiutl applies here to the urban poor: it would be absurd to reduce their economic, cultural, political, and social reality to the "Procrustean bed of some catchword characterization." In part, our job in this book was to avoid a single characterization and show this ambivalence as it is expressed in everyday life. We were interested in both identifying the set of objective relationships that the marginalized establish in order to survive and understanding how these relationships were lived, understood, and experienced. Once this subjective dimension is scrutinized, ambivalence is further amplified.

Think, for example, about the place that politics occupies in the neighborhoods. There is, as we saw in chapter 4, a rather skeptical shared understanding of politics. This view does not stem from an alternative "value system" but from the repeated negative experiences with a way of doing politics that does not seek to build collective actors and community power (despite the rhetoric that claims so) but rather particular personal advantages ("business"). In the rough terrain of everyday neighborhood life—not on television, not on Twitter, Instagram, or Facebook but in the day-to-day life full of risks, urgencies, and uncertainties—popular politics is embodied in politicians who are perceived as corrupt or, at best, opportunists. Neighbors believe they must take whatever advantage they can from those politicians. Politics tends to be understood as driven by pure interest. It is perceived as an instrumental activity that—on more than one occasion—is either illegal or immoral.

But along with this skepticism about politics, there are also beliefs and practices that indicate shared aspirations to change the material conditions of existence: to eat better food, to have a better-paying job, to improve housing and neighborhood infrastructure, to "give a future" to their children. These hopes, as we saw in chapter 2, are materialized in the very origin of the neighborhood (what, if not an expression of collective will and longing, is the land occupation?) and in its development (what, if not the manifestation of an aspiration for progress, is the collective construction of sidewalks, streets, and the successful claims for a school, a plaza, and a health center?). Paradoxically, many of these hopes were and are permeated by politics—from the land occupation to the provision of infrastructure, the soup kitchens, and the welfare programs that help people survive. In other words, shelter and food are, in part, made possible by the action of political actors who are suspected and disbelieved. Party politics and everyday life are deeply intertwined, folded into each other.

Despite the difficulties in making ends meet, despite being overwhelmed and feeling unprotected, despite the lack of infrastructure, the frequent floods, and the surrounding violence, many inhabitants in these marginalized areas claim to have experienced improvements in their living conditions. This should not surprise us: Since the beginning of the settlement, and thanks to their individual and collective efforts, the material conditions of existence have been radically transformed. That trajectory was informed by their aspirations for progress. These aspirations shape their actions in the present—not only the determination with which they approach the daily task of making ends meet but also their yearnings to "get ahead." Part of this text was an attempt to interrogate the form and origins of hope as a constitutive element of the livelihood strategies of the marginalized. Years of fieldwork taught us that subsisting at the bottom of the social structure also implies aspiring to a better future—if not for oneself, then for one's daughters, sons, granddaughters, and grandsons. In practice, in the act of hope (Moore, Eiró, and Koster 2022; see also Holston 1991), these yearnings are expressed in self-construction and in the collective work of infrastructural improvements. They are also manifested in their eagerness to be able to "eat milanesas more often," to go to the supermarket and be able to "fill their carts," and to eat their meals at home (rather than relying on soup kitchens).

The state at the margins appears in more complex ways than usually thematized (in terms of punitive presence or absence and abandonment). The state as an institution, anthropologists Aradhana Sharma and Akhil Gupta argue (2006, 11), expresses itself in people's lives through the seemingly banal practices of bureaucracies. People experience the state when they wait in line to receive a social benefit (Auyero 2012); attend a court hearing (Desmond 2017) or local council meeting (Sullivan 2018; see also Bleger and Stella 2020; Fainstein 2020); invade land, build their homes, or work (underpaid) in soup kitchens; see a police officer make an "arrangement" with the local drug dealer; choose a private parochial school over the public one; or seek (and fail to find) treatment for a child suffering from a drug addiction. These lived experiences matter because they make the state what it is and constitute the workings of its many "hands" (Morgan and Orloff 2017), and they also serve as a basis for criticizing it or making claims against it.

Thus far we reviewed some of the more general substantive lessons from these years of intensive fieldwork. Our collaboration also provided us with methodological and epistemological lessons. Let us review them before bringing all these (substantive and methodological) learnings together.

"The point," writes journalist Ted Conover (2016, 209) in *Immersion: A Writer's Guide to Going Deep*, "is that by simply spending time with people, being at their sides as they encounter challenging situations—by hanging out, in other words—you learn a lot more about them than you might by only conducting interviews. By eating with them, traveling with them, breathing their air, you get more than just information. You gain shared experience. And often you get powerful true stories" (209). As we explained in the introduction, our text is based on Sofía's immersion in the everyday life of the neighborhood. But this ethnographic immersion had, it is important to recognize, different levels of depth. She lives in La Paz, a neighborhood adjacent to La Matera, where she conducted the interviews, observations, and the survey whose results we presented in chapters 2 and 3. From her home she walked to the Comedor de Virginia, located in Barrio El Tala, where she conducted the participant observation that serves as the basis for chapter 8. The reconstruction of Pocho's actions is based on observations at his place in La Matera but above all on in-depth interviews with him, his collaborators, his followers, and his critics. The harsh realities of violence in the streets and in police stations and jails were reconstructed based on a series of life stories and on formal and informal interviews with neighbors and with different members of two extended families.

In order to produce "good-enough" ethnographic work (Scheper-Hughes 1993), the "immersion" described by Conover and advised by many ethnography manuals is not enough. Nor does it suffice to look at social things "with character" or to "try to understand," as journalist Leila Guerriero says. It is necessary to dive in "armed" with theoretical and conceptual tools. These (outlined schematically in chapter 1) allowed us to construct a socioanthropological object (in our case, the intertwining of livelihood strategies and forms of domination) and to focus on issues such as persistence and hope. Without that toolbox, immersion would have led us into "a bottomless ocean of stimuli [and we would have been] caught in a blizzard of factoids, swept by a continuous flow of impressions without rhyme or reason," as Loïc Wacquant puts it (Wacquant and Vandebroeck 2023, 17).

In our case, existing scholarship on marginalization, subsistence strategies, and urban violence provided us with a "principle of pertinence and proto-model of the phenomenon at hand" (Wacquant 2002, 1524), indicating which material should be examined in detail and which should not. The granularity of our analysis, then, should not be confused with crude empiricism. We paid particular attention to the minute details of daily life on the margins, to residents' seemingly circumstantial interactions with a neighborhood broker, with an official or political leader, with a cellmate, with a relative, with a neighbor during a land occupation—attending, with equal consideration, to the care put into a child's schoolwork, to the direction with which a son directs a fan toward the bed in which his violent father sleeps, or to the words of a president in a political act. We exercised this granular, specific gaze because our theoretical tools urged us to search, in these supposedly trivial details of the difficult terrain of daily life on the margins, for partial answers to the more general questions that occupy sociology and anthropology—from how those who have the least make ends meet to how domination works. Immerse yourself, yes. Observe "with character," yes. "Seek to understand," sure. But do all this equipped with theory, and through a sustained exercise of reflexivity: This effort enabled us to produce better data and better comprehend daily life at the urban margins.

One final caveat and three general takeaway points: Our historical and ethnographic reconstruction may have all the trappings of a "standard story" (Tilly 2002), a set of tales of independent, self-motivated, and conscious actors in a particular time and place in which making ends meet (acquiring shelter, procuring food, etc.) happened as the direct result of poor people's actions. This misunderstanding might be an artifact of ethnographic and historical writing but does not reflect the way in which we think about the important relations and mechanisms behind poor people's persistence strategies. Recall our reconstruction of the land occupation and our attention to the role played by grassroots activists and local officials. Now remember our detailed examination of residents' budgets and the operation of political brokers. We focus on these not because we see strategies as the direct consequences of the actions, intentions, deliberations, or impulses of squatters, brokers, or politicians, but because it is our way of inspecting the relevant political mechanisms behind persistence strategies: the mobilization of resources, the brokering of connections, the appropriation of opportunities.

In other words, we couched our analysis in storied form—because, although we agree with Tilly that standard stories are "execrable" (2002, 35) guides to social explanation, we think that narrative has an important place in social science writing (Kramer and Call 2007). Poor people have, undoubtedly, motivations; they engage in self-propelled actions; they aim for certain outcomes. But their "subsistence bricolage" results, like most significant social processes, from incremental, interactive, unintended, and collective causes (Tilly 2002): a labor market that becomes more fragmented and informal, illicit markets that count on police protection, a state that barely ameliorates the deleterious effects of impoverishment, a political field that relies more and more on patronage relationships, and an existing repertoire of (more or less transgressive) joint action on which poor people rely to address some of their basic needs. Altogether these provide the structure of opportunities—"the relationship between the population's interest and the current state of the world around it" (Tilly 1978, 55)—for persistence strategies to unfold.

Three General Lessons

Had we only conducted ethnographic work, we would have missed the centrality of transgressive collective action and patronage politics as strategies to obtain shelter. We would also have confused what is more likely a pause in popular contention with acquiescence and resignation (Desmond and Travis 2018). Had we only carried out historical research, we would have missed the key role of the interplay between state aid, clientelist networks, and mutual aid in procuring sustenance. So, there is then the *first general lesson* that our historical and ethnographic account offers for those interested in studying poverty and marginality in other contexts: Poor people's strategies need to be examined both synchronically and diachronically, in present tense and across time. Doing so not only affords a better view of the strategies' deeply political character and diversity, but also dissolves the distinction between what it means "to survive" and "to make progress." This distinction does not do justice to what those strategies are all about—even amid deep material scarcity, most of our interlocutors think (and consequently act) about making ends meet *and* improving their living conditions, if not for themselves then for their children at least—as attested in the effort they put into their children's academics and extracurricular activities. Strategies thereby should be examined as they span across generations. The notion of *persistence strategies* captures the dynamics uncovered during our field research. Securing material subsistence is hard in several ways: physically (long lines, excruciating wait times), emotionally (the many instances in which parents have nothing more than bread and tea to feed their children), and morally (the contortions one must make to please a local broker to obtain needed resources). And, yet, this effort is never—at least in the practices we witnessed or reconstructed— divorced from attempts to be recognized or respected as a person or member of a specific community (a family, a group, neighborhood center, etc.). This effort should not be separated from the individual (and sometimes collective) endeavor to secure a better future. In other words, satisfying urgent needs and nurturing hopes in the future are, in the logic of poor people's strategies, inextricable.

The second general lesson is that strategies of persistence are about material and symbolic reproduction and, notably, also about physical security. Given the widespread violence at the urban margins, individuals and families relationally manage, not only to "get stuff" but also to "stay safe." We need to examine poor people's ways of dealing with scarcity and violence simultaneously. Doing so unveils the occasionally ambivalent character of kin and friend networks. Sometimes these relationships help people obtain food and protection. But other times, the very same connections that are instrumental in procuring the material resources that are indispensable to a family's mere reproduction may bring violence to households.

This brings us to the *third general lesson*: Strategies never work in a vacuum. As bundles of operative ties, they are deployed in a relational context pervaded by direct and mediated forms of domination. In and through a plethora of practices, poor residents construct strategies out of objective circumstances "immediately given in the immediate present" (Bourdieu and Wacquant 1992, 129): a highly exploitative labor market, a meager (and oftentimes malfunctioning) state safety net, and a durable and highly extortive and manipulative set of political practices. To resort to an old, but still useful, paraphrasis, poor people strategize, and they engage in subsistence bricolage, but not under the economic and political conditions of their own choosing. Consequently, relations of domination and exploitation at the margins are produced and reproduced simultaneously by the actions of brokers, politicians, cops, criminals, and bosses (who are themselves hustling to make do and get ahead) and by the poor themselves who, out of (often desperate) need and their own strategic choices, partake in those relationships.

We did not begin our research by intending to provide detailed documentation of all the things the poor do daily, their strenuous efforts to provide for themselves and their loved ones, or the fact that poverty is not (contrary to an increasingly prevalent perception in Argentina, and one enduring in the United States [Rank et al. 2021]) the result of individual failures or inadequacies. Our impetus was not to disprove, once more, that the poor lack motivation, that they are being rewarded by welfare programs or any such moral/political valuations.[1] Nor did we seek, as some scholars are fond of insisting these days (Benach and Delgado 2022), to portray the margins as spaces potentially generative of alternatives to the current highly exclusionary regimes of capitalist accumulation, creativity, and/or social, cultural, and political experimentation. We decided to first research and then write about poor people's strategies as a point of entry to what really matters to us: How and why do people put up with, perpetuate, or push back against the conditions that produce their suffering? How are forms of political domination and precarious exploitation sustained and reproduced at the bottom of the social order? For Sofía, these questions were first encountered in the classroom and then expanded and problematized during the course of this research. For Javier, these interrogations have been present throughout his more than two-decades-long scholarly work. This book integrates the many aspects of this research agenda and (hopefully) improves on the (always tentative) answers provided thus far.

INTRODUCTION

1 The Conurbano Bonaerense is an area comprising thirty-three districts
that surround the city of Buenos Aires. Roughly fourteen million people
reside in the Conurbano. Although geographically small (just 0.5 percent
of the national territory), 29 percent of the total population lives there and
40 percent of its residents fall below the national poverty line (Zarazaga
and Ronconi 2017). Unless noted otherwise, all names of people and places
are real.

2 SUBE is the Unique Electronic Ticket System, implemented in the country
since 2011. The SUBE card allows each user to pay for state-subsidized trips on
buses, subways, and trains.

3 In Argentina, beef symbolizes good (and longed-for) food not just for those at
the bottom of the social scale. In an interview between the sociologist Mariana Heredia and a university student, the latter told her that she "thought of a
barbecue and her eyes filled with tears." Some of the material deprivations that
affect the most dispossessed are becoming, according to Heredia, more transversal to social groups that are losing purchasing power or income (Mariana
Heredia, personal communication).

4 The AUH (Asignación Universal por Hijo), a federal welfare program, provides
families with USD $30 per child per month as of 2019.

5 We thank Loïc Wacquant (personal communication) for making us aware of
the multidimensionality of persistence.

6 Cravino and Vommaro (2018) describe the origins of these settlements.

7 We selected La Matera as a field site because of our interest in poor people's
strategies to make ends meet and their ways of dealing with violence. We conducted research in La Paz and El Tala because, as we will examine in the following chapters, the networks and organizations on which the inhabitants of

La Matera depend either originated there (as in the case of land squatting) or extend to those neighborhoods (as with the exchange of resources between relatives or the community kitchen that residents of the settlement attend). We selected our research sites for both theoretical reasons (in the case of La Matera) and empirical reasons (in the case of the two adjacent neighborhoods). This then is not a comparative study, but a case study that presents an analytically luminous example of the diversity of strategies, the role of the state, and the collective action and clientelism within them. The fact that La Matera is not a representative neighborhood of urban marginality does not detract from the sociological relevance of our work. The case we dissect in this book is important because what happens there exposes the complex workings of strategies in particularly clear form (see Zussman 2004 on the logic of the case study). In other words, this is not a study of La Matera, La Paz, or El Tala, but of the forms and experiences of everyday subsistence. It is not a study of the neighborhoods, but a study of persistence in the neighborhoods. See the classic text by Geertz (1973) on this important and often-ignored distinction.

8 We believe that the dichotomy between "insider" and "outsider" that is sometimes used as a criterion for evaluating urban ethnography is simplistic and misleading—no one is completely one or the other. The intellectual collaboration between an anthropology student who was born and lives in the place where the research is being carried out and a sociologist who lives outside the country seeks to demonstrate that, in order to carry out sound ethnographic research, what really matters is neither the social or geographical position of the researcher nor categorical attributes (age, gender, etc.) but rather the time invested in it, the constant epistemological vigilance, and the reflexivity applied during the research process (see Miller 2021).

9 We sought to minimize as much as the possible external intrusion (residents see Sofía as "the daughter of Susana," "the cousin of...," "the neighbor of..."), the distance, or the asymmetry that is typical in relationships between interviewers and interviewees, observers and observed. On more than one occasion, our fieldwork produced moments of "induced and accompanied self-analysis" (Bourdieu et al. 2000, 615) when people like Chela, Soledad, Luis, Eliana, and Sofía herself took the opportunity provided by an interview or a conversation to conduct a self-examination. They "took advantage of the permission or prompting afforded by our questions or suggestions...to carry out a task of clarification—simultaneously gratifying and painful—and to give vent, at times with extraordinary expressive intensity, to experiences and thoughts long kept unsaid or repressed" (615).

1. EXPLICATING SUBSISTENCE AT THE MARGINS

1 Following most of the recent literature on the subject, we here use *clientelist* and *patronage politics* as interchangeable terms (Kitschelt and Wilkinson

2007; Levitsky 2003). For a thorough review of the vast literature on poor people's strategies in the Americas, see Deckard and Auyero (2022).

2 A now-classic statement on the intricate ways in which deprivation generates these horizontal and vertical, cooperative and conflictive entanglements was made by anthropologist Nancy Scheper-Hughes (1993) in her masterful ethnography of suffering in Brazil.

3 Argentine sociologist Susana Hintze (2004) offers an insightful overview of the use of this and related concepts (estrategias familiares de vida, estrategias de existencia, estrategias de reproducción) in Latin American social sciences. She states that the term *estrategias de supervivencia* (survival strategies) was first used by Joaquín Duque and Ernesto Pastrana (1973) in their study of Santiago de Chile's poor. For a detailed study of food strategies of survival, see Hintze (1989).

4 Again, we thank Loïc Wacquant for identifying this shortcoming in the notion of "strategy of survival" and for suggesting the notion of "strategy of persistence" as a superior alternative.

5 A strand of scholarship in Latin America groups the many relational strategies through which poor people seek to make ends meet under the term *social economy* or *popular economy* (Coraggio 2014; Salvia and Chávez Molina 2013).

6 According to Lubbers and colleagues (2020), the reasons behind these different diagnoses range from the substantive (i.e., the various populations under study) to the contextual (different political and economic conditions) and methodological (ethnographic fieldwork, survey research, etc.). For a study of the tension within reciprocity networks between support and exploitation, see Rosales (2020).

7 We draw on a classic distinction between direct and indirect modes of domination outlined by Pierre Bourdieu (1977). According to the French sociologist, relationships of domination could be "made, unmade, and remade in and by the interactions between persons" (exercised and renewed in a direct and personal manner) or they can be "mediated by objective and institutionalized mechanisms" (184). In the latter case, in which those prevailing in the school system were the object of Bourdieu's careful analyses, relations of domination "have the opacity and permanence of things and escape the grasp of individual consciousness and power" (184).

8 On the collective longing of subaltern groups, see the excellent work of María Ximena Dávila (2020).

9 Here we draw on Annemarie Mol (2003, 33) when she asserts that "the ethnographic study of practices does not search for knowledge in subjects who have it in their minds and may talk about it. Instead, it locates knowledge primarily in activities, events, buildings, instruments, procedures, and so on." See also Ochs (2011).

10 On the mechanisms that produce and reproduce social inequality, see Tilly (1999). For Latin America, see Reygadas (2008) and Benza and Kessler (2020). For the case of Argentina, see Salvia and Chávez Molina (2013); Svampa (2005); Heredia, Pereyra, and Svampa (2020); Poy and Salvia (2019); and Salvia (2012).

2. COLLECTIVE ACTION AND PARTY POLITICS IN THE MAKINGS OF A SQUATTER SETTLEMENT

1 La Matera, and before it La Paz and El Tala, is an example of what Teresa Caldeira (2017) calls "peripheral urbanization" (see also Holston 1991). What makes the process peripheral "is not its physical location but rather the crucial role of residents in the production of space and how as a mode of urbanization it unfolds slowly, transversally in relation to official logics, and amidst political contestations" (Caldeira 2017, 4). As we will see, similar to the cases examined by Caldeira, La Matera, La Paz, and El Tala "offer a model of social mobility, as they become the material embodiments of the notions of progress" (Caldeira 2017, 6).

2 On auto-construction as a concrete expression of hope, see the recent study by Moore, Eiró, and Koster (2022) on popular housing in Medellín, Colombia. Like us, they approach hope as a practice to be ethnographically observed. Habitat improvement through auto-construction is "an experience of future-oriented agency, as it acts towards and gives expression to a particular imagination of the future" (96). Hauer, Nielsen, and Niewöhner (2018, 60) also analyze hope as practice that "takes place" in and is "co-constitutive of" the urban landscape.

3 In 2018, the median monthly income of informal workers was 41 percent lower than the income of all employed workers. Half of the households that have workers in informal or precarious jobs are below the poverty line (Observatorio de la Deuda Social Argentina [ODSA] 2021).

4 As Almeida and Perez Martín (2022) note, in the late 1980s and early 1990s all these policies (more or less realized, depending on the country) came to be known as the "Washington Consensus."

5 According to the ODSA, these programs together reduced income poverty by approximately 9 percent. As Díaz Langou and others find in a detailed analysis of these programs, together "these policies probably prevented around 1.2 million more people from falling below the poverty line" in the country (2021, 21).

6 This same period saw a gradual reduction in "multidimensional poverty" (due to the progressive improvement of indicators such as the availability of running water inside homes, access to gas, school attendance rates, and overall quality of housing). The fact that poverty increased since the return of democracy does not necessarily invalidate Huber and Stephens's (2012) authoritative and insightful cross-national quantitative and comparative historical analysis of the impact of political forces on poverty and inequality. Building on power constellations theory and studying five countries (Argentina, Brazil, Chile, Costa Rica, and Uruguay) over seven decades (until 2010), they argue that "democracy is one of the most important determinants of redistributive social policy. One mechanism by which democracy promotes egalitarian social policy is that it is a precondition for the development of left parties and their access to governmental power" (3). In their view, democracy allows "social movements, civil society organizations, and parties of the left to form,

grow, and slowly gain influence on policy to shape it in a more egalitarian direction. Democracy does not guarantee uniform movement toward lower poverty and inequality, but it makes gradual movement in this direction possible" (12). In emphasizing that "politics matter fundamentally and have the potential of modifying seemingly immutable structures of inequality in Latin America" (13), Huber and Stephens agree with Brady (2009) about the key role politics play in deepening or remedying misery. Poverty, as Brady convincingly shows through a historical, cross-national comparison of eighteen affluent Western democracies, "is ultimately a political problem, the fundamental cause of poverty is politics" (2009, 9). The works of Brady and Huber and Stephens are powerful antidotes against individualistic explanations of poverty prevailing in US social sciences that emphasize cultural, behavioral, demographic, or labor-market characteristics of the poor (see also Wacquant 2022).

7   On this earlier cycle of mobilization, see Izaguirre and Aristizabal (1988) and Fara (1988). See also Cravino and Vommaro (2018) on the political processes behind land occupations.

8   In her insightful book about squatter settlements, political mobilization, and marginality in urban Montevideo, Uruguay, sociologist María José Álvarez-Rivadulla (2017) argues that economic hardship is a necessary but insufficient condition for explaining the occurrence of land occupations. Squatter settlements emerge when conditions such as housing scarcity and overcrowding, for example, interact with particular political factors. These factors (strength of clientelist arrangements being one of them) shape the specific form in which the occupation unfolds. Classic and contemporary works (Collier 1976; Holland 2017) document the variety of state responses to land occupations (repression, forbearance, neglect—or a combination of them). See also Schneider (1995).

9   Desmond and Travis (2018) assert that the urban poor in the United States do not challenge the depth and expanse of their poverty. Poor people are, according to them, cynical and unmobilized. Misery shapes their perceptions of efficacy and capacity for political action. Far from this fatalism, quiescence, and lack of political participation, the land occupation and the subsequent protests—as well as the high levels of mobilization by, for example, unemployed workers (Rossi 2017; Perez 2022)—illustrate the intense political involvement of poor people in Buenos Aires. Reflecting on the first time they squatted, Maria told us "we did politics even without knowing it." This high level of political participation happened despite extremely precarious (and spatially concentrated) material conditions of existence—two factors that, according to Desmond and Travis, would feed fatalism and discourage political action.

10 The estallido refers to the financial and political collapse of December 2001 and the massive street mobilizations that followed.

11 We identified these major concerns through a series of 105 short interviews. Ours was a convenience sample, and interviewees were chosen to maximize variation (Weiss 1994). Fifty-one interviews were carried out in the eight

blocks that surround the school and the health center. Fifty-four were conducted in the blocks that are farther away from the center. In terms of basic infrastructure, La Matera is not that different from other slums, squatter settlements, and low-income neighborhoods in the Conurbano. As Zarazaga (2017) describes, less than 10 percent of the families living in those areas of the Conurbano have a formal connection to the potable water network, most families heat their homes with gas canisters, and only 38 percent of households have garbage collection services.

3. PERSISTENCE STRATEGIES

1 Why do they choose private schools over public ones? The answer is straightforward: because public schools are deemed unreliable. Based on qualitative research on the operation of the public education system, Emilio Tenti Fanfani (2005, 2021), one of the foremost experts on sociology of education in Argentina, confirms and elaborates on parents' critical evaluation of public schools and the reasons behind it:

> The slow decline of the public school seems to have no end.... Perhaps one of the most dramatic situations occurred in many schools in Greater Buenos Aires since, according to a widely held opinion of parents, the public school is widely criticized for its intermittent operation.... The complaint is a plain and simple absence of service for various reasons. The first is the closed school, i.e., the lack of classes due to teacher conflict. The second is teacher absenteeism. If to these two reasons we add student absenteeism, the resulting picture is more than worrying.... Faced with this critical situation, the private school is seen as "better" not so much because of its intrinsic qualities, but because it simply offers a normal service, that is, it guarantees class time and a basic institutional order. It could be said that the privately managed school is preferred not so much because of its virtues, but because of the serious defects that are blamed on many public schools. (Tenti Fanfani 2005, 45)

2 One US dollar equaled 65 Argentine pesos in early 2020. At the time of the writing of our final draft, in January 2023, one US dollar equaled 300 Argentine pesos. When we submitted the final manuscript for publication, one US dollar equaled 870 Argentina pesos.

3 Forty-seven out of our 105 interviewees said that they receive some form of state aid (IFE, AUH, Tarjeta Alimentaria, etc.).

4 This federal program provides funds for six months and seeks to, according to the government's website, "strengthen the economic independence of women and LGBTI+ in situations of gender violence." Olga asked Gustavo if she should apply, to which he replied, "Just make sure they don't come looking for me." She remembers laughing, and then adds: "Some neighbors told me about it. It was easy to apply and nobody controlled anything." On the program, see "Accompany Program," Argentine State portal, accessed May 4,

2024, https://www.argentina.gob.ar/generos/plan_nacional_de_accion
_contra_las_violencias_por_motivos_de_genero/programa-acompanar.

5 On the theoretical and analytic limitations of the term *precariat* to understand
   the reality of workers and the urban poor in general in the Global South, see
   Munck (2013).

6 Here we heed Charles Tilly's (1999, 10) definition of *exploitation* as that mechanism which "operates when powerful, connected people command resources
   from which they draw significantly increased returns by coordinating efforts
   of outsiders whom they exclude from the full value added by that effort."

4. BROKERS AND THEIR FOLLOWERS

1 Political scientist Rebecca Weitz-Shapiro (2014, 5) captures this recent shift well
   when she writes, "Earlier definitions of clientelism within the social sciences emphasized that the practice was embedded in social ties and encompassed the exchange of a broad range of services and support between patrons and their clients,
   which were not necessarily political in nature.... Increases in urbanization, economic development, and the salience of competitive politics in much of the developing world eventually led scholars to shift their attention to examining how these
   exchange relationships functioned within the context of competitive politics."

2 See Auyero and Benzecry (2017) for both a theoretical and empirical elabora-
   tion of this point.

3 This case does not seem to be exceptional. About 70 percent of the brokers interviewed by Zarazaga (2017, 50) "consider that it is common for certain services to be compensated" with marijuana, paco, or other drugs.

4 Known as bazuco in Colombia, baserolo in Ecuador, and mono in Chile, paco
   is a cheap, highly addictive form of cocaine.

5. LIVES AT RISK

1 See Sampson, Raudenbush, and Earls (1997); Ousey and Lee (2002); Imbusch,
   Misse, and Carrión (2011); G. Willis (2015); Cruz (2016); Klinenberg (2018);
   and Auyero and Sobering (2019).

2 Ana Villarreal (2024) develops this argument with great analytical depth and
   illuminating empirical evidence.

6. VICTIMS AND PERPETRATORS

1 Violence is here understood as "the intentional use of physical force or power,
   threatened or actual, against oneself, another person, or against a group or
   community, that either results in or has a high likelihood of resulting in injury,
   death, [or] psychological harm" (WHO 2002, 4).

2 The various accounts of what occurred can be found in the section titled
   "Cuestiones" (Matters of the Case) in the court ruling.

1 For a description of the dynamics of collusion between police and "transas,"
see Auyero and Sobering (2019). Clandestine relationships between members
of the security forces and participants in the criminalized drug market are an
open secret in Buenos Aires neighborhoods. A recent example is recounted by
Juan Diego Britos (2022): "Those who live in neighborhoods with a lot of drug
dealing say that the silence [about trafficking] is guaranteed by police complicity, through the street boss who receives a percentage of money every week in
exchange for protection. Narcos call this payment a *'cuota,'* and the police define it as *'la juntada.'"*

8. WOMEN AT WORK

This chapter was inspired by Vrinda Marwah's excellent work on female health
workers in India. See Marwah (2021a, 2021b).

1 Data are, as Geertz (1973, 9) reminds us, "really our own constructions of
other people's constructions of what they and their compatriots are up to."

2 We want to thank Mo Hume for alerting us about Moser's classic work on
gender and development.

3 As Paul Willis puts it in his classic *Learning to Labor* (2017, 126), "The cultural
forms may not say what they know, nor know what they say, but they mean
what they do—at least in the logic of their praxis. There is no dishonesty in in-
terpreting that."

4 SOFÍA'S FIELDNOTES, AUGUST 5, 2021. *Silvia tells us about the amount of
money she is spending on her son, Germán, who plays soccer in a local club:
"The bus fare, the boots, the thermal leggings, the socks, everything.... I'm
broke. Yesterday he called me and told me that they called him to play against
an AFA club [Argentine Football Association]. I told him, 'Oh, son, that's great,'
but inside I was crying thinking about all the money I will have to spend, because on top of everything I have to buy him a team uniform just for practice,
they don't even use it to play games. But after thinking about the money I have
to spend, I think that it is much better that he is in the club than in the streets."*

5 The National Food Program (PAN for Programa Alimentario Nacional) was a
policy implemented during the presidency of Raúl Alfonsín. PAN boxes were
distributed monthly to poor families. The boxes contained flour, oil, noodles,
rice, beans, powdered milk, and canned meat.

CONCLUSIONS

1 On these nonscholarly reasons animating academic work on the dispossessed
and their pernicious outcomes, see Wacquant (2002).

Abello Colak, Alexandra, Heidy Cristina Gómez Ramírez, and María Isela Quintero Valencia. 2014. "Iniciativas comunitarias y su incidencia en la seguridad humana." In *Nuestras voces sobre seguridad humana en Medellín: Diálogos sobre seguridad*, 145–84. Medellín: Universidad de Antioquia.

Adams, Tani Marilena. 2017. "How Chronic Violence Affects Human Development, Social Relations, and the Practice of Citizenship." Woodrow Wilson Center Reports on the Americas 36. Washington, DC: Woodrow Wilson International Center for Scholars.

Aimetta, Corina, and Juliana Santa María. 2007. "Sobre las estrategias laborales: Las huellas de la precariedad en el mundo del trabajo." In *Los significados de la pobreza*, edited by Amalia Eguía and Susana Ortale, 35–48. Buenos Aires: Biblos.

Almeida, Paul, and Amalia Pérez Martín. 2022. *Collective Resistance to Neoliberalism*. New York: Cambridge University Press.

Álvarez-Rivadulla, María José. 2017. *Squatters and the Politics of Marginality in Uruguay*. New York: Palgrave Macmillan, 2017.

Alzugaray, Lucas. 2007. "Redes sociales y relaciones comunitarias en Barrio Esperanza." In *Los significados de la pobreza*, edited by Amalia Eguía and Susana Ortale, 121–32. Buenos Aires: Biblos.

Anderson, Jeanine. 2007. "Urban Poverty Reborn: A Gender and Generational Analysis." *Journal of Developing Societies* 23, no. 1–2 (January 2007): 221–41. https://www.doi.org/10.1177/0169796X0602300213.

Arias, Enrique Desmond. 2009. *Drugs and Democracy in Rio de Janeiro: Trafficking, Social Networks, and Public Security*. Chapel Hill: University of North Carolina Press.

Auyero, Javier. 2001. *Poor People's Politics: Peronist Survival Networks and the Legacy of Evita*. Durham, NC: Duke University Press.

Auyero, Javier. 2012. *Patients of the State: The Politics of Waiting in Argentina*. Durham, NC: Duke University Press.

Auyero, Javier, and Claudio Benzecry. 2017. "The Practical Logic of Political Domination: Conceptualizing the Clientelist Habitus." *Sociological Theory* 35 (3): 179–99. https://www.doi.org/10.1177/0735275117725767.

Auyero, Javier, and María Fernanda Berti. 2016. *In Harm's Way: The Dynamics of Urban Violence*. Princeton, NJ: Princeton University Press.

Auyero, Javier, and Kristine Kilanski. 2015. "From 'Making Toast' to 'Splitting Apples': Dissecting 'Care' in the Midst of Chronic Violence." *Theory and Society* 44 (5): 393–414. https://www.doi.org/10.1007/s11186-015-9255-6.

Auyero, Javier, Pablo Lapegna, and Fernanda Page Poma. 2009. "Patronage Politics and Contentious Collective Action: A Recursive Relationship." *Latin American Politics and Society* 51 (3): 1–31. https://www.doi.org/10.1111/j.1548-2456.2009.00054.x.

Auyero, Javier, and Sofía Servián. 2021. "Vidas en Riesgo." *Cuestiones Criminales* 4 (7–8): 89–118.

Auyero, Javier, and Katherine Sobering. 2019. *The Ambivalent State*. New York: Oxford University Press.

Auyero, Javier, and Debora Alejandra Swistun. 2009. *Flammable: Environmental Suffering in an Argentine Shantytown*. New York: Oxford University Press.

Benach, Núria, and Manuel Delgado. 2022. *Márgenes y umbrales: Revuelta y desorden en la colonización capitalista del espacio*. Barcelona: Virus Editorial.

Benedict, Ruth. 2006. *Patterns of Culture*. Boston: Mariner.

Benza, Gabriela, and Gabriel Kessler. 2020. *Uneven Trajectories: Latin American Societies in the Twenty-First Century*. Cambridge: Cambridge University Press.

Bleger, Mariel, and Valentina Stella. 2020. "La espera desobediente: Análisis de un caso etnográfico sobre una comunidad Mapuche en Bariloche (Río Negro)." *Avá Revista de Antropología* 36 (6): 43–64.

Bonfiglio, Juan Ignacio. 2018. "Evolución de capacidades de subsistencia de los hogares." Informe técnico. Pontificia Universidad Católica Argentina. Observatorio de la Deuda Social Argentina. Barómetro de la Deuda Social Argentina.

Bourdieu, Pierre. 1977. *Outline of a Theory of Practice*. Cambridge: Cambridge University Press.

Bourdieu, Pierre. 1990. *Homo Academicus*. Stanford, CA: Stanford University Press.

Bourdieu, Pierre. 1996. "Understanding." *Theory, Culture & Society* 13 (2): 17–37.

Bourdieu, Pierre. 1998. *Acts of Resistance: Against the Tyranny of the Market*. New York: New Press.

Bourdieu, Pierre. 2000. *Pascalian Meditations*. Stanford, CA: Stanford University Press.

Bourdieu, Pierre. 2020. *On the State: Lectures at the Collège de France, 1989–1992*. New York: Polity.

Bourdieu, Pierre, Jean-Claude Chamboderon, and Jean-Claude Passeron. 1991. *The Craft of Sociology*. New York: de Gruyter.

Bourdieu, Pierre, and Loïc Wacquant. 1992. *An Invitation to Reflexive Sociology*. Chicago: University of Chicago Press.

Bourdieu, Pierre, et al. 2000. *The Weight of the World: Social Suffering in Contemporary Society*. Stanford, CA: Stanford University Press.

Bourgois, Philippe. 2003. *In Search of Respect: Selling Crack in El Barrio*. Cambridge: Cambridge University Press.

Bourgois, Philippe, Laurie Hart, George Karandinos, and Fernando Montero. 2019. "Coming of Age in the Concrete Killing Fields of the US Inner City." In *Exotic No More: Anthropology for the Contemporary World*, edited by Jeremy MacClancy, 7–28. Chicago: University of Chicago Press.

Brady, David. 2009. *Rich Democracies, Poor People: How Politics Explain Poverty*. New York: Oxford University Press.

Brady, David. 2019. "Theories of the Causes of Poverty." *Annual Review of Sociology* 45 (1): 155–75. https://www.doi.org/10.1146/annurev-soc-073018–022550.

Braithwaite, Valerie. 2004. "Collective Hope." ANNALS *of the American Academy of Political and Social Science* 592 (1): 6–15. https://www.doi.org/10.1177/0002716203262049.

Britos, Juan Diego. 2022. "Narcomenudeo en el Conurbano: El principio de la historia." *Cordón: Revista Conurbana: Universidad Nacional de Lomas de Zamora*, February 8. http://cordon.unlz.edu.ar/2022/02/08/narcomenudeo-en-el-conurbano-el-principio-de-la-historia/.

Burawoy, Michael. 2016. "Sociology as a Vocation." *Contemporary Sociology* 45 (4) 379–93.

Burdick-Will, Julia. 2017. "Neighbors but Not Classmates: Neighborhood Disadvantage, Local Violent Crime, and the Heterogeneity of Educational Experiences in Chicago." *American Journal of Education* 124 (1): 37–65. https://www.doi.org/10.1086/693958.

Caldeira, Teresa. 2001. *City of Walls: Crime, Segregation, and Citizenship in São Paulo*. Berkeley: University of California Press.

Caldeira, Teresa. 2017. "Peripheral Urbanization: Autoconstruction, Transversal Logics, and Politics in Cities of the Global South." *Environment and Planning D: Society and Space* 35 (1): 3–20. https://www.doi.org/10.1177/0263775816658479.

Calvo, Ernesto, and María Victoria Murillo. 2004. "Who Delivers? Partisan Clients in the Argentine Electoral Market." *American Journal of Political Science* 48 (4): 742–57. https://www.doi.org/10.2307/1519931.

Centeno, Miguel, and Joseph Cohen. 2012. "The Arc of Neoliberalism." *Annual Review of Sociology* 38:317–40. https://doi.org/10.1146/annurev-soc-081309-150235.

Centro de Estudios Legales y Sociales (CELS). 2019. *Derechos humanos en la Argentina: Informe 2019*. Buenos Aires: Siglo XXI Editores.

Chant, Sylvia. 2002. "Researching Gender, Families and Households in Latin America: From the 20th into the 21st Century." *Bulletin of Latin American Research* 21 (4): 545–75. https://www.doi.org/10.1111/1470-9856.00059.

Christin, Rosine. 2000. "A Silent Witness." In *The Weight of the World*, edited by Pierre Bourdieu et al., 354–60. Stanford, CA: Stanford University Press.

Collier, David. 1976. *Squatters and Oligarchs: Authoritarian Rule and Policy Change in Peru*. Baltimore, MD: Johns Hopkins University Press.

Collins, Caytlin, Katherine Jensen, and Javier Auyero. 2017. "A Proposal for Public Sociology as Localized Intervention and Collective Enterprise: The Makings and Impact of *Invisible in Austin*." *Qualitative Sociology* 40:191–214. https://doi .org/10.1007/s11133-017-9353-z

Collins, Randall. 2008. *Violence: A Micro-Sociological Theory*. Princeton, NJ: Princeton University Press.

Conley, Dalton. 2005. *The Pecking Order: A Bold New Look at How Family and Society Determine Who We Become*. New York: Vintage.

Conover, Ted. 2016. *Immersion: A Writer's Guide to Going Deep*. Chicago: University of Chicago Press.

Coraggio, José Luis. 2014. "*La presencia de la economía social y solidaria y su institucionalización en América Latina no. 7.*" UNRISD Occasional Paper: Potential and Limits of Social and Solidarity Economy.

Cortina, Adela. 2022. *Aporophobia: Why We Reject the Poor Instead of Helping Them*. Princeton, NJ: Princeton University Press.

Cravino, Maria Cristina, and Pablo Ariel Vommaro. 2018. "Asentamientos en el sur de la periferia de Buenos Aires: Orígenes, entramados organizativos y políticas de hábitat." *Política & Sociedad* 25 (2): 1–27.

Cruz, José Miguel. 2016. "State and Criminal Violence in Latin America." *Crime, Law and Social Change* 66 (4): 375–96. https://www.doi.org/10.1007/s10611-016 -9631-9.

Cvetkovich, Ann. 2012. *Depression: A Public Feeling*. Durham, NC: Duke University Press.

Das, Veena. 2012. "Ordinary Ethics: The Perils and Pleasures of Everyday Life." In *A Companion to Moral Anthropology*, edited by Didier Fassin, 133–49. New York: Wiley-Blackwell.

Dávila, María Ximena. 2020. "El anhelo del Estado: Lideresas sociales y estado local en Montes de María, Colombia." MA thesis, Universidad de los Andes.

Deckard, Faith, and Javier Auyero. 2022. "Poor People's Survival Strategies: Two Decades of Research in the Americas." *Annual Review of Sociology* 48:373–95. https://www.doi.org/10.1146/annurev-soc-031021-034449.

Del Real, Deisy. 2019. "Toxic Ties: The Reproduction of Legal Violence within Mixed-Status Intimate Partners, Relatives, and Friends." *International Migration Review* 53 (2): 548–70. https://www.doi.org/10.1177/0197918318769313.

Denice, Patrick, and Betheny Gross. 2016. "Choice, Preferences, and Constraints: Evidence from Public School Applications in Denver." *Sociology of Education* 89 (4): 300–20. https://www.doi.org/10.1177/0038040716664395.

Desmond, Matthew. 2009. *On the Fireline: Living and Dying with Wildland Firefighters*. Illustrated ed. Chicago: University of Chicago Press.

Desmond, Matthew. 2012. "Eviction and the Reproduction of Urban Poverty." *American Journal of Sociology* 118 (1): 88–133. https://www.doi.org/10.1086/666082.

Desmond, Matthew. 2015. "Severe Deprivation in America: An Introduction." *RSF: The Russell Sage Foundation Journal of the Social Sciences* 1 (1): 1–11. https://www.doi.org/10.7758/RSF.2015.1.2.01.

Desmond, Matthew. 2017. *Evicted: Poverty and Profit in the American City*. New York: Crown.

Desmond, Matthew. 2023. *Poverty, by America*. New York: Crown.

Desmond, Matthew, and Adam Travis. 2018. "Political Consequences of Survival Strategies among the Urban Poor." *American Sociological Review* 83 (5): 869–96. https://www.doi.org/10.1177/0003122418792836.

Desmond, Matthew, and Bruce Western. 2018. "Poverty in America: New Directions and Debates." *Annual Review of Sociology* 44 (1): 305–18. https://www.doi.org/10.1146/annurev-soc-060116-053411.

Diani, Mario, and Doug McAdam, eds. 2003. *Social Movements and Networks: Relational Approaches to Collective Action*. Oxford: Oxford University Press.

Díaz Langou, Gala, Gabriel Kessler, Carola della Paolera, and Matilde Karczmarczyk. 2021. "Impacto social del COVID-19 en Argentina: Balance del primer semestre del 2020." Buenos Aires: CIPPEC. https://www.cippec.org/publicacion/impacto-social-del-covid-19-en-argentina-balance-del-primer-semestre-del-2020/.

Di Nunzio, Marco. 2019. *The Act of Living: Street Life, Marginality, and Development in Urban Ethiopia*. Ithaca: Cornell University Press.

Duque, Joaquín, and Ernesto Patrana. 1973. "Las estrategias de supervivencia económica de las unidades familiares del sector popular urbano: una investigación exploratoria." Santiago, Chile: ELAS-CELADE.

Edin, Kathryn, Laura Lein, and Christopher Jencks. 1997. *Making Ends Meet: How Single Mothers Survive Welfare and Low-Wage Work*. New York: Russell Sage Foundation.

Edin, Kathryn, and H. Luke Shaefer. 2016. *$2.00 a Day: Living on Almost Nothing in America*. Boston: Mariner.

Eguía, Amalia Cristina, and María Susana Ortale. 2004. "Reproducción social y pobreza urbana." *Cuestiones de Sociología* 2:21–49.

Eguía, Amalia, and María Susana Ortale, eds. 2007. *Los significados de la pobreza*. Buenos Aires: Biblos.

Elias, Norbert. 2000. *The Civilizing Process: Sociogenetic and Psychogenetic Investigations*. Oxford: Blackwell.

Emerson, Robert M. 2011. *Writing Ethnographic Fieldnotes*. Chicago: University of Chicago Press.

Ernaux, Annie. 2022. *La Vergüenza*. Madrid: Tusquets.

Fainstein, Carla. 2020. "Problemas del mientras tanto: Espera y justicia en la causa 'Mendoza.'" *Avá Revista de Antropología* 36:165–93.

Fara, Luis. 1988. "Luchas reivindicativas en un contexto autoritario: Los asentamientos de San Francisco Solano." In *Los nuevos movimientos sociales*, edited by Elizabeth Jelin, 120–39. Buenos Aires: CEAL.

Fassin, Didier. 2021. *Death of a Traveller: A Counter-Investigation*. New York: Polity.

Fernández-Kelly, Patricia. 2015. *The Hero's Fight: African Americans in West Baltimore and the Shadow of the State*. Princeton, NJ: Princeton University Press.

Fischer, Brodwyn, Bryan McCann, and Javier Auyero, eds. 2014. *Cities from Scratch: Poverty and Informality in Urban Latin America*. Durham, NC: Duke University Press.

Fontaine, Laurence, and Jürgen Schlumbohm. 2000. "Household Strategies for Survival: An Introduction." *International Review of Social History* 45 (s8): 1–17. https://www.doi.org/10.1017/S0020859000115263.

Gasparini, Leonardo, Leopoldo Tornarolli, and Pablo Gluzman. 2019. "El desafío de la pobreza en la Argentina." Buenos Aires: CEDLAS, CIPPEC, PNUD, 2019. https://www.cippec.org/publicacion/el-desafio-de-la-pobreza-en-la -argentina/.

Gay, Robert. 2005. *Lucia: Testimonies of a Brazilian Drug Dealer's Woman*. Philadelphia: Temple University Press.

Geertz, Clifford. 1973. *The Interpretation of Cultures*. New York: Basic Books.

Geertz, Clifford. 1996. *After the Fact: Two Countries, Four Decades, One Anthropologist*. Cambridge, MA: Harvard University Press, 1996.

Glenn, Evelyn Nakano. 2000. "Creating a Caring Society." *Contemporary Sociology* 29 (1): 84–94. https://www.doi.org/10.2307/2654934.

Goldstein, Donna M. 2013. *Laughter Out of Place: Race, Class, Violence, and Sexuality in a Rio Shantytown*. Berkeley: University of California Press.

Goldstein, Paul. 1985. "The Drugs/Violence Nexus: A Tripartite Conceptual Framework." *Journal of Drug Issues* 15 (4): 493–506. https://www.doi.org/10.1177 /002204268501500406.

González de la Rocha, Mercedes. 2001. "From the Resources of Poverty to the Poverty of Resources? The Erosion of a Survival Model." *Latin American Perspectives* 28 (4): 72–100.

González de la Rocha, Mercedes. 2020. "Of Morals and Markets: Social Exchange and Poverty in Contemporary Urban Mexico." *ANNALS of the American Academy of Political and Social Science* 689 (1): 26–45. https://www.doi.org/10.1177 /0002716220916700.

Gould, Roger V. 2003. *Collision of Wills: How Ambiguity about Social Rank Breeds Conflict*. Chicago: University of Chicago Press.

Guerriero, Leila. 2015. *Zona de obras*. Buenos Aires: Anagrama.

Gutiérrez, Alicia B. 2004. *'Pobre,' como siempre . . . Estrategias de reproducción social en la pobreza*. Córdoba: Ferreyra Editor.

Hailey, Chantal. 2020. "Choosing Schools, Choosing Safety: The Role of School Safety in School Choice." PhD diss., New York University. https://www.proquest .com/docview/2427528236.

Harding, David J. 2010. *Living the Drama: Community, Conflict, and Culture among Inner-City Boys*. Chicago: University of Chicago Press.

Hauer, Janine, Jonas Østergaard Nielsen, and Jörg Niewöhner. 2018. "Landscapes of Hoping—Urban Expansion and Emerging Futures in Ouagadougou, Burkina Faso." *Anthropological Theory* 18 (1): 59–80. https://www.doi.org/10.1177 /1463499617747176.

Helmke, Gretchen, and Stephen Levitsky. 2004. "Informal Institutions and Comparative Politics: A Research Agenda." *Perspectives in Politics* 2 (4): 725–40. https://www.doi.org/10.1017/S1537592704040472.

Heredia, Mariana, Sebastián Pereyra, and Maristella Svampa. 2020. *José Nun y las ciencias sociales: Aportes que perduran.* Buenos Aires: Biblos.

Hicken, Allen. 2011. "Clientelism." *Annual Review of Political Science* 14:289–310. https://www.doi.org/10.1146/annurev.polisci.031908.220508.

Hilgers, Tina. 2012a. "Clientelistic Democracy or Democratic Clientelism: A Matter of Context." In *Clientelism in Everyday Latin American Politics*, edited by T. Hilgers, 161–86. New York: Palgrave.

Hilgers, Tina. 2012b. "Democratic Processes, Clientelistic Relationships, and the Material Goods Problem." In *Clientelism in Everyday Latin American Politics*, edited by T. Hilgers, 3–24. New York: Palgrave.

Hintze, Susana. 1989. *Estrategias alimentarias de sobrevivencia: Un estudio de caso en el Gran Buenos Aires.* Buenos Aires: Centro Editor de América Latina.

Hintze, Susana. 2004. "Capital social y estrategias de supervivencia: Reflexiones sobre el 'Capital Social de Los Pobres.'" In *Políticas sociales y economía social: Debates fundamentales*, edited by Claudia Danani, 1–19. Buenos Aires: UNGS-Altamira-Fundación OSDE.

Hoang, Kimberly Key. 2015. *Dealing in Desire: Asian Ascendancy, Western Decline, and the Hidden Currencies of Global Sex Work.* Berkeley: University of California Press.

Holland, Alisha C. 2017. *Forbearance as Redistribution: The Politics of Informal Welfare in Latin America.* New York: Cambridge University Press.

Holston, James. 1991. "Autoconstruction in Working-Class Brazil." *Cultural Anthropology* 6 (4): 447–65. https://www.doi.org/10.1525/can.1991.6.4.02a00020.

Holston, James. 2009. *Insurgent Citizenship: Disjunctions of Democracy and Modernity in Brazil.* Princeton, NJ: Princeton University Press.

Huber, Evelyne, and John D. Stephens. 2012. *Democracy and the Left: Social Policy and Inequality in Latin America.* Chicago: University of Chicago Press.

Hume, Mo. 2009. *The Politics of Violence: Gender, Conflict and Community in El Salvador.* Hoboken: Wiley-Blackwell.

Hunter, Wendy, and Natasha Borges Sugiyama. 2014. "Transforming Subjects into Citizens: Insights from Brazil's Bolsa Família." *Perspectives on Politics* 12 (4): 829–45. https://www.doi.org/10.1017/S1537592714002151.

Imbusch, Peter, Michel Misse, and Fernando Carrión. 2011. "Violence Research in Latin America and the Caribbean: A Literature Review." *International Journal of Conflict and Violence* 5 (1) 87–154. https://www.doi.org/10.4119/ijcv-2851.

Izaguirre, Inés, and Zulema Aristizabal. 1988. *Las tomas de tierras en la zona sur del Gran Buenos Aires.* Buenos Aires: CEAL.

Jackman, Mary. 2002. "Violence in Social Life." *Annual Review of Sociology* 28:387–415. https://www.doi.org/10.1146/annurev.soc.28.110601.140936.

Jacobs, Bruce. 2004. "A Typology of Street Criminal Retaliation." *Journal of Research in Crime and Delinquency* 41 (3): 295–323. https://www.doi.org/10.1177/0022427803262058.

Jaffe, Rivke, Eveline Dürr, Gareth Jones, Alessandro Angelini, Alana Osbourne, and Barbara Vodopivec. 2020. "What Does Poverty Feel Like? Urban Inequality and the Politics of Sensation." *Urban Studies* 57 (5): 1015–31. https://www.doi .org/10.1177/0042098018820177.

Jarrett, Robin, Ozge Sensoy Bahar, and Angela Odoms-Young. 2014. "'You Just Have to Build a Bridge and Get Over It': Low-Income African American Care-givers' Coping Strategies to Manage Inadequate Food Supplies." *Journal of Poverty* 18 (2): 188–219. https://doi.org/10.1080/10875549.2014.896306.

Jensen, Katherine, and Javier Auyero. 2019. "Teaching and Learning the Craft: The Construction of Ethnographic Objects." *Urban Ethnography* 16:69–87. https:// www.doi.org/10.1108/S1047-004220190000016007.

Jensen, Steffen, and Dennis Rodgers. 2022. "The Intimacies of Drug Dealing: Nar-cotics, Kinship and Embeddedness in Nicaragua and South Africa." *Third World Quarterly* 43 (11): 2618–36. https://www.doi.org/10.1080/01436597.2021.1985450.

Katz, Jack. 1982. *Poor People's Lawyers in Transition.* New Brunswick, NJ: Rutgers University Press.

Kitschelt, Herbert, and Steven I. Wilkinson, eds. 2007. *Patrons, Clients and Policies: Patterns of Democratic Accountability and Political Competition.* New York: Cambridge University Press.

Klinenberg, Eric. 2018. *Palaces for the People.* New York: Crown.

Kramer, Mark, and Wendy Call. 2007. *Telling True Stories: A Nonfiction Writers' Guide from the Nieman Foundation at Harvard University.* Telford: Plum.

Lamaison, Pierre, and Pierre Bourdieu. 1986. "From Rules to Strategies: An In-terview with Pierre Bourdieu." *Cultural Anthropology* 1, no. 1 (February 1986): 110–20. http://www.jstor.org/stable/656327.

Lambek, Michael, ed. 2010. *Ordinary Ethics: Anthropology, Language, and Action.* New York: Fordham University Press.

Lamont, Michele. 2009. *The Dignity of Working Men: Morality and the Boundaries of Race, Class, and Immigration.* Boston: Harvard University Press.

Lapegna, Pablo. 2016. *Soybeans and Power: Genetically Modified Crops, Environ-mental Politics, and Social Movements in Argentina.* New York: Oxford Univer-sity Press.

Lareau, Annette. 2003. *Unequal Childhoods: Class, Race, and Family Life.* Berke-ley, CA: University of California Press.

Lareau, Annette. 2021. *Listening to People: A Practical Guide to Interviewing, Par-ticipant Observation, Data Analysis, and Writing It All Up.* Chicago: University of Chicago Press.

Lareau, Annette, and Kimberly Goyette, eds. 2014. *Choosing Homes, Choosing Schools.* New York: Russell Sage Foundation.

Larkins, Erika Mary Robb. 2015. *The Spectacular Favela: Violence in Modern Bra-zil.* Berkeley: University of California Press.

Lawson, Chappell, and Kenneth Greene. 2011. "Self-enforcing Clientelism." Paper presented at the Conferencia Clientelism and Electoral Fraud. Madrid: Instituto Juan March, June 22.

Levien, Michael. 2018. *Dispossession without Development: Land Grabs in Neoliberal India*. New York: Oxford University Press.

Levitsky, Steven. 2003. *Transforming Labor-Based Parties in Latin America: Argentine Peronism in Comparative Perspective*. Cambridge: Cambridge University Press.

Lomnitz, Larissa Adler. 1977. *Networks and Marginality: Life in a Mexican Shantytown*. New York: Academic Press.

Lomnitz, Larissa Adler. 1993. *¿Cómo sobreviven los marginados?* 15th ed. México City, México: Siglo XXI de España Editores. Siglo XXI de España Editores.

Lubbers, Miranda J., Mario Luis Small, and Hugo Valenzuela García. 2020. "Do Networks Help People to Manage Poverty? Perspectives from the Field." *ANNALS of the American Academy of Political and Social Science* 689 (1): 7–25. https://www.doi.org/10.1177/0002716220923959.

Marwah, Vrinda. 2021a. "For Love of Money: Rewards of Care for India's Women Community Health Workers." *Social Problems* 70 (4): 1104–22. https://www.doi.org/10.1093/socpro/spab062.

Marwah, Vrinda. 2021b. "Promissory Capital: State Legitimacy among Women Community Health Workers in India." *Qualitative Sociology* 44:403–18. https://www.doi.org/10.1007/s11133-021-09487-y.

Massey, Douglas, and Nancy Denton. 1994. *American Apartheid: Segregation and the Making of the Underclass*. Boston: Harvard University Press.

Maurel, Valentina, dir. 2022. *Tengo Sueños Eléctricos [I Have Electric Dreams]*. Brussels, Belgium: Wrong Men.

McAdam, Doug. 1988. *Freedom Summer*. New York: Oxford University Press.

McCann, Colum. 2018. *Letters to a Young Writer*. New York: Bloomsbury.

McCurn, Alexis S. 2018. *The Grind: Black Women and Survival in the Inner City*. New Brunswick, NJ: Rutgers University Press.

Menjívar, Cecilia. 2000. *Fragmented Ties: Salvadoran Immigrant Networks in America*. Berkeley, CA: University of California Press.

Merklen, Denis. 1991. *Asentamientos en La Matanza: La terquedad de lo nuestro*. Buenos Aires: Catálogos Editora.

Mesa, Sara. 2019. *Silencio administrativo: La pobreza en el laberinto democrático*. Barcelona: Anagrama.

Miller, Reuben Jonathan. 2021. *Halfway Home: Race, Punishment, and the Afterlife of Mass Incarceration*. New York: Back Bay.

Mol, Annemarie. 2003. *The Body Multiple: Ontology in Medical Practice*. Durham, NC: Duke University Press.

Moncada, Eduardo. 2022. *Resisting Extortion*. New York: Cambridge University Press.

Moore, A., F. Eiró, and M. Koster. 2022. "Illegal Housing in Medellín: Autoconstruction and the Materiality of Hope." *Latin American Politics and Society* 64 (4): 94–118. https://www.doi.org/10.1017/lap.2022.31.

Morgan, Kimberly J., and Ann Shola Orloff, eds. 2017. *The Many Hands of the State: Theorizing Political Authority and Social Control*. New York: Cambridge University Press.

Moser, Caroline. 1993. *Gender Planning and Development: Theory, Practice and Training.* New York: Routledge.

Moser, Caroline, and Cathy McIlwaine. 2000. *Urban Poor Perceptions of Violence and Exclusion in Colombia.* Washington, DC: World Bank Publications.

Müller, Markus M. 2016. *The Punitive City: Privatized Policing and Protection in Neoliberal Mexico.* New York: Zed.

Mullins, Christopher, Richard Wright, and Bruce Jacobs. 2004. "Gender, Street Life and Criminal Retaliation." *Criminology* 42 (4): 911–40.

Munck, Ronaldo. 2013. "The Precariat: A View from the South." *Third World Quarterly* 34 (5): 747–62.

Municipalidad de Quilmes. 2010. *Censo Social Quilmes.* Municipalidad de Quilmes.

Nardin, Santiago. 2019. "Memorias sobre tomas de tierras en San Francisco Solano: Acción directa, vínculo de ciudadanía y distinciones sociales." MA thesis, Universidad Nacional de General Sarmiento. https://repositorio.ungs.edu.ar/handle/UNGS/720.

Newman, Katherine S. 2020. "Ties That Bind/Unwind: The Social, Economic, and Organizational Contexts of Sharing Networks." ANNALS *of the American Academy of Political and Social Science* 689 (1): 192–201. https://www.doi.org/10.1177/0002716220923335.

Ngozi Adichie, Chimamanda. 2009. "The Danger of a Single Story." TED Talk, July 2009. https://www.ted.com/talks/chimamanda_ngozi_adichie_the_danger_of_a_single_story.

Nichter, Simeon. 2008. "Vote Buying or Turnout Buying? Machine Politics and the Secret Ballot." *American Political Science Review* 102 (1): 19–31. https://www.doi.org/10.1017/S0003055408080106.

Nun, José. 2001. *Marginalidad y exclusión social.* Buenos Aires: Fondo de Cultura Económica.

Nussbaum, Martha. 2006. "Poverty and Human Functioning: Capabilities as Fundamental Entitlements." In *Poverty and Inequality*, edited by David B. Grusky and Ravi Kanbur, 47–75. Stanford, CA: Stanford University Press.

Observatorio de la Deuda Social Argentina (ODSA). 2021. *Efectos de la pandemia COVID-19 sobre la dinámica del bienestar en la Argentina urbana: Una mirada multidimensional acerca de impacto heterogéneo de la crisis tras una década de estancamiento económico (2010–2020).* Buenos Aires: Universidad Católica Argentina, 2021.

Ochs, Juliana. 2011. *Security and Suspicion: An Ethnography of Everyday Life in Israel.* Philadelphia: University of Pennsylvania Press.

Ortner, Sherry B. 2016. "Dark Anthropology and Its Others: Theory since the Eighties." *HAU: Journal of Ethnographic Theory* 6 (1): 47–73. https://www.doi.org/10.14318/hau6.1.004.

Østby, Gudrun. 2016. "Violence Begets Violence: Armed Conflict and Domestic Sexual Violence in Sub-Saharan Africa." HiCN working paper 233. Households in Conflict Network. https://econpapers.repec.org/paper/hicwpaper/233.htm.

Ousey, Graham C., and Matthew R. Lee. 2002. "Examining the Conditional Nature of the Illicit Drug Market–Homicide Relationship: A Partial Test of the Theory of Contingent Causation." *Criminology* 40 (1): 73–102. https://www.doi.org/10.1111/j.1745-9125.2002.tb00950.x.

Papachristos, Andrew. 2009. "Murder by Structure: Dominance Relations and the Social Structure of Gang Homicide." *American Journal of Sociology* 115 (1): 74–128. https://www.doi.org/10.1086/597791.

Pearce, Jenny. 2019. "Introducción: Un aporte conceptual y empírico para resignificar la seguridad en México." In *Seguridad humana y violencia crónica en México: Nuevas lecturas y propuestas desde abajo*, edited by Gema Kloppe Santamaría and Alexandra Abello Colak, 5–33. Mexico City: Instituto Tecnológico Autónomo de México, Editorial Miguel Ángel Porrua.

Penglase, R. Ben. 2014. *Living with Insecurity in a Brazilian Favela: Urban Violence and Daily Life*. New Brunswick, NJ: Rutgers University Press.

Perez, Marcos Emilio. 2018. "Institutional Strengthening in a Receding Movement: The Trajectory of *Piquetero* Organizations between 2003 and 2015." *Latin American Research Review* 53 (2): 287–302. https://www.doi.org/10.25222/larr.336.

Perez, Marcos Emilio. 2022. *Proletarian Lives: Routines, Identities, and Culture in Contentious Politics*. New York: Cambridge University Press.

Perlman, Janice. 2011. *Favela: Four Decades of Living on the Edge in Rio de Janeiro*. New York: Oxford University Press.

Phillips, Kristin. 2018. *An Ethnography of Hunger: Politics, Subsistence, and the Unpredictable Grace of the Sun*. Bloomington: Indiana University Press.

Piñeiro, Claudia. 2020. *Catedrales*. Buenos Aires: Alfaguara.

Pitt-Rivers, Julian Alfred. 1954. *The People of the Sierra*. New York: Criterion.

Piven, Frances Fox, and Richard Cloward. 1978. *Poor People's Movements: Why They Succeed, How They Fail*. New York: Vintage.

Portes, Alejandro, and Kelly Hoffman. 2003. "Latin American Class Structures: Their Composition and Change during the Neoliberal Era." *Latin American Research Review* 38:41–82. http://dx.doi.org/10.1353/lar.2003.0011.

Poy, Santiago, and Agustin Salvia. 2019. *Estratificación social, movilidad intergeneracional y distribución de resultados de bienestar en la Argentina*. Informe técnico. Pontificia Universidad Católica Argentina. Observatorio de la Deuda Social Argentina. Barómetro de la Deuda Social Argentina. https://www.doi.org/10.13140/RG.2.2.14281.49764.

Ralph, Laurence. 2014. *Renegade Dreams: Living through Injury in Gangland Chicago*. Chicago: University of Chicago Press.

Rank, Mark Robert, Lawrence Eppard, and Heather Bullock. 2021. *Poorly Understood: What America Gets Wrong about Poverty*. New York: Oxford University Press.

Raudenbush, Danielle T. 2016. "'I Stay by Myself': Social Support, Distrust, and Selective Solidarity among the Urban Poor." *Sociological Forum* 31 (4): 1018–39. https://www.doi.org/10.1111/socf.12294.

Raudenbush, Danielle T. 2020. *Health Care Off the Books: Poverty, Illness, and Strategies for Survival in Urban America*. Berkeley: University of California Press.

Reinarman, Craig, and Harry G. Levine, eds. 1997. *Crack in America: Demon Drugs and Social Justice*. Berkeley: University of California Press.

Reygadas, Luis. 2008. *La apropiación: Destejiendo las redes de la desigualdad*. Barcelona, Mexico: Anthropos.

Rodgers, D., J. Beall, and R. Kanbur, eds. 2012. *Latin American Urban Development into the Twenty-First Century: Towards a Renewed Perspective on the City*. New York: Palgrave Macmillan.

Rodgers, Dennis. 2000. "Living in the Shadow of Death: Violence, Pandillas, and Social Disintegration in Contemporary Urban Nicaragua." PhD diss., Department of Social Anthropology, University of Cambridge.

Rodgers, Dennis. 2004. "'Disembedding' the City: Crime, Insecurity and Spatial Organization in Managua, Nicaragua." *Environment and Urbanization* 16 (2): 113–24. https://www.doi.org/10.1177/095624780401600202.

Rodgers, Dennis. 2007. "'Each to Their Own': Ethnographic Notes on the Economic Organisation of Poor Households in Urban Nicaragua." *Journal of Development Studies* 43 (3): 391–419. https://www.doi.org/10.1080 /00220380701204240.

Rosales, Rocío. 2020. *Fruteros: Street Vending, Illegality, and Ethnic Community in Los Angeles*. Berkeley, CA: University of California Press.

Rossi, Federico M. 2017. *The Poor's Struggle for Political Incorporation: The Piquetero Movement in Argentina*. New York: Cambridge University Press.

Rubinich, Lucas. 2022. *Contra el homo resignatus: Siete ensayos para reinventar la rebeldía política en un mundo invadido por el desencanto*. Buenos Aires: Siglo Veintiuno Editores.

Ruddick, Sara. 1998. "Care as Labor and Relationship." In *Norms and Values: Essays on the Work of Virginia Held*, edited by Joram G. Haber and Mark S. Halfon, 3–25. Lanham, MD: Rowman and Littlefield.

Salvia, Agustín. 2012. *La trampa neoliberal: Un estudio sobre los cambios en la heterogeneidad estructural y la distribución del ingreso en la Argentina: 1992–2003*. Buenos Aires: Eudeba.

Salvia, Agustín, and Eduardo Chávez Molina. 2013. *Sombras de una marginalidad fragmentada*. Buenos Aires: Miño y Davila.

Sampson, Robert J., Stephen W. Raudenbush, and Felton Earls. 1997. "Neighborhoods and Violent Crime: A Multilevel Study of Collective Efficacy." *Science* 277 (5328): 918–24. https://www.doi.org/10.1126/science.277.5328.918.

Sánchez-Jankowski, Martín. 2008. *Cracks in the Pavement*. Berkeley: University of California Press.

Saporito, Salvatore. 2003. "Private Choices, Public Consequences: Magnet School Choice and Segregation by Race and Poverty." *Social Problems* 50 (2): 181–203. https://www.doi.org/10.1525/sp.2003.50.2.181.

Scheper-Hughes, Nancy. 1993. *Death without Weeping: The Violence of Everyday Life in Brazil*. Berkeley: University of California Press.

Scheper-Hughes, Nancy, and Philippe I. Bourgois, eds. 2004. *Violence in War and Peace: An Anthology*. Oxford: Blackwell.

Schneider, Cathy. 1995. *Shantytown Protest in Pinochet's Chile*. Philadelphia, Penn: Temple University Press.

Schweblin, Samanta. 2020. *Distancia de Rescate*. Buenos Aires: Random House.

Sen, Amartya. 1983. *Poverty and Famines: An Essay on Entitlement and Deprivation*. Reprint edition. Oxford: Oxford University Press.

Sharkey, Patrick. 2018. *Uneasy Peace: The Great Crime Decline, the Renewal of City Life, and the Next War on Violence*. New York: W. W. Norton.

Sharma, Aradhana, and Akhil Gupta, eds. 2006. *The Anthropology of the State: A Reader*. Malden, MA: Wiley-Blackwell.

Simmel, Georg. 1964. *The Sociology of Georg Simmel*. Edited by Kurt H. Wolff. New York: Free Press.

Small, Mario Luis. 2004. *Villa Victoria: The Transformation of Social Capital in a Boston Barrio*. Chicago: University of Chicago Press.

Small, Mario Luis, and Leah E. Gose. 2020. "How Do Low-Income People Form Survival Networks? Routine Organizations as Brokers." ANNALS *of the American Academy of Political and Social Science* 689 (1): 89–109. https://www.doi .org/10.1177/0002716220915431.

Smith, Nicholas Rush. 2019. *Contradictions of Democracy: Vigilantism and Rights in Post-Apartheid South Africa*. New York: Oxford University Press.

Smith, Sandra. 2016. "Job-Finding among the Poor: Do Social Ties Matter?" In *The Oxford Handbook of the Social Science of Poverty*, edited by David Brady and Linda Burton, 438–61. New York: Oxford University Press.

Soss, Joe, and Vesla Weaver. "Police Are Our Government: Politics, Political Science, and the Policing of Race–Class Subjugated Communities." *Annual Review of Political Science* 20, no. 1 (2017): 565–91. https://doi.org/10.1146/annurev -polisci-060415-093825.

Stack, Carol B. 1974. *All Our Kin: Strategies for Survival in a Black Community*. 2nd ed. New York: Basic Books.

Stitt, Mary Ellen, and Javier Auyero. 2018. "Drug Market Violence Comes Home: Three Sequential Pathways." *Social Forces* 97 (2): 823–40. https://doi.org/10.1093 /sf/soy035.

Stokes, Susan. 2005. "Perverse Accountability: A Formal Model of Machine Politics with Evidence from Argentina." *American Political Science Review* 99 (3): 315–25. https://www.doi.org/10.1017/S0003055405051683.

Stokes, Susan, Thad Dunning, and Marcelo Nazareno. 2013. *Brokers, Voters, and Clientelism: The Puzzle of Distributive Politics*. New York: Cambridge University Press.

Stuart, Forrest. 2020. *Ballad of the Bullet: Gangs, Drill Music, and the Power of Online Infamy*. Princeton, NJ: Princeton University Press.

Sullivan, Esther. 2018. *Manufactured Insecurity: Mobile Home Parks and Americans' Tenuous Right to Place*. Berkeley: University of California Press.

Svampa, Maristella. 2005. *La sociedad excluyente*. Buenos Aires: Taurus.

Svampa, Maristella. 2008. *Los que ganaron: La vida en los countries y barrios privados*. Buenos Aires: Biblos.

Szwarcberg, Mariela. 2015. *Mobilizing Poor Voters: Machine Politics, Clientelism, and Social Networks in Argentina*. Cambridge: Cambridge University Press.

Tenti Fanfani, Emilio. 2005. "La educación escolar y la nueva 'cuestión social.'" *Punto de Vista* 81:42–48.

Tenti Fanfani, Emilio. 2021. *La escuela bajo sospecha: Sociología progresista y crítica para pensar la educación para todos*. Buenos Aires: Siglo XXI.

Thompson, Edward P. 1993. "The Moral Economy of the English Crowd in the Eighteenth Century." In *Customs in Common*, 120–65. New York: New Press.

Tilly, Charles. 1978. *From Mobilization of Revolution*. New York: Longman.

Tilly, Charles. 1992. "How to Detect, Describe, and Explain Repertoires of Contention." Working paper 150. New School Archives. New York: Center for Studies of Social Change.

Tilly, Charles. 1999. *Durable Inequality*. Berkeley: University of California Press.

Tilly, Charles. 2002. *Stories, Identities, and Political Change*. Lanham, MD: Rowman & Littlefield.

Tilly, Charles. 2003. *The Politics of Collective Violence*. New York: Cambridge University Press.

Tilly, Charles. 2006. *Regimes and Repertoires*. Chicago: University of Chicago Press.

Tilly, Charles. 2008. *Contentious Performances*. Illustrated ed. Cambridge: Cambridge University Press.

Vega, Nohora, Luis Antonio Flores, and Brenda Raquel Velásquez. 2019. "Narrativas de la violencia en la colonia Sánchez Taboada en Tijuana: Entre el desamparo y la ciudadanía activa." In *Seguridad humana y violencia crónica en México: Nuevas lecturas y propuestas desde abajo*, edited by Gema Kloppe Santamaría and Alexandra Abello Colak, 103–36. Mexico: Instituto Tecnológico Autónomo de México, Editorial Miguel Ángel Porrua.

Venkatesh, Sudhir. 2008. *Gang Leader for a Day: A Rogue Sociologist Takes to the Streets*. New York: Penguin.

Villarreal, Ana. 2024. *The Two Faces of Fear: Violence and Inequality in the Mexican Metropolis*. New York: Oxford University Press.

Vommaro, Gabriel, and Helene Combes. 2016. *El clientelismo político*. Buenos Aires: Siglo XXI.

Wacquant, Loïc. 2002. "Scrutinizing the Street: Poverty, Morality, and the Pitfalls of Urban Ethnography." *American Journal of Sociology* 107 (6): 1468–532. https://www.doi.org/10.1086/340461.

Wacquant, Loïc. 2006. *Body and Soul: Notebooks of an Apprentice Boxer*. Illustrated ed. Oxford: Oxford University Press.

Wacquant, Loïc. 2007. *Urban Outcasts: A Comparative Sociology of Advanced Marginality*. New York: Polity.

Wacquant, Loïc. 2015. "Afterword: Plumbing the Social Underbelly of the Dual City." In *Invisible in Austin: Life and Labor in an American City*, 264–71. Austin: University of Texas Press.

Wacquant, Loïc. 2022. *The Invention of the "Underclass": A Study in the Politics of Knowledge*. Medford, MA: Polity.

Wacquant, Loïc. Forthcoming. *The Zone: Making Do in the Hyperghetto at Century's End*.

Wacquant, Loïc, and Dieter Vandebroeck. 2023. "Carnal Concepts in Action: The Diagonal Sociology of Loïc Wacquant." *Thesis Eleven*, 1–33. https://www.doi.org/10.1177/07255136221149782.

Wallace, Harvey, Cliff Roberson, and Julie L. Globokar. 2019. *Family Violence: Legal, Medical, and Social Perspectives*. New York: Routledge.

Ward, Jesmyn. 2022. *Mother Swamp*. Seattle: Amazon Original Stories.

Ward, Peter M. 2012. "'A Patrimony for the Children': Low-Income Homeownership and Housing (Im)Mobility in Latin American Cities." *Annals of the Association of American Geographers* 102 (6): 1489–510. https://www.doi.org/10.1080/00045608.2011.628260.

Ward, Peter. 2019. "Self-help Housing." In *The Wiley Blackwell Encyclopedia of Urban and Regional Studies*, 1–6. New York: Wiley-Blackwell.

Way, Lucan A., and Steven Levitsky. 2007. "Linkage, Leverage and the Post-Communist Divide." *East European Politics and Societies* 27 (21): 48–66. https://www.doi.org/10.1177/0888325406297134.

Weingrod, Alex. 1977. "Patrons, Patronage, and Political Parties." In *Friends, Followers, and Factions: A Reader in Political Clientelism*, edited by S. Schmidt, L. Guasti, C. Landé, and J. Scott, 323–37. Berkeley: University of California Press.

Weiss, Robert. 1994. *Learning from Strangers: The Art and Method of Qualitative Interview Studies*. New York: Free Press.

Weitz-Shapiro, Rebecca. 2014. *Curbing Clientelism in Argentina: Politics, Poverty, and Social Policy*. New York: Cambridge University Press.

Weyland, Kurt, Raul Madrid, and Wendy Hunter. 2010. *Leftists Governments in Latin America: Successes and Shortcomings*. New York: Cambridge University Press.

Wilding, Polly. 2012. *Negotiating Boundaries: Gender, Violence and Transformation in Brazil*. New York: Palgrave Macmillan.

Wilkinson, Steven. 2007. "Explaining Changing Patterns of Party-Voter Linkages in India." In *Patrons, Clients, and Policies: Patterns of Democratic Accountability and Political Competition*, edited by H. Kitschelt and S. Wilkinson, 110–40. New York: Cambridge University Press.

Willis, Graham Denyer. 2015. *The Killing Consensus: Police, Organized Crime, and the Regulation of Life and Death in Urban Brazil*. Berkeley: University of California Press.

Willis, Paul. 2017. *Learning to Labor: How Working-Class Kids Get Working-Class Jobs*. New York: Columbia University Press.

Wolcott, Harry. 2008. *Ethnography: A Way of Seeing*. Lanham, MD: AltaMira.

World Health Organization (WHO). 2002. *World Report on Violence and Health*. Geneva: World Health Organization.

Wright, Erik Olin. 2021. *How to Be an Anticapitalist in the Twenty-First Century*. New York: Verso.

Zarazaga, Rodrigo. 2014. "Brokers beyond Clientelism: A New Perspective through the Argentine Case." *Latin American Politics and Society* 56 (3): 23–45. https://www.doi.org/10.1111/j.1548-2456.2014.00238.x.

Zarazaga, Rodrigo. 2017. "Punteros, el rostro del estado frente a los pobres." In *Conurbano infinito*, edited by Lucas Ronconi and Rodrigo Zarazaga, 38–57. Buenos Aires: Siglo XXI Editores.

Zarazaga, Rodrigo, and Lucas Ronconi, eds. 2017. *Conurbano infinito*. Buenos Aires: Siglo XXI Editores.

Zubillaga, Verónica, Manuel Llorens, and John Souto. 2019. "Micropolitics in a Caracas Barrio: The Political Survival Strategies of Mothers in a Context of Armed Violence." *Latin American Research Review* 54 (2): 429–43.

Zussman, Robert. 2004. "People in Places." *Qualitative Sociology* 27 (4): 351–63.

mutual aid, x, 18–19, 152. *See also* subsistence

neoliberalism, 24
Networks and Marginality: Life in a Mexican Shantytown (Lomnitz), 13
networks: reciprocal exchange, 13–15, 18–20, 41, 43–44, 57, 152–53; informal, 15, 18, 41; kin and friend, 15, 18, 86–88, 141, 152–53; protest, 15. *See also* social ties; subsistence

Ortale, Susana, 27

patronage. *See* clientelism
Penglase, Ben, 80, 87
pensions, 26
Perón, Juan, 36
Peronist party, 28, 26, 37, 65, 73–74. *See also* clientelism
persistence: strategies of 4, 16–17, 139, 152, 156–58; relational 124
Phillips, Kristin, 16
pibes, 21, 26, 46, 85, 114, 145
pink tide, 25
piqueteros, 61, 74
police, 21, 30, 36, 152; involvement in illicit activities, 103–4, 105, 107, 115, 168n1
politics, 9–10, 16, 20, 67, 76–78, 153–54; partisan 36–37, 49, 56, 73. *See also* brokers; clientelism; Peronist Party
Poor People's Politics, x, 57–58, 74
poverty: democracy and, 164n6, multidimensional approach to, 15–16, 18; political participation and, 165n9, rates in Argentina, 25–27; violence and, 115
precarious exploitation, 20, 49, 152
prisons, 105–6; violence inside, 107–10
protectors, of neighborhood children, 128–30, 149–50
protests, 37–39, 58

recognition: material, 120–21, 149, 152; social and symbolic, 120–21, 125, 128, 134, 139, 149, 152, 158
Rocha, Mercedes González de la, 18

Sharma Aradhana, 154
Simmel, Georg, 132
social media 76
social structure, bottom of the 27, 42, 76, 105, 138, 154
social ties, 18, 19, 87–88. *See also* networks
socorro, 20
soguero, 72–73
solidarity, 14, 18, 19, 37, 57
soup kitchens, 1, 36, 41, 75–76, 109, 117–37, 143, 154. *See also* community center
squatter settlements, 4, 23–39, 165n8; flooding in 30–31, 35, 64, 142; infrastructural precarity in 29–36, 65, 141; versus slums, 36, 66, 137–38; state negotiations and, 37–38. *See also* land occupation
Stack, Carol, 13–14, 17, 86
state: absence of, x, 154; bureaucracies, 39, 147–48, 154; daily experiences of 154–55; domination by, 158; many hands of, 155; as space of struggle, 39, 152–53. *See also* clientelism; welfare subsidies; violence
subsistence, strategies of, x, 3–5, 9, 19, 67, 156–58; politics and 45, 62, 153; violence as risk to, 87–88, 90, 144–47; welfare and, 67. *See also* brokers; household budgets; illicit activities; mutual aid; networks
survival, strategies of, x, 4–5, 16–17, 87–88, 163n3
survival question, the, x
synchronic analysis, 48, 157

Tarjeta Alimentar, 26, 42, 166n3
Thompson, E. P., 144
Tilly, Charles, 37, 157

unemployment, 24, 25, 27, 57, 85
upper classes, 80, 146
urban poor, 3, 5–6, 13–14, 16–18, 29, 57, 79; stereotypes of, 151, 153
urbanization, peripheral, 164n1

violence: in the Americas, 79, 85–86; concatenated, 90–98, 104–13; interpersonal, 3, 27, 79–88, 90–101, 124, 145; multiple uses of, 115; as repertoire of (inter)action, 101; responses to, 79–81, 85–88, 121–24;